Approaches to Teaching
Shakespeare's English History Plays

Approaches to Teaching Shakespeare's English History Plays

Edited by

Laurie Ellinghausen

The Modern Language Association of America
New York   2017

MLA and the MODERN LANGUAGE ASSOCIATION are trademarks owned by the
Modern Language Association of America. For information about obtaining permission
to reprint material from MLA book publications, send your request
by mail (see address below) or e-mail (permissions@mla.org).

Library of Congress Cataloging-in-Publication Data

Names: Ellinghausen, Laurie, 1972– editor.
Title: Approaches to teaching Shakespeare's English history plays / edited by Laurie
    Ellinghausen.
Description: New York : The Modern Language Association of America, 2017. | Series:
    Approaches to teaching world literature ; 145 | Includes
    bibliographical references and index.
Identifiers: LCCN 2016054827 | ISBN 9781603292993 (hardback) | ISBN 9781603293006
    (paper) | ISBN 978-1-60329-301-3 (EPUB) | ISBN 978-1-60329-302-0 (Kindle)
Subjects: LCSH: Shakespeare, William, 1564–1616—Histories. | Shakespeare, William,
    1564–1616—Study and teaching. | Historical drama, English—Study and teaching. |
    Literature and history—Great Britain. | BISAC: LANGUAGE ARTS & DISCIPLINES /
    Study & Teaching. | LITERARY CRITICISM / Shakespeare. | LITERARY CRITICISM /
    European / English, Irish, Scottish, Welsh.
Classification: LCC PR2982 .A76 2017 | DDC 822.3/3—dc23
LC record available at https://lccn.loc.gov/2016054827

ISSN 1059-1133

Cover illustration of the paperback and electronic editions:
Henry (Harry) A. Payne (1868–1940), *Choosing the Red and White Roses in the Temple
Garden*, 1910, fresco. Houses of Parliament, Westminster, London, UK / Bridgeman Images.

Published by The Modern Language Association of America
85 Broad Street, suite 500, New York, New York 10004-2434
www.mla.org

CONTENTS

Political, Intellectual, and International Contexts

Theory and Criticism

Gender

Teaching through Research, Writing, and Performance

ACKNOWLEDGMENTS

I would like to thank the MLA's senior acquisitions editor, James C. Hatch, for his careful and conscientious stewardship of the project throughout its various stages. Thanks also to the MLA Publications Committee and the project's anonymous readers for their thoughtful responses. I wish to thank the colleagues who shared their experiences and insights in a survey about teaching Shakespeare's English history plays. Mark Aune and Virginia Blanton provided feedback and advice on the early stages of the proposal. The volume also has profited from the experience of Peter Herman, who provided invaluable feedback on part 1 and advice at other stages. Ann Christensen and Mark Aune read early drafts of part 2, which improved in response to their suggestions. Thanks also to my colleagues at the University of Missouri, Kansas City, and throughout the field who expressed interest in and support for the project during all stages.

Finally, my gratitude goes to my husband, Jeff Callan, for his continual love and support.

Part One

MATERIALS

This resource guide, as well as the introduction to part 2 that follows, reflects the responses of the 130 colleagues at institutions throughout the world who responded to the MLA's survey on teaching Shakespeare's English history plays. The survey prompted respondents to reflect on the rewards and challenges of teaching the histories; it also asked them to share recommended editions, supplementary resources, and specific pedagogical approaches.

Editions

Complete Works

Stephen Greenblatt, Walter Cohen, Jean E. Howard, and Katharine Eisaman Maus's *The Norton Shakespeare* and G. Blakemore Evans's *The Riverside Shakespeare* emerge as the most popular complete works in the survey, the Norton with a substantial edge. Instructors see it as offering the best value for the student, with copious information about history, society, the material theater, and performance practices, including an essay by Andrew Gurr. Respondents describe introductions "unrivaled with their blend of erudition and accessibility," bibliographies arranged by subject matter, "comprehensive yet accessible" footnotes, and single-column text with "informative" marginal glosses that "keep students' eyes on the text." Norton's one-volume second edition includes all ten English history plays, as well as *The Reign of King Edward III* and passages attributed to Shakespeare from *Sir Thomas More*. The paperback *Essential Plays* includes *Richard III*, *Richard II*, *1 Henry IV*, and *Henry V*. These are prefaced with an essay by Howard that covers the probable order of the plays' authorship, the differences among the tetralogies, and political and literary contexts. The "Shakespearean Chronicle" correlates Shakespeare's life and writings with such nationally important occasions as the defeat of the Spanish Armada, the execution of the Earl of Essex, and the accession of James I. The front of the volume presents a genealogy of monarchs from Henry II through Elizabeth I, followed by a brief summary of each monarch's reign. An appendix on "early modern map culture"—containing full-page reproductions of maps of London, the British Isles, and the Mediterranean region—helps students track significant locations. Norton's four-volume genre set also includes a histories volume. The notoriously thin paper, however, poses a major drawback, making note-taking difficult. (Note that at the time of the survey, respondents based their answers on the then most recent Norton editions, which used the *Oxford Shakespeare* texts described below and introductions and ancillary materials written by the Norton team. However, Norton has released new editions since the survey; these do not use the Oxford texts.)

The second most popular complete works, the one-volume hardcover *Riverside Shakespeare*, has not seen a new edition since 1996. It also costs more than the *Norton*. Still, instructors who prefer the *Riverside* extol it for its textual rigor, especially its extensive glosses and notes. Those who find the *Norton's* attention to contemporary theory "faddish" (in the word of one respondent) might prefer the *Riverside's* emphasis on texts, sources, and influences. The *Riverside* offers sturdier pages than the *Norton*, which facilitates easier reading and note-taking. Like the *Norton*, the *Riverside* contains all ten histories, *Edward III*, and the *More* passages. Respondents praise its clear genealogical tables, especially the "Edward's sacred blood" genealogy. The "Scene of the History Plays" map helps students situate the action geographically. Herschel Baker's introductions attend to the plays' authorship (particularly complicated in the case of the *Henry VI* plays), sources, language, and structure. The histories section also features illustrations of animals, coins, gardens, inns and taverns, knightly combat, and military technology.

Survey respondents to earlier Approaches volumes embraced David Bevington's *Complete Works of Shakespeare* (Longman) along with the *Riverside*, when the *Norton* had not yet achieved its current status. This survey reflects a marked change. Yet since several respondents noted that the Bevington edition had not been updated recently, I attribute the difference in part to the date of the survey, which closed just before the seventh edition appeared in January 2013. Here I will report the survey responses and also describe the features of the 2013 edition.

Bevington's "uniformly excellent" general introduction—covering Shakespeare's life and work, language, and the London stage—draws praise from respondents. The seventh edition updates these materials by adding a section titled "Reading Shakespeare in the Twenty-First Century" and a revised section on language keyed to the needs of novice readers. Other new features include an updated film and video guide and "Shakespeare's World: A Visual Portfolio," containing sixteen pages of full-color illustrations depicting Renaissance culture as well as significant performances. Although the speech prefixes are spelled out in full, the margins of the text still allow plenty of room for readers to take notes. While one respondent calls Bevington's notes "too elementary," this remark contrasts with others who describe them as helpful, particularly when they gloss words and explain cultural phenomena. One respondent "prefers" Bevington's introductions, which provide overviews of the plays' most widely discussed themes. The "Royal Genealogy of England, 1154–1625" appears after the appendixes, followed by one map of London and another of England and western France. Like the *Norton*, Bevington's edition also comes in a four-volume paperback genre set. Bevington's paperback *Necessary Shakespeare* extracts *Richard III, Richard II, 1 Henry IV*, and *Henry V*, among other plays, from the *Complete Works*.

A handful of respondents assign Stanley Wells and Gary Taylor's *Oxford Shakespeare*, particularly when they wish to incorporate textual study. These instructors value the *Oxford*'s "complete" yet "inexpensive" format. Other honorable mentions include the *Arden Shakespeare* (also for textual study, mostly at the graduate level), the *Complete Pelican Shakespeare* ("light and easy to carry" with "rather good" introductions and "reliable" text), and the Royal Shakespeare Company's *Complete Works* (inexpensive and popular for performance work). Since the survey, the first edition of the *Bedford Shakespeare*, edited by Russ McDonald and Lena Cowen Orlin, has been published.

Single Editions

Instructors assign single editions mainly for their relatively low cost and portability. Respondents also report that students tend to prefer them over complete works. The Folger Shakespeare Library and Arden editions stand out as the most widely adopted.

The Folger offers all ten English histories, each up to date and well edited by Barbara Mowat and Paul Werstine. Described by one respondent as "the most student-friendly among the reputable editions," they are popular for lower-division and survey courses. They contain explanatory notes facing each page and scene summaries to aid students in comprehension. Students like the price and overall "simplicity" of these volumes, which do not weigh students down too heavily with textual apparatus. A few respondents see these editions as too elementary or, in the words of one, "edited down to the level of high school students." Another complains that "the notes tend to be misleading for first-time readers." Yet others find this same level of direction valuable for students new to Shakespeare.

Arden also offers all ten English histories, edited by distinguished scholars such as James Siemon (*Richard III*), Charles Forker (*Richard II*), David Scott Kastan (*1 Henry IV*), and T. W. Craik (*Henry V*). While the Folger volumes seem aimed at beginners, instructors commonly adopt the Arden texts for graduate and upper-division undergraduate classes, particularly text-based, theoretical, and genre classes. They cost more than the Folger editions yet offer more in the way of textual apparatus. Although the editors intervene little in the text itself, they offer "thoroughly edited, very informative footnotes"; "excellent introductions"; and "exhaustive supplementary materials," including genealogical tables, casting and doubling charts, and appendixes addressing quartos, folios, and variants. Because of this level of detail, one respondent feels Arden to be most fitting "for matters of great scrutiny," such as textual scholarship and dramaturgical work. Others see the Arden volumes' extensive apparatus as excessive for undergraduates who struggle with understanding the basics of language and plot.

Beyond these two series, respondents assign editions according to differing criteria. Those seeking a wealth of supplementary material look to the Oxford World's Classics, the Norton Critical Editions, the Bedford/St. Martin's Texts and

Contexts series, and the Longman Cultural Editions. The Oxford works feature introductions by eminent scholars, rich contextual information, secondary readings, and copious annotations (hailed in particular by one instructor who teaches in a non-English speaking country). Oxford offers all ten histories, and respondents singled out Bevington's *Henry IV, Part I* and John Jowett's *The Tragedy of King Richard III* as especially good. The two Norton histories—*1 Henry IV* (Gordon McMullan) and *Richard III* (Thomas Cartelli)—receive specific mentions for their "useful and interesting" introductions, as well as their excerpts from contemporary documents and criticism. Described as a "favorite" and a "gem for contextualizing" the play, Barbara Hodgdon's Texts and Contexts edition of *1 Henry IV* offers "fantastic" supplementary materials, including excerpts from Holinshed's *Chronicles* and chapters on military culture and tavern life. From Longman, Ronald Levao's *Henry IV Parts One and Two* includes the complete texts from Bevington as well as a timeline, genealogical tables, and contextual material.

The Signet and Pelican series, both published by Penguin, are popular mainly for their accessibility and low price. Yet they too contain helpful introductions; "useful" but "not intrusive" notes; and "legible, uncluttered, and spacious" pages. Other editions mentioned include Bantam, New Kittredge, Modern Library/ RSC, Oxford School Shakespeare, Cambridge, and Dover Thrift. Adopters of the Bantam series describe them as "cheap" and "easy to carry" while still containing some textual, source, and production history material to help students with further reading and research. Like the Folger text, the Bantam books feature notes on the verso page, making them easy to consult. Those who use the New Kittredge and Modern Library/RSC series value them for performance work, given their attention to staging matters and production history.

Resources for Historical and Cultural Background

While the history plays can be read simply as great stories, students no doubt benefit from delving into the intricacies of early modern idiom as well as the other written histories that shaped Shakespeare's representations of events. This section will guide further study of those topics.

Language

Although most modern editions contain glossaries, they differ from one to another and cannot possibly address all questions students may have about language. Thus other resources should be enlisted. The third edition of E. A. Abbott's important nineteenth-century reference work, *A Shakespearean Grammar*, was reprinted as recently as 2003; the *Perseus Digital Library* offers it online. Jonathan Hope's *Shakespeare's Grammar*, commissioned by Arden as a replacement for Abbott, is more coherent and easier to use. Other resources include C. T. Onions and Robert D. Eagleson's *A Shakespeare Glossary* and David Crystal and Ben Crystal's *Shakespeare's Words: A Glossary and Language Companion*. The Crystals enhance study of the histories through attention to British dialects as well to places mentioned in the plays. The *Oxford English Dictionary* remains indispensable for researching etymology.

Those seeking commentary on Shakespeare's language can begin with Arden's *Reading Shakespeare's Dramatic Language: A Guide*, edited by Sylvia Adamson, Lynette Hunter, Lynne Magnusson, Ann Thompson, and Katie Wales. It contains sixteen essays exploring Shakespeare's rhetoric, including heightened language (Thompson), descriptiveness (William B. Carroll), narrative (Kastan), theatrical dimensions (Peter Lichtenfels), and linguistic variation, including regional dialects and sociolects for parsing differences among social classes (Wales). Wales's "A–Z of Rhetorical Terms" and an annotated guide to further reading complete the volume.

Shakespeare's Sources

Geoffrey Bullough's *Narrative and Dramatic Sources of Shakespeare* remains the first stop for source study. Volumes 3 and 4 discuss the histories and provide excerpts from chronicles, drama, and poetry. Students undertaking further research can consult Stuart Gillespie's *Shakespeare's Books: A Dictionary of Shakespeare's Sources*, Kenneth Muir's *Shakespeare's Sources*, Selma Guttman's *The Foreign Sources of Shakespeare's Works*, John W. Velz's *Shakespeare and the Classical Tradition*, and Emrys Jones's *The Origins of Shakespeare*, which devotes seven chapters to the histories.

These resources introduce readers to the material Shakespeare consulted. Holinshed's *Chronicles of England, Scotland, and Ireland* stands out as Shakespeare's principal source. *Early English Books Online (EEBO)* offers the full text in facsimile. Students also can access both the 1577 and 1587 texts, presented in parallel for easy comparison, through Oxford University's *The Holinshed Project*; students likely will find this edition more navigable than the basic HTML version at *Project Gutenberg*. For a modern print edition, Henry Ellis's six-volume edition of Holinshed was reprinted in 1965; Richard Hosley also compiled and edited the chronicles for a 1968 edition. Allardyce Nicoll and Josephine Nicoll's *Holinshed's Chronicle as Used in Shakespeare's Plays* presents excerpts corresponding to episodes in the plays, as does Walter George Boswell-Stone's *Shakespeare's Holinshed: The Chronicle and the Historical Plays Compared*.

Because the chronicles of "Holinshed" in fact reflect many different authorial hands, some supplementary guidance is recommended. Resources include Stephen Booth's *The Book Called* Holinshed's Chronicles, Annabel Patterson's *Reading* Holinshed's Chronicles, Igor Djordjevic's *Holinshed's Nation: Ideals, Memory, and Practical Policy in the Chronicles*, and *The Oxford Handbook of* Holinshed's Chronicles, edited by Paulina Kewes, Ian W. Archer, and Felicity Heal, which contains the essays "Shakespeare and Medieval History" (Djordjevic) and "Shakespeare and British History" (Richard Dutton). *The Holinshed Project* Web site also features a comprehensive introduction and a bibliography.

Another source for Shakespeare's histories is Edward Hall's *The Union of the Two Noble and Illustre Families of Lancastre and Yorke* (1550), which reflects the influence of earlier texts such as Polydore Vergil's *Anglica Historica* and Robert Fabian's *New Chronicles of England and France*. Hall chronicles Henry IV's accession, traces the ensuing conflict known as the Wars of the Roses, and concludes with the 1547 death of Henry VIII. The printer Richard Grafton extensively plagiarized his own *Chronicle* (1568) from Hall, making it possible that Shakespeare consulted it as well as, or even instead of, Hall. *Internet Shakespeare Editions* features a free peer-reviewed selection of Hall; *EEBO* offers the full text in digital facsimile. Those who prefer print can consult Ellis's complete edition.

In addition to Holinshed and Hall, scholars generally acknowledge Samuel Daniel's poem *The Civil Wars between the Two Houses of York and Lancaster* as a source for Shakespeare's second tetralogy, also known as the Henriad (*Richard II, 1* and *2 Henry IV*, and *Henry V*). Other sources for the Henriad include the antiquarian John Stow's *Chronicles of England* (1588) and *Annales of England* (1592), which contain apocryphal stories of Prince Hal's wild youth. The collection of poems compiled by William Baldwin and titled *A Myrroure for Magistrates* (1559), which didactically relates the fall of political figures from England's past, supplies material for *1 Henry IV* and *Richard III*. As a source for *Richard III*, Thomas More's 1513 *History of King Richard the Thirde* also offers a portrait of life under tyranny. Shakespeare's portrayal of the reigns of John and Henry VIII draws on John Foxe's Protestant martyrology *Acts and Monuments* (1583), popularly known as the *Book of Martyrs*.

Other Primary Texts

Because Shakespeare wrote during a vogue for chronicle history drama, Tudor plays by other writers helped shape his approach. Plays associated with the Henriad include the anonymous *The Life and Death of Jack Straw*, *Thomas of Woodstock* (also known as *Richard the Second Part One*), *The Famous Victories of Henry the Fifth*, Anthony Munday's *Sir John Oldcastle*, and Christopher Marlowe's *Edward II*. *Edmund Ironside; or, War Hath Made All Friends* has been linked to *3 Henry VI*. Thomas Legge's Latin play *Richardus Tertius* and the anonymous *True Tragedy of Richard III* may have alerted Shakespeare to Richard's potential as a dramatic villain. Scholars identify the anonymous *The Troublesome Reign of King John* as a probable source for Shakespeare's *King John*, although the plays display very different attitudes toward John's personality, his political legacy, and the significance of his reign for English Protestantism. Shakespeare also likely drew on John Bale's *King Johan*. While the exact relationship between these plays and Shakespeare's remains a matter of debate, incorporating them into the classroom can provide context for Shakespeare's handling of nation and kingship, as well as specific people and events. Comparison between plays also reveals the specificity of Shakespeare's own approach, showing his viewpoint to be one of many enacted on stage.

As for nondramatic influences, the survey respondents offer many recommendations. For understanding literary traditions and traditions of historiography, instructors might incorporate medieval texts such as the romances of Chrétien de Troyes, the *lais* of Marie de France, and Bede's *Ecclesiastical History of the English People*. All are regularly excerpted in British literature anthologies as well as available in modern English editions online. Tudor and Jacobean prose, poetry, and literary criticism can introduce students to issues of history, historiography, nostalgia, and anachronism. For example, *The Faerie Queene*, Edmund Spenser's medievalist epic, blends poetry and chronicle into a mythical account of the English nation; Philip Sidney's *Defence of Poesy* features a widely influential treatment of poetry versus history. Instructors who wish to convey the early modern political philosophies of royal absolutism and obedience to hierarchy can choose from a wide range of materials, including sermons like the "Homily against Disobedience and Wilful Rebellion" and political treatises such as James I's *True Law of Free Monarchies* and *Basilikon Doron* and John Ponet's *A Short Treatise of Politique Power*. Segments from Machiavelli's *The Prince* can provide an intellectual framework for Shakespeare's examination of political power and statecraft.

Scholarship on Primary Texts and Contexts

Several respondents recommend "Politics and Religion: Early Modern Ideologies" from Russ McDonald's *Bedford Companion to Shakespeare*. McDonald's overview of political power—defined as the mutually supporting relationship between religion and monarchy—samples a range of important primary texts, including Thomas Smith's *De Republica Anglorum*; Elizabeth I's "Tilbury Speech"; James I's "Speech to the Lords and Commons of the Parliament at Whitehall," "Secret Letter to Sir Robert Cecil," and "Letter to George Villiers, Duke of Buckingham"; John Harrington's "Letter Describing the Revels at King James's Court"; Machiavelli's *The Prince*; James I's *Basilikon Doron*; Simon Forman's *His Diary*; John Field and Thomas Wilcox's "An Admonition to the Parliament"; "The Catholics' Supplication" and "An Answer to the Catholics'

Supplication"; "An Homily against Disobedience and Willful Rebellion"; Richard Hooker's *Of the Laws of Ecclesiastical Polity*; and Phillip Stubbes's *Anatomy of Abuses*. McDonald's attention to royal counselors makes this resource particularly valuable, since counselors play critical roles in the histories.

Anthologies offer modern critical overviews to specific topics and plays. Dutton and Howard's *A Companion to Shakespeare's Works: The Histories* contains twenty-two essays introducing recent perspectives and methodologies, including archipelagic studies (Willy Maley), film (Peter J. Smith), gender studies (Rebecca Ann Bach), and reading practices (Siemon). Kastan's *A Companion to Shakespeare* includes essays titled "Shakespeare's Political Thought" (Martin Dzelzainis), "Political Culture" (David Harris Sacks), "The Shapes of History" (D. R. Woolf), and "Shakespeare and Genre" (Howard). Together, these essays introduce students to the political philosophies shaping the plays, tensions between governors and governed, and instabilities in the genre itself. Margreta de Grazia and Wells's *New Cambridge Companion to Shakespeare* also contains essays by individual scholars, including Ton Hoenselaars's piece on the histories, which covers the plays' authorship, their chronology, their historical and thematic scope, and the struggle they depict between dominant and marginal elements, including differences between Shakespeare's handling of these topics and those of his contemporaries. *The Cambridge Companion to Shakespeare's History Plays*, edited by Michael Hattaway, presents a range of approaches in essays on political and theatrical context (part 1) as well as close readings of the plays (part 2). The *Oxford Companion to Shakespeare*, edited by Michael Dobson and Wells, contains entries on all ten histories, their characters (from major ones such as Hal to minor figures such as Young Talbot and Simon Simpcox's wife), and places significant to the action.

Students frequently are curious about characters and their historical counterparts. W. H. Thomson's *Shakespeare's Characters: A Historical Dictionary* keys each entry to a list of plays, acts, and scenes where that character appears. The volume also features thirty-two genealogical tables, including all the English royal houses significant to the plays, the French kings and dauphins, the empire of Charles V, and Henry V's claim to the French crown. For a narrative account of the kings, with attention to Shakespeare's dramatic innovations, Peter Saccio's *Shakespeare's English Kings* remains a widely used resource. John Julius Norwich's *Shakespeare's Kings: The Great Plays and the History of England in the Middle Ages, 1337–1485* fills a similar niche with readable accounts of the late medieval reigns. For more details on the monarchs, Yale University Press's English Monarchs Series features biographies of nearly all the Plantagenets and Tudors: *Henry V* (Christopher Allmand), *Henry VII* (S. B. Chrimes), *Mary I* (John Edwards), *Edward III* (W. Mark Ormrod), *Edward IV* and *Richard III* (Charles Ross), *Richard II* (Nigel Saul), *Henry VIII* (J. J. Scarisbrick), and *Henry VI* (Bertram Wolffe). The New Oxford History of England offers three volumes placing the monarchs in political, social, religious, and economic context: Gerald Harriss's *Shaping the Nation: England, 1360–1461*, Michael Prestwick's *Plantagenet England, 1225–1360*, and Penry Williams's *The Later Tudors: England, 1547–1603*. Peter C. Herman's *Short History of Early Modern England* features a chapter, "From Richard II and Henry VII," that gives literature students necessary background on the histories' main players.

Other studies treating history and politics include Christine Carpenter's *The Wars of the Roses: Politics and the Constitution in England, c. 1437–1509*, Ernst Kantorowicz's *The King's Two Bodies: A Study in Medieval Political Theology*, F. J. Levy's *Tudor Historical Thought*, Carol Levin's *The Heart and Stomach of a King: Elizabeth I and the Politics of Sex and Power*, Linda Levy Peck's *Court Patronage and Corruption in Early Stuart England*, J. G. A. Pocock's *The Ancient Constitution and the Feudal Law: A Study of English Historical Thought in the Seventeenth Century*, A. J. Pollard's *The Wars of the Roses*, Lawrence Stone's *Crisis of the Aristocracy, 1558–1641*, and Joan Thirsk's *Economic Policy and Projects: The Development of a Consumer Society in Early Modern England*. Recommended works of literary history include David J. Baker and Maley's edited collection *British Identities and English Renaissance Literature*, Carroll's "Theories of Kingship in Shakespeare's England" (in Dutton and Howard's *Companion*), Jonathan Goldberg's *James I and the Politics of Literature: Jonson, Shakespeare, Donne, and Their Contemporaries*, Richard Helgerson's *Forms of Nationhood: The Elizabethan Writing of England* and "Writing Empire and Nation" (in *The Cambridge Companion to English Literature, 1500–1600*, edited by Arthur F. Kinney), and Annabel Patterson's *Censorship and Interpretation: The Conditions of Reading and Writing in Early Modern England*.

Critical Tradition

Because of the sheer amount of criticism on the histories, this section cannot be comprehensive. Instead, it will recommend specific texts and approaches for instructors to consider depending on their pedagogical goals. Those new to the plays may wish to begin with the critical companions discussed above; those volumes represent relatively recent scholarship.

Two studies that reinvigorated twentieth-century interest in the histories are E. M. W. Tillyard's *Elizabethan World Picture* (1944) and *Shakespeare's History Plays* (1946). In the former, Tillyard describes a Tudor worldview of a divinely ordained top-down hierarchy in which everything in the universe exists in vertical relation to everything else. His later volume demonstrates how the histories stress the necessity of divine order and degree, and Tillyard concludes that Shakespeare was sympathetic to the conservative social aims of "world picture" ideology. Another influential mid-twentieth-century study is Lily B. Campbell's *Shakespeare's Histories: Mirrors of Elizabethan Policy* (1947), which focuses primarily on Elizabethan conceptions of history as a source of wisdom. Campbell reads *King John, Richard II, Richard III, Henry IV,* and *Henry V* as reflections of Tudor thought about contemporary realities of rebellion, threatened usurpation, and war.

Critics since have exploded the providentialism outlined by Tillyard and Campbell by giving the idea of "history" itself a wider berth; some of the first to do so include Derek Traversi, Irving Ribner, Robert Ornstein, Michael Manheim, Edward I. Berry, Joseph A. Porter, and James Calderwood. This body of work uncovers different, but still "universal," values through close reading of language, pattern, and structure (Traversi, Ornstein, Calderwood, Porter) and links the plays, and by implication Shakespeare's thinking, to a range of historical patterns and influences, some of which reflect a sense of decay rather than the divine hand of Providence (Ribner, Manheim, Berry). For a succinct view of how the plays capture contradiction, Norman Rabkin's classic essay "Rabbits, Ducks, and *Henry V*" comes highly recommended by respondents. One respondent notes that Rabkin's sense of "the perception of reality as intransigently multivalent" (295) resonates with postmodern students, accustomed as they are to the play of "truths" across media.

The new historicism and cultural materialism of the early 1980s challenge earlier approaches in two major ways. First, under the influence of Michel Foucault's discursive analyses of culture, new historicists (such as Stephen Greenblatt, Louis Adrian Montrose, Steven Mullaney, and Stephen Orgel) and cultural materialists (such as Jonathan Dollimore, Alan Sinfield, and Graham Holderness) bring a keen interest in power, subversion, and material culture to early modern texts. Second, these critics place literary and nonliterary texts in the same analytic framework, a move inspired by the work of Hayden White, who approaches history in terms of narrative structure. The effect is to collapse the distinction between art and history in favor of putting all "texts" on a single continuum of discourse, each narrative telling a necessarily incomplete story. Power becomes responsive, manipulable, and, most of all, theatrical. Identity becomes performative and situational, rather than unitary or transcendent. Several survey respondents assign the work of Greenblatt, whose seminal *Renaissance Self-Fashioning* analyzes figures who find mobility within Tudor ideologies of "natural" social fixity. Greenblatt's classic "Invisible Bullets: Renaissance Authority and Its Subversion: *Henry IV* and *Henry V*" also comes highly recommended. The essay introduces the concepts of subversion and containment to describe how power both creates and contains its own demise. While new historicism tends to detect the eventual containment of subversive energies, cultural materialism focuses on human interventions, particularly those originating from marginal populations. Dollimore and Sinfield's collection *Political Shakespeare: Essays in Cultural Materialism* illustrates these commitments. In addition to its reprinted "Invisible Bullets," readers of the history plays also can consult Leonard Tennenhouse's "Tragedies of State and Political Plays: *A Midsummer Night's Dream, Henry IV, Henry V, Henry VIII*" and Sinfield's "Royal Shakespeare: Theatre and the Making of Ideology." Both essays apply cultural materialist analyses to such themes as statehood, monarchy, and political self-presentation.

Criticism of the late 1980s and 1990s reflects the influence of new historicism and cultural materialism, even as it departs from or argues with the movements' approaches to politics, power, and representation. Studies include Walter Cohen's *Drama of a Nation: Public Theater in Renaissance England and Spain*, Larry S. Champion's *Perspective in Shakespeare's English Histories* and *The Noise of Threatening Drum: Dramatic Strategy and Political Ideology in Shakespeare and the English Chronicle Plays*, Phyllis Rackin's *Stages of History: Shakespeare's English Chronicles*, Christopher Pye's *The Regal Phantasm: Shakespeare and the Politics of Spectacle*, Alexander Leggatt's *Shakespeare's Political Drama: The History Plays and the Roman Plays*, Robert C. Jones's *These Valiant Dead: Renewing the Past in Shakespeare's Histories*, Barbara Hodgdon's *The End Crowns All: Closure and Contradiction in Shakespeare's History*, Helgerson's *Forms of Nationhood*, and Paola Pugliatti's *Shakespeare the Historian*. These works present varying perspectives on Shakespeare's brand of history, whether seen as conservative and royalist, subversive and sympathetic to the marginal, or as a blend of perspectives.

Indeed, criticism after Tillyard takes history to be contested ground, where dominant and marginal narratives compete for articulation. To convey this idea to students, several respondents recommend two chapters from Kastan's *Shakespeare after Theory*: "'The King Hath Many Marching in His Coats'; or, What Did You Do in the War, Daddy?" and "Proud Majesty Made a Subject" (originally published in *Shakespeare Quarterly*). Kastan opposes formalist accounts that subordinate the tavern to the aristocracy in *1 Henry IV*, arguing that Falstaff refuses to be assimilated by the power of the unifying state, itself resting on a fantasy that kingship can truly represent power without also calling attention to its own inadequacy as representation. "Divine" kingship, in the hands of Henry V, emerges as something ultimately constructed, a thing founded and maintained by conquest, violence, and force—a fact that Henry V acknowledges to himself and uses, which therefore makes him successful.

Gender points the way toward further areas of contested history. Students and instructors interested in the roles of women are encouraged to begin with Rackin's essay in the *Cambridge Companion* and explore further the work of Howard and Rackin (especially the chapter on "Gender and Nation" in *Engendering a Nation*), Nina S. Levine (*Women's Matters: Politics, Gender, and Nation in Shakespeare's Early History Plays*), Katherine Eggert (*Showing Like a Queen: Female Authority and Literary Experiment in Spenser, Shakespeare, and Milton*), and Kathryn Schwarz (especially the chapter on the chronicle plays in *Tough Love: Amazon Encounters in the English Renaissance*). In addition to feminist scholarship, studies of masculinity illuminate the histories' preoccupation with heroism and honor. Useful readings include Dollimore and Sinfield's "History and Ideology, Masculinity and Miscegenation" (in Sinfield's *Faultlines: Cultural Materialism and the Politics of Dissident Reading*), Coppélia Kahn's *Man's Estate: Masculine Identity in Shakespeare* ("'The Shadow of the Male': Masculine Identity in the History Plays"), Bruce R. Smith's *Shakespeare and Masculinity*, and Jennifer A. Low's *Manhood and the Duel: Masculinity in Early Modern Drama and Culture*. Goldberg's chapter "Desiring Hal" (*Sodometries: Renaissance Texts, Modern Sexualities*) illuminates the figure of Hal as a monarch whose image depends in part on absorbing—and then discarding—the traits of the men around him, namely Hotspur and Falstaff. Smith's *Homosexual Desire in Shakespeare's England: A Cultural Poetics* also explores the Elizabethan sex-gender system—generally acknowledged as less stable than modern regimes—to account for relations between men as combatants, comrades, and knights. Alan Bray's *Homosexuality in Renaissance England* presents a series of models by which to study relations between men, deepening our sense of how the bonds that sustain patriarchy depend on economies of male-to-male desire and the subordination of the female.

Citizens, commoners, and the working classes also challenge official narratives of history, making lasting dramatic impact even when their efforts meet with defeat. While monarchy remains at the center of the history plays, Shakespeare does give popular elements a voice in them: Henry V's interrogation at the hands of Bates and Williams, Jack Cade's rebellion, the silent citizens refusing to cheer Richard of Gloucester's nomination, Londoners jeering at the disgraced Richard II, pirates executing the Duke of Suffolk, and of course the denizens of the Boar's Head Tavern. Much critical writing on these episodes appeared with the rise of social history and its attention to the domestic, the marginal, and the anecdotal. Recommended readings include Greenblatt's "Murdering Peasants: Status, Genre, and the Representation of Rebellion," Carroll's *Fat King, Lean Beggar: Representations of Poverty in the Age of Shakespeare* ("'The Perill of Infection': Vagrancy, Sedition, and 2 *Henry VI*"), Annabel Patterson's *Shakespeare and the Popular Voice*, Michael D. Bristol's *Carnival and Theatre: Plebeian Culture and the Structure of Authority in Renaissance Britain*, and the essays by Siemon, Carroll, and Cartelli in Richard Burt and John Michael Archer's *Enclosure Acts: Sexuality, Property, and Culture in Early Modern England*.

While England may occupy the center of Shakespeare's historical drama, the recent influence of British studies reminds us of England's status as an "imagined community" (to borrow Benedict Anderson's term) in close proximity with nearby others—namely Ireland, Scotland, Wales, and, directly across the Channel, France. Teachers and students can get an overview of British and archipelagic perspectives from Baker and Maley's *British Identities and English Renaissance Literature*, which features essays on Holinshed's treatment of Ireland (Richard McCabe), *Henry IV* (Matthew Greenfield), and Welshness in *Henry V* (Patricia Parker). These essays effectively dislocate the centrality of England and problematize the idea of the sovereign nation with stable borders. Teachers seeking to develop discussions of Welsh, Irish, and Scottish presences in the plays also can consult the work of Lisa Hopkins, Philip Schwyzer, and Michael Neill.

Over the past two generations, two Iraq wars and one in Afghanistan have vivified critical interest in war and military culture. Studies by Nina Taunton (*1590s Drama and Militarism: Portrayals of War in Marlowe, Chapman, and Shakespeare's* Henry V), Nick de Somogyi (*Shakespeare's Theatre of War*), Simon Barker (*War and Nation in the Theatre of Shakespeare and His Contemporaries*), and Patricia Cahill (*Unto the Breach: Martial Formations, Historical Trauma, and the Early Modern Stage*) examine underexplored primary materials—manuals, treatises, military correspondence, maps, and newsletters—detailing Elizabethan conversations about war, its technologies, and its ethics. These studies provide a material basis for studying the discursive and ideological nature of war and how wartime culture influenced the theater. The wars of recent decades also have reawakened the "just war" debate, versions of which appear from Shakespeare's lifetime all the way to our own. Pugliatti's *Shakespeare and the Just War Tradition* details the Tudor debate in the light of ongoing conflicts abroad. Her analysis not only bears directly on plays such as *Henry V* but also provides a bridge to the rhetoric of current justifications, showing how "just war" discourse carries and changes over time.

As Pugliatti shows, Tudor debates about war resonate with our own time and, therefore, in our classrooms. Several respondents express interest in the possibilities of presentist approaches for making Shakespeare's English histories relevant to modern students. Presentism represents an alternative to historicist reading, which treats the literary and cultural contexts of a text's original production, by refusing to privilege originary moments and instead studies each instantiation of a text over time, including the moment in which the critic writes. Readers may sample presentist approaches in Hugh Grady and Terence Hawkes's collection *Presentist Shakespeares*, which includes an essay by Ewan Fernie on *Henry V*. Evelyn Gajowski's collection *Presentism, Gender, and Sexuality in Shakespeare* offers a section titled "Politics/War," which focuses on military and masculine culture in the histories. *Shakespeare's English Histories and Their Afterlives*, edited by Peter Holland, attends to English histories in performance and in other contexts around the world.

New work comes out every year. Readers can consult the *World Shakespeare Bibliography Online* (published for *Shakespeare Quarterly*), *The Year's Work in English Studies*, the *Annual Bibliography of English Language and Literature*, and the *MLA International Bibliography* for the latest publications. *SEL's* annual review essay, "Recent Studies in Tudor and Stuart Drama," surveys new monographs, collections, and editions, situating them in a broader discussion of the field's current directions.

Performance

Theater, film, and television unfold the afterlives of the English histories. The best of them make convincing arguments for why these plays remain vital and important today. The increasing availability of productions on DVD and streaming video makes it easier than ever for instructors to incorporate performance into the classroom by juxtaposing several versions of the same scene, contrasting modern versus traditional adaptations, or having students watch, discuss, and write about entire productions.

Teachers who wish to assign a production sequence have two options. First is *Shakespeare's An Age of Kings*, produced by the BBC for live television in 1960, which presents the eight plays of the two tetralogies in order of their reigns (*Richard II*; *1* and *2 Henry IV*; *Henry V*; *1, 2*, and *3 Henry VI*; and *Richard III*). A valuable aid to viewing these productions is Susan Willis's *The BBC Shakespeare Plays: Making the Televised Canon*. Willis addresses the ways in which the series' directors take advantage of the television medium to interpret the material; notable directorial choices include repertory casting across the tetralogies, characters confiding directly to the camera, and battle scenes outside scripted dialogue.

While *An Age of Kings* represents an extraordinary achievement for its time, viewers accustomed to more recent recording technologies and acting styles might respond more readily to the BBC's *The Hollow Crown* (2012). This series covers the second tetralogy with one film-length episode per play. The *Richard II* episode, directed by Rupert Goold and widely regarded as the best of the four, features Ben Whishaw in a performance that earned him a BAFTA award for Best Leading Actor. The remaining three episodes, directed by Richard Eyre ("Henry IV, Part 1"; "Henry IV, Part 2") and Thea Sharrock ("Henry V"), while less highly praised, offer beautiful settings and musical scores alongside compelling performances by Simon Russell Beale (Falstaff), Jeremy Irons (Henry IV), and Tom Hiddleston (Prince Hal/Henry V). The six-part BBC series *Shakespeare Uncovered* features two episodes treating the *The Hollow Crown*'s production of *Richard II*, *Henry IV*, and *Henry V* (narrated by Derek Jacobi and Irons, respectively). These episodes make for good background viewing, as they situate the plays in discussions of each king's historical legacy as well as other important productions. Just before this volume's publication, a second series appeared, *The Hollow Crown: The Wars of the Roses*, with three episodes: two episodes devoted to the three *Henry VI* plays and a third episode covering *Richard III* (2016).

Apart from *An Age of Kings*, the first tetralogy has not been well served by film and television, *Richard III* being the exception. The 1912 *Richard III*, directed by Andre Calmettes and James Keane, is considered the first feature-length film adaptation of Shakespeare. Laurence Olivier's *Richard III* (1955) incorporates some elements of *3 Henry VI* into a production that popularized

Shakespeare for filmgoers. Two more films emerged in the 1990s: Al Pacino's documentary *Looking for Richard* and Richard Loncraine's *Richard III*, featuring Ian McKellen in the title role. *Looking for Richard* offers an entertaining take on the challenge of Shakespeare for American film and television actors working in the shadow of the British stage tradition. While hammy at times and prone to comically misguided decisions (such as substituting "C" for "G" in the prophecy impugning George Duke of Clarence), the film offers helpful perspective for students without a performance background. Loncraine's *Richard III* adapts the story to pre–World War II Britain, with Richard as would-be dictator complete with Hitler-like mustache and military uniform. As a pedagogical tool, the film encourages students to consider the business of adapting Shakespeare as a comment on specific historical moments.

Instructors seeking to incorporate film and video of the Henriad will find more choices. David Giles's *Richard II* (1978) appears in the BBC's *Complete Dramatic Works of William Shakespeare*, which also aired originally on television. Outstanding performances—Jacobi as a vain, petulant Richard and John Gielgud as an angry and embittered John of Gaunt—make this production one of the best of the history plays available on video. William Woodman's 1982 *Richard II*, performed on a bare stage by American actors, is less highly praised than Giles's production, but it still gives students the opportunity to witness a stage production if one cannot be seen nearby. Orson Welles's masterful *Chimes at Midnight* (1965) is the first adaptation of the Henriad to fully use the medium of film as distinct from live theater. Welles's reconstruction—arguably a more fitting term here than *adaptation*—centers on the *Henry IV* plays but also incorporates *Richard II*, *Henry V*, and *Merry Wives of Windsor*, with Ralph Richardson narrating from Holinshed's *Chronicles*. *Chimes at Midnight* influenced later films such as Gus Van Sant's *My Own Private Idaho* (1991). Van Sant loosely incorporates the Henriad into a story of two gay street hustlers; the complex friendship between Scott (the Hal figure, played by Keanu Reeves) and Mike (the Poins figure, played by River Phoenix) draws on the drama of Hal's betrayal of friendship in favor of a life better aligned with his father's vision.

Apart from *The Hollow Crown*, the two major *Henry V* films are those of Olivier (1944) and Kenneth Branagh (1989). Olivier's film, intended to boost British morale at the end of World War II, makes an excellent case study of how a production can speak to and reflect on the moment in which it is produced. Because theaters released it to coincide with the Allied invasion of Normandy, critics frequently dismiss it as jingoistic propaganda, especially since the film omits the play's less-than-flattering details (e.g., Henry's brutal threats at the gates of Harfleur, the hanging of Bardolph, and the mention of Henry VI's eventually losing of France). But these facts should not overshadow Olivier's achievement, as the popular and critically acclaimed production changed the status of Shakespeare on film, previously regarded as box office poison. The film adapts the play to several perspectives, from the opening and closing scenes at the Globe Theatre, to book of hours medieval compositions, to the panoramic scope of the Battle of Agincourt. Branagh's version, released around the time of the first Gulf War, offers a more critical take on Henry and the war, featuring a mud-spattered and violent Battle of Agincourt as counterpoint to Olivier's sunny and expansive scene. The Globe scenes of Olivier's film are replaced by Jacobi as Chorus, speaking of the deficiencies of the "wooden O" while strolling through a film set. Falstaff also appears in a flashback incorporating dialogue from the *Henry IV* plays.

Performance history and criticism provides insight into these and other productions. Hoenslaars's *Shakespeare's History Plays: Performance, Adaptation and Translation in Britain and Abroad* examines performance contexts from Ireland, Wales, France, Japan, Italy, Bulgaria, Belgium, and Spain, and also includes essays on Brecht and early modern historiography. Although the collection begins by considering matters of translation and appropriation, it moves toward treatments of Shakespeare as something to be taken on, even destroyed, by visionary contemporary artists. Among much else available, respondents single out two journal articles they find useful for teaching. Roberta Barker's essay on stage versions of Hotspur is the first. In this piece of performance history, Barker describes how Hotspur can be variously played as heroic, boorish, or even clownish depending on the needs of the moment, thus destabilizing Hotspur's heroicization as the brave face of chivalry in *1 Henry IV*. The second is Robert Lane's essay on Branagh's *Henry V*. Lane sees Branagh's production as flattening out the provocative questions about Henry's character and governance raised by Shakespeare. One respondent recommends teaching this essay alongside Kastan's "What Did You Do in the War, Daddy?" as a way to stimulate discussions about Shakespeare's ambiguous representations of kingly power. Teachers seeking to include performance also might consider Emma Smith's edition of *King Henry V*—which uses promptbooks, actors' memories, photographs, and reviews—from Cambridge's Shakespeare in Production series.

Textbooks and guides to teaching performance also abound, especially as instructors increasingly embrace "getting students on their feet." Volume 2 of the Folger Shakespeare Library's three-volume *Shakespeare Set Free* offers performance-based lesson plans for *1 Henry IV* (O'Brien). Edward L. Rocklin's *Performance Approaches to Teaching Shakespeare* covers three plays, *Richard III* being one. Rocklin emphasizes that the plays should be taught as theater as well as literature, particularly since performance approaches always return students to the text. For introducing students to Shakespeare on film, two resources stand out. First is Samuel Crowl's *Shakespeare and Film: A Norton Guide*, which serves as a fine introduction to film adaptation, presenting careful models of close reading, discussions of specific terms (supported by a glossary), and chapters devoted to influential directors (including Olivier, Welles, and Branagh). Second is from Kenneth S. Rothwell's *A History of Shakespeare on Screen: A Century of Film and Television*, a volume international in scope and updated in 2004.

Digital Resources

The Internet has revolutionized reading, writing, and research in favor of non-linear relationships between readers and writers, new structures of authority, and greater openness toward what counts as legitimate knowledge. But with this openness also come the perils of inaccuracy and even outright quackery. Bad Shakespearean texts proliferate on the Internet, with misinformation about these texts, their author(s), and the cultures that produced them. This unreliability may account, at least in part, for why most respondents balk at assigning an Internet edition as the main classroom text, although a handful report using online texts as supplementary resources for editing work, for comparing quartos and folios, or for examining facsimiles. The general reluctance also may reflect bewilderment at the sheer volume of options, as well as uncertainty about how to gauge quality in a relatively new medium. Much scholarship addressing these questions has emerged from the field's recent turn toward textuality and away from the search for an authoritative Shakespeare. The "Contemporary Media" section of part 2 will provide some examples of how to bring digital texts into the classroom; Hugh Macrae Richmond's essay in the "Guide to Internet Resources" section at the end of part 2 offers an overview of material available on the Web. Here, I add to those resources by sharing supplementary information from the survey.

While ten respondents report using a digital edition in some capacity, only half mention one by name: *Internet Shakespeare Editions* (*ISE*). Under the general editorship of Michael Best, *ISE* has established scholars—including Bevington, Helen Ostovich, Anthony Dawson, and Paul Yachnin—as well as younger scholars editing individual plays. The site provides an advanced search tool for concordance work as well as contextual information on Shakespeare's life and early modern theater (including a directory of sites on Shakespeare and the Renaissance), bibliographies, and an archive of performance information. The actual texts and their critical apparatus, however, remain in various states of completion as of this writing. While the site provides old-spelling editions for all the plays, it only offers modern editions for some plays. Some come with an abundance of additional features, while others do not. For example, James Mardock's edition of *Henry V* includes modernized and old-spelling editions of both quarto and folio, as well as a general introduction, chronology, family tree, supplementary materials (including excerpts of Holinshed, Hall, Lyly, and Drayton), and a list of performances and performance artifacts. Catherine Lisack's edition of *Richard II* also offers modern and old-spelling editions, facsimiles, and performance histories, yet with a far less comprehensive editor's introduction. No one seems to be working on the *Henry VI* texts at the time of this writing. As a whole, *ISE* shows real attempts at standardization, even if those attempts, predictably enough, seem weighted toward the more popular history plays.

ISE's Queen's Men Editions also can aid in the study of history plays. Under Ostovich's general editorship, the series provides electronic editions of plays owned or performed by the Queen's Men, including *Famous Victories of Henry V*, *The Troublesome Reign of King John*, and *The True Tragedy of Richard III*. The site also links texts to production resources and images wherever possible, demonstrating a current trend in electronic editions that highlights the relation between text and performance.

Open Source Shakespeare, a site built on the principles of "power, flexibility, friendliness, and openness," features the full range of history plays and superior search tools for concordance work, even if, because of copyright laws barring the use of modern editions, it does use the old Globe edition of Shakespeare from the nineteenth century. (This standard Internet edition also appears in two relatively primitive sites that come up at the top of *Google* searches: James Matthew Farrow's *The Works of the Bard* and Jeremy Hylton's *The Complete Works of William Shakespeare*.) *Folger Digital Texts*, based on the Folger editions, offers a search tool; a tool allowing readers to jump to act, scene, or line numbers; page numbers from the print edition; and the "Folger through Line Numbers" (FTLN) that number each line sequentially. The site also makes its source code available for noncommercial projects.

Web sites facilitating general Shakespeare study are numerous and of varying quality, but a few recommendations will help readers get started. The well-curated Web site *The Shakespeare Resource Center* offers annotated links on Shakespeare's biography, language, the Globe, theater companies, Elizabethan England, and resources for study. *PlayShakespeare.com*, "the ultimate free Shakespeare resource," offers massive amounts of material. Users who register can access synopses, character lists, scenes, and related documents for all the plays and poems (including apocrypha such as *Edward III* and *Double Falsehood*), as well as a discussion forum, podcasts, video, a directory of theater companies and festivals, reviews, and a glossary. *Shakespeare's Staging: Shakespeare's Performance and His Globe Theatre*, from the University of California, Berkeley, offers performance bibliographies of individual plays, annotated image galleries, video clips, and links to forty other sites about Shakespeare in performance.

Part Two

APPROACHES

Introduction

Laurie Ellinghausen

Why teach Shakespeare's English histories? That was the primary question posed to survey respondents, who answered it with arresting clarity and conviction. One colleague points out that to ignore the histories in favor of more accessible fare is to ignore one-third of Shakespeare's total output. Another insists that the vogue for history plays and history writing in late Tudor England makes the histories Shakespeare's most popular and impactful work. As such, they merit special pedagogical consideration. Another respondent articulates the plays' importance for understanding both Shakespeare and early modern cultural life:

> The history plays are an important part of Shakespeare's own development and a reflection of the larger evolution of early modern theater. History plays are directly related to early modern educational practices and reflect Shakespeare's early responses to his fellow playwrights and his audiences.

Additionally, many respondents embrace the histories' usefulness in making students savvy readers of historical narrative, a skill important not only for reading history plays and their sources but for parsing the cultural narratives shaping our present moment. The histories, more than any other dramatic genre, demonstrate "how politics weave into 'everyday' life and affect 'ordinary' people." The plays' relevance to political life, in all its complexity, draws students into "the multivalent nature of these plays, by what Annabel Patterson has termed 'functional ambiguity,' the ways the plays may be speaking from truth to power but always in ways that allow some form of deniability." Above all, respondents feel that the histories contain some of the best Shakespeare has to offer—famous soliloquies, fascinating perspectives on real figures, stunning poetry interspersed with lively comedy, and the pathos of intergenerational civil war. As Gail Kern Paster comments in the video series *Shakespeare Uncovered*, *1 Henry IV* is one of "the greatest plays Shakespeare ever writes" because "it's got so much for the actors . . . so much for the audience," including "some trace element" from nearly every other play he wrote.

Yet respondents were equally eloquent on the histories' challenges for students. Typically, students lack familiarity with the genre and know only "the reputation that histories have for boredom and difficulty." Another instructor elaborates:

> With tragedies, students seem to come to class knowing they are important and that they will be good. With comedies, students seem to have

fewer preconceived ideas. With history plays, it just seems like students don't see why they will want to read them or understand them as much.

Confusion joins this reluctance once students delve into the plays' intricate plotting and characterization, much of which relies on historical knowledge that Shakespeare's audiences possessed but that modern students do not. Much class time gets spent sorting out their primary questions: "who are all these people and what is going on?" Indeed, one respondent recently spent two hours disentangling the "Edward's sacred blood" genealogy printed in the *Riverside Shakespeare*, trying to help her baffled students work through "the broad cast of characters and the broad range of events." The histories deal with long-term and long-over events, as multiple Henrys, Edwards, and Richards war over something as archaic as a crown. Even the stakes of these battles can be lost on modern students. As one respondent observes, "The transfers of power and the overlapping political systems are difficult for them to grasp, especially given residual and emergent elements of feudalism, primogeniture, etc." In contrast to the "universal" themes of the more familiar comedies and tragedies, the histories seem to speak a time-bound foreign language.

These responses, which encapsulate both the histories' rewards and challenges, permeate *Approaches to Teaching Shakespeare's English History Plays* and drive its purpose, which is to offer pedagogical groundwork that instructors may adapt to their own needs. The selection of essays required taking up the thorny issue of history as a genre that, at least in Shakespeare's hands, seems to challenge the idea of genre itself. Bawdy jests juxtapose poetic dramas of kingship and state, as comic and tragic conventions mix in historical retellings. The plays, furthermore, contain many linguistic registers, from high lyricism to tavern slang, from English insults to Welsh songs. "These linguistic hurdles appear in other plays, of course," writes one instructor, "but in these other plays the density or obscurity of the language often becomes part of the allure of the characters with whom the students otherwise feel certain connections." In addition to the language, students encounter the diversity of historical writing itself. The plays' amalgamation of different kinds of history—medieval *fabulae*, urban history, chronicle history, classical allusion, and typological biblical history, to cite some examples—frustrates generic classification. As one respondent proposes, these plays "are not necessarily a genre in their own right but a display of Shakespeare's interest in genres." Certainly the Roman plays (including *Cymbeline*), *Macbeth*, and *King Lear* can be claimed as historical, and several essays here reference them as points of comparison. Furthermore, throughout the corpus of early modern drama, title pages featuring phrases such as "comical history" regularly appear. The main goal of this volume, however, is to address the unique features of the English chronicle plays, as these plays receive less classroom attention than those typically classified as comedy and tragedy. We aim to offer user-friendly, specific approaches, examples, assignments, and resources, which would not be possible with a broader focus. The pages that follow outline the main sections of part 2 and show how the essays form cohesive units, if not uniform arguments, addressing particular methods and concerns.

Among the English histories, certain ones—*Richard III, Richard II, 1* and *2 Henry IV,* and *Henry V*—are more likely to be taught than others—*1, 2,* and *3 Henry VI; King John;* and *Henry VIII.* Readers will notice that the first group receives more attention than the second, because most contributors and survey respondents have drawn on their own experiences with the tetralogies. Yet readers seeking guidance on the less taught plays will nonetheless find suggestions here. The essays by Glenn Odom, M. G. Aune, Phyllis Rackin, and Ronda Arab all focus on those plays; Hugh Macrae Richmond lists resources for them; and the suggestions in nearly every essay can be applied to plays outside the ones immediately addressed. We hope these approaches will not only expand teachers' options for *Richard III* and the Henriad but will inspire them to consider teaching the other histories as well.

For some contributors, and quite a few survey respondents, it makes sense to begin by immersing students in that "foreign" language endemic to the histories: that is, in the idioms of early British life. Timelines and genealogical charts outline basic plots and relationships, but these tools cannot illuminate the cultural and political contexts that made the plays compelling for audiences. One approach is to consider Shakespeare not only as a writer but as a reader of printed material that proliferated during the Tudor rage for history. This emphasis shows, in Peter C. Herman's words, Shakespeare's "imagination in action" as well as the "range of interpretations" open to him. This collection, therefore, opens with "Primary Sources," which describes ways to teach the plays in tandem with the chronicles and other historical texts. Odom begins the section by describing his course on the history plays and early modern historiography. Reading a wide range of texts understood by early moderns as historical—such as Walter Raleigh's *History of the World,* John Foxe's *Acts and Monuments,* Thomas More's *History of King Richard III,* Thomas North's translation of Plutarch's *Lives,* and Herodotus's *Histories*—Odom's students discover history as something always in process and actively negotiated. Likewise the plays demonstrate not one, but many approaches to history, as Odom's students learn when they read the collection of vignettes informing *Henry VIII.*

In Odom's example, history becomes not just one authoritative account but a convergence of multiple narratives. The dynamism of overlapping and even competing versions invites students into the central debates of Elizabethan political life. These "arguments of the histories," one respondent observes, stem from enduring questions: "What makes a good ruler? What are the ruler's responsibilities to his subjects?" In the next two essays, Aune and Herman show that the plays' ambiguity on these subjects stems from the sources themselves, texts that variously display what another respondent calls the "dangers" of writing history in a censorious age. Aune's lessons on *King John* ask students to investigate the play's seeming confusion about the deaths of two principal characters—King John and his nephew, Prince Arthur. Reading corresponding passages from Holinshed's *Chronicles* and Foxe's *Acts and Monuments*, Aune's students learn that the play's apparent inconsistencies in fact reflect differences among historians. Students soon realize that Shakespeare's artistic choices are shaped by, and responsive to, the political and philosophical questions that define the historical moment. By juxtaposing chronicle accounts of Richard II from Holinshed and Edward Hall, Herman shows Richard's attachment to divine right in Shakespeare's play was only one point of view in a larger debate about the ancient constitution and the role of "the people" (itself a debated term) in conferring authority. Together, these essays illustrate a shift from mundane questions of "what really happened" to a deeper discussion about, in the words of one respondent, "who gets to write history and what the goals of history writing, either as prose or drama, might be."

The next section, "Political, Intellectual, and International Contexts," expands the historiographical focus to encompass a broader selection of primary texts and cultural phenomena. Many respondents recommend the use of historical documents to create a sense of context; the essays in this section demonstrate several ways to do so. In the first essay, William A. Oram and Howard Nenner describe a team-taught course that uses an array of primary materials on the topics of authority and legitimacy as they unfold in the Henriad and *Richard III*. Jonathan Hart follows with an exploration of rhetoric in the history plays, placing a special emphasis on tracing the relation between rhetoric and theatricality. "Acting and performance are part of politics and history," Hart writes, and students who read the history plays receive an intensive education in the performativity of politics. In the next essay the focus shifts to early modern philosophical tradition. Here Mary Janell Metzger employs Montaigne to introduce the topic of skepticism and apply skeptical reading to the crumbling foundations of authority in *Richard III*. Metzger's use of Montaigne in the classroom prompts students to connect *Richard III* to the history of influential ideas circulating in Europe during Shakespeare's lifetime.

Next, Matthew J. Smith tackles the dense, but undoubtedly key, topic of religion's influence on the histories. While acknowledging that one could teach religion in a topical way, by connecting the plays to specific religious events, Smith offers a series of exercises to help students explore the "characterological, dramaturgical, and philosophical" uses that Shakespeare makes of religion, uses that deeply inform how Shakespeare draws his historical characters. Kathleen Kalpin Smith presents Hal in a similar, but slightly different, vein; returning to the concept of political self-presentation, Smith offers Hal as a rich study in "the difficulty of knowing a person's true identity, especially when that person attempts to manipulate the way that others view him."

While England is the apparent subject of the histories, David J. Baker and Barbara Sebek remind us that the world of the history plays is in fact much larger. This expansion corrects conceptions of the plays as insular, revealing instead that they engage not only multiple temporalities but territories beyond English borders. One respondent, speaking to the struggle to give students a sense of meaningful context, suggests "map[ping] out major spaces" to help students understand the genre's engagement with nationhood as physical space. "Start with a map," Baker similarly advises, referencing the scene in *1 Henry IV* where the rebels pore over their own map, dividing up imagined future spoils. To teach students about "the matter of Britain," as it figures throughout the Henriad, is to reveal something crucial about the mindset of the characters, who view "British" land not just as an arbitrary set of borders but as a political construct under continual revision. Sebek expands the plays' geographical reach even further to include "global consciousness," a discursive framework that reflects early modern England's increasing involvement in worldwide trade. Sebek recommends sections from the second edition of the *Norton Shakespeare*, critical readings, and podcasts to give students a sense of England's global reach and equip them with a perspective that raises new and provocative questions about what "national identity" actually signified in Shakespeare's time.

While the first two sections offer teachers and students things to talk about and ways to talk about them, the section "Theory and Criticism" develops methodology in greater detail. The survey results indicate that assigning literary criticism remains a widespread practice; however, instructors hope to have students develop independent insight about both the plays and the published commentary addressing them. Likewise, Neema Parvini's essay expresses a commitment to helping students grow beyond passive and obsequious consumers of criticism toward thoughtful evaluators of the scholarly "authorities" they might otherwise simply quote in their essays. Arguing that "students learn best through reaching their own conclusions rather than through the repetition of someone else's," Parvini describes a structure that allows students to arrive at their own discoveries about the plays' treatment of history, politics, and power; this strategy, Parvini reports, yields higher quality discussion and writing than when he began by lecturing on the historicist work of Althusser, Foucault, Greenblatt, Dollimore, and Sinfield. Lynne Bruckner's essay brings a different kind of critical awareness—that is, a critical evaluation of the present—to bear on students' reading of the histories. Bruckner describes a presentist approach to teaching *Richard II* in which she places the king's wasteful habits into dialogue with the local practice of hydraulic fracturing—or "fracking"—thus bringing ecocriticism to bear on her teaching of the play as well.

Phyllis Rackin opens the next section, "Gender," by exploring the roles of women in the histories. Several survey respondents view the lack of well-drawn female roles as an obstacle to teaching the histories. Rackin argues, however, that focusing on the women—including, crucially, Joan of Arc and Margaret of Anjou from the *Henry VI* plays—"offers unique opportunities to explore issues central to the dynamics of the plays and to the historical contexts in which the plays were first produced and subsequently reproduced." These powerfully transgressive figures, when examined alongside the relatively passive female characters in *Richard III* and the second tetralogy, show how representations of women change between the two tetralogies and over the course of the 1590s.

In the next three essays, Rebecca Ann Bach, Ronda Arab, and Joyce Green MacDonald examine the gendered relations that underwrite social and political bonds. Noting "how immediately queer social and sexual relations appear in [the histories] if they are looked at carefully," Bach guides her students through readings of *Richard II* that destabilize today's familiar categories of heterosexual, homosexual, and bisexual. Mining students' natural fascination with the charismatic Jack Cade, Arab contextualizes the artisan rebels in *2 Henry VI* in early modern anxieties about working men—their unruly masculinity, their brawn, and their alleged restiveness. MacDonald's essay examines the bonds between men—specifically, the relationships between sons and fathers—to alert students to the themes of memory and memorialization so key to Shakespeare's histories. In their respective ways, these essays illustrate the role of gender in creating, sustaining, and disrupting political systems. They also highlight the plays' preoccupation with the themes of heroism and masculine identity.

The next section, "Teaching through Research, Writing, and Performance," echoes Parvini's goal of stimulating independent thought but develops it in new directions. Joshua Calhoun, Paula Marantz Cohen, Yu Jin Ko, and Patricia Marchesi activate student insights into the reading by having students create scholarly and artistic productions of their own. Calhoun structures student research with specific exercises that guide students into archives and bibliographical resources, familiarize students with these tools, ease students into their own original insights, and translate those insights into essays that draw on original discoveries rather than hastily digested criticism. In addition to various kinds of writing, student performances remain popular among the survey respondents; Cohen, Ko, and Marchesi offer ideas about how to structure such assignments. Cohen describes a successful three-term course, taught with faculty members in theater, that brings students from reading to dramaturgy to their own performance of the *Henry IV* plays. Political calculation informs Yu Jin Ko's take on Richard III, a character that deploys complicated rhetorical tropes in his version of the recognizably modern art of the "sell." Ko's classroom strategy combines close reading as well as performance study. Marchesi also uses performance to investigate politics, inviting students to think of Hal and Hotspur as "candidates" with specific ideological platforms—as well as campaign posters and slogans—presenting themselves to skeptical audiences. All four instructors maintain that these approaches helped transform students from passive readers to creative interpreters.

The contributors in this volume regularly draw on film, streaming video, and Internet editions to facilitate their teaching. Likewise, nearly all the survey respondents report relying on video and the Internet to some degree. These are media with which students are already familiar, although students do not necessarily possess a working vocabulary for discussing film as a unique performance medium. While the essays throughout this volume regularly reference film, the first two essays in "Contemporary Media" focus on film and television by homing in on the particularities of the media. Covering adaptations of *1 Henry IV*, Maya

Mathur and Lisa Siefker Bailey treat film and television productions as artistic visions in their own right—an important corrective given many undergraduates' initial expectation that productions be "faithful to the text." Their respective approaches stress editing, camera angles, and other features that uncover unique perspectives—relations between monarch and subject in Mathur's case, relations between men in Bailey's—on the play's much-discussed characters. Catherine E. Thomas carries the politics of adaptation into the digital realm with a series of assignments asking students to analyze and catalog political cartoons of figures such as Richard III, Henry V, and Cardinal Wolsey. Her lessons, which speak to the several dozen respondents who express interest in incorporating visual imagery into the classroom, not only draw on artistic and political revisions of Shakespeare but also teach students to be critical readers—and users—of new media and innovations in bibliography. Christy Desmet follows by describing lessons that use digital editions of Holinshed's *Chronicles* and John Foxe's *Acts and Monuments* and bring the ancient question of Falstaff's true historical identity to the forefront while showing why it matters. Vimala C. Pasupathi writes of how she took advantage of Hofstra University's hosting of the 2012 United States Presidential debates to present the Henriad through word cloud tools that reveal thematic preoccupations by highlighting the reoccurrence of certain words. If students are put off by the historical distance of the Wars of the Roses, they undoubtedly understand the relevance of the digital. These innovative scholarly tools invite them into scholarship through a medium they already know.

In the next section, "Classroom Contexts," three contributors demonstrate possibilities for teaching the histories in special or nontraditional situations. The goal of this section is not to showcase these particular settings so much as to stimulate dialogue and complicate common assumptions about where the histories best fit within certain curricula and academic settings. Caroline McManus's essay proposes that "Shakespeare's English histories, frequently assumed to be arcane and inaccessible to students, may be, paradoxically, even more likely to engage them than the tragedies." McManus tests this thesis in her Shakespeare for Teachers course, where undergraduates pursuing single-subject credentials in English experiment with strategies that surpass the "tedious genealogical charts and convoluted narratives" that stereotype these plays. Diane K. Jakacki and Ruben Espinosa also find that special contexts cast fresh light on teachers' as well as students' perspectives. Jakacki recounts the challenge of teaching the histories both in a first-year composition course and to students majoring in the STEM disciplines with ostensibly little investment in studying the humanities. Espinosa's essay, which describes the experience of teaching *Henry V* to first-generation Americans at the University of Texas, El Paso, uncovers fascinating differences among student populations that do not all understand the concept of "nation" in the same way.

The volume concludes with a "Guide to Internet Resources" from Hugh Macrae Richmond, director of the *Shakespeare's Staging* digital project at the

University of California, Berkeley. Richmond's comprehensive survey includes specific resources for teaching all ten histories.

While each contributor in this book shares what has worked, many also describe what has not worked and what they learned from it. Their stories confirm that good teaching is an experiment that calls for continual revisitation and refinement. *Approaches to Teaching Shakespeare's English History Plays* offers reflections in this spirit, while at the same time eagerly anticipates discoveries yet to come.

Unless otherwise noted, all citations from Shakespeare's history plays are from the *Norton Shakespeare*, second edition.

Shakespeare's History Plays and Historiography

Glenn Odom

When reading the *Norton Shakespeare*'s introduction to *Henry VIII*, I was struck by Stephen Greenblatt's suggestion of the political implications of the play's historiographic modes (3111). For Greenblatt, there is an unresolvable ambiguity between the contrasting political projects implied by the different modes of history. Greenblatt's introduction suggests both the value and difficulty in reading Shakespeare's plays in the light of historiographic practice.

The potentially unanswerable question of how to deploy varying historiographic practices in the plays' political frameworks provides the perfect ground for an upper-division class. This course examined different Elizabethan and Jacobean historiographic modes, analyzed how these modes were staged in various history plays, and charted the political implications of the genre's evolution between the two monarchs (particularly considering that the genre arguably died out with *Perkin Warbeck* and that Shakespeare only wrote one English history play under the reign of King James).

I taught the class as an exploration where I was also actively engaged in its questions. I opened with the premise that, in addition to whatever specific political, social, and emotional critiques a history play might make, what united this genre was a critique of the idea of history itself, and that such critiques are necessarily political in some manner. I presented this claim as a hypothesis alongside materials students could use in combatting or supporting this hypothesis.

A significant portion of the course was devoted to reading primary historical documents, but we also read a selection of Shakespeare's plays (the Henriad,

Richard III, Henry VIII, and, for potential contrast, *Julius Caesar* and *Macbeth*); plays by Christopher Marlowe and John Ford; and Anthony Munday and others' *Sir John Oldcastle* (as a piece of the Shakespeare apocrypha). These readings helped students home in on potentially distinctive qualities of Shakespeare's history plays and of the genre, as well as potential changes in the genre over time.

The course's value was not in the conclusions we reached, however, but in the process. This course taught students about the nature of historiography as opposed to history, about using primary sources, about incorporating theory into their writing, and, most important, about the vast terrain of questions that remain unanswered in our field. Because the generic features of the history play remain underexplained, they make a perfect vehicle for experiencing the joy of discovery and exploration. This course positioned undergraduates as producers rather than consumers of knowledge.

The course examined historiographic practice in early modern England through texts written or studied during the period, including Walter Raleigh's *History of the World*, Thomas North's translation of Plutarch's *Lives of the Noble Greeks and Romans*, Thomas More's *History of King Richard III*, John Foxe's *Book of Martyrs*, Holinshed's *Chronicles*, such classical histories as Herodotus's *The Histories* and a brief selection of Thucydides, and philosophical texts that deployed the concept of history without claiming to be histories such as Machiavelli's *Discourses on Livy* and St. Augustine's *City of God*. We also focused on connections between theater and history by reading Philip Sidney's *The Defense of Poesy*, the medieval *A Treatise on Miracles Playing*, and Aristotle's *Poetics*. The goal was to compile diverse selections from the "greatest hits" list that Shakespeare's contemporaries would have been most likely to read. I noted that I had tried to select one text from each major "school" of history and encouraged students to challenge these classifications.

Through the first half of the class, each session was divided between a brief introductory lecture, some guided questions, and then free discussion among the students (generally starting with the question, What did you notice in this reading?). The students posed and answered questions such as the following: What is the boundary between explicitly political tracts in the vein of Machiavelli and less explicitly political histories like Holinshed's *Chronicles*? Where is the boundary between a book like Foxe's *Acts and Monuments*, which might be considered history, and St. Augustine's *City of God*, which is often read as a religious tract? Both texts are clearly driven by spiritual impulses, yet both generate a conception of history.

Thus, for each text in this section, we began with the ontological and functional questions "what is this?" and "what does it do?" With the first few texts, students wanted to critique these ideas of history (e.g., it is foolish to assume history can be told through vignettes of great men because the common man is "obviously" part of history) before they had completely articulated what these ideas were (e.g., why did history focus on great men?). By the end of the semester, however, they were able to read a text's position in a discursive field as well as its specific content. While working through passages from Raleigh, the class had an epiphany: Raleigh did not have a precise answer to the questions we were posing any more than we did. History and historiography, for early modern England, were concepts in flux, in development. While the classical tradition provided some models, these models were hardly taken as gospel.

From this hard-won epiphany the students realized that Shakespeare's history plays would have to position themselves amid these various arguments. The class synthesized the historiographic debate into a provisional taxonomy—an epistemological rather than an ontological taxonomy—that described a fluid, nonexclusive, overlapping set of categories. This taxonomy was created at the midpoint in the semester, when I asked each student to explain how one of the texts we read treated history. After students presented on the texts, we worked as a group to organize the important points of these presentations. The student-created taxonomy that follows preserves contradictory impulses of the historiographic modes we studied. It provided us with a vocabulary we used to determine what counted as a history play and what sort of history was in these plays. Since the students created this list, they were able to deploy it with much more fluency than they would have with anything that I provided for them. We then returned to some of the history plays we had read earlier and analyzed them anew with this tool.

Student-Created Taxonomy

Great Man Theory (see Machiavelli, Herodotus, North/Plutarch, and Foxe): This is the familiar concept that history is shaped by great individuals taking actions worthy of imitation. Simultaneously, however, these people are participating in a specific, special moment in history; thus the possibility for emulation is muted. In its purest form, the actions and virtues of the "great man" are not contingent on the historical moment: the great man's greatness would have made him great at any time. We discussed the connection of action to virtue (with Aristotle firmly in mind) and debated how we could figure out which were the truly great actions and which were imitations.

Unknowable Teleology (see Augustine): This understanding of history is based on the idea that God has a plan. We can only retroactively understand the plan's function, and even this understanding is provisional. This led not only to the standard fate versus free will debates but also to discussions of the simultaneity of history (if God can see it all, is it all occurring at once? is the synchronicity across seemingly unrelated locales? etc.).

Knowable Teleology (see Raleigh, Herodotus, and Foxe): This mode of history advocates the idea that God has a plan and we can understand it as it unfolds if we work hard enough. We can understand it because the entire world reflects the unfolding of a singular historical truth. Discovering this mode of history in Raleigh led us on a quest to find early modern history plays based on the lives of everyday citizens rather than the nobility (if history is all around us, it is the story of "us" and not just great men): John Ford's *Perkin Warbeck* (1634) provided an interesting case, given its status as one of the final history plays of the era, the critical reception arguing that it is an "antihistory," and the fact that its plot explicitly focuses on the line between commoner and noble. *Perkin Warbeck* was not initially on the syllabus, but, given the class's interest in pursuing this matter, we added it.

Multivocal History (see Holinshed): In what some of my students argued was a direct contrast to the singularity of the two teleological modes of historiography, this mode argues that history is the compilation of all possible opinions on a subject. It is not one narrative but many, even if such narratives are collected by a single writer. Discussing this mode led us to question the extent to which the history plays are uni- or multivocal (in terms of authorship—as in Holinshed—and in terms of plot) and to examine Shakespeare and others' *Sir Thomas More* as a potential example of multivocality.

Empirical History (see Herodotus, Machiavelli, and More): This historiographic mode argues that history is a series of precise events that can be observed, recorded, and used to make further predictions. There are limited possibilities and variables, many of which we can control. Students debated the place of God in such a framework.

History as Action (see Aristotle and Sidney): This idea circulates through several of the above modes and claims that history is nothing more or less than a series of actions—it is not leading anywhere "meaningful" beyond the effects of actions. This action may be reproduced in artistic forms. One acts in reproducing action, and thus art has the power to recreate history. This active art is stronger than reinterpretation and only possible if history is contained in a series of actions. Art can make us better (or worse) than we are by changing history. As with some of the theologically grounded readings of history, students found this conception foreign and difficult to articulate.

History as Recorded Action (see More): This is essentially a subset of the above mode, but it insists that history is the written—and therefore interpreted and shaped—version of action. In writing and shaping the action, one shapes history.

De casibus / Moral History (see Foxe and North): We discussed the notion that history is essentially a listing of moral vignettes—self-contained episodes that each make a moral point. Students recognized a conflict between the moral vignette and the strong teleology of Augustine.

"Medical" History: At the repeated insistence of one student, we added this category to suggest that, while we hadn't read anything that explicitly linked science to history, scientific metaphors (the four humors, for instance) might be found as explanations for the overall functioning of history.

The final category above suggests one of the limitations and joys of this exploration. I had to select many of the texts in advance, and most of the additions to the syllabus were from a list of texts that I had read to prepare for the class. By the end of the semester, the students were trained to consider everything for themselves rather than accept the received wisdom and thus began to question, and research, the extent to which I had accurately represented the field. They pointed out that early modern studies of history were often paired with an interest in the sciences. Some combination of Cicero, Galen, and the Scholastics would fill this gap in the syllabus should I teach this class again.

There was an additional, unexpected step in the learning process. As we began to read our first plays, the students were able to pick out elements of these historical modes. The difficulty, however, was that, despite our class's dynamic construction of historiographic practices, these practices became static for the students in their application. Students were participating in a process of matching play to practice without being able to articulate what was at stake. While we were able to debate the merits of each historiographic mode abstractly, the students had difficulty imagining the plays as doing anything other than representing one or more of them—2 *Henry IV* became an emblem of great man history. To move students away from this notion of static representation to something more analytic, I encouraged them to list the ideas or paradoxes that they could use to critique the above modes of history. In other words, I asked the students to anticipate the historiographic critiques the plays might make. After we expanded our taxonomy to include these paradoxes, we read *Henry VIII*, and the students were able to recognize the disjointed nature of the play as a critique of historiographic practice: the *De casibus* mode of history limits any attempt at teleology and, by stringing together vignettes in a single play, Shakespeare calls attention to this fact.

Once *Henry VIII* opened the floodgates, the students began to apply a number of tensions in the historiographic practices to our readings. The students' evolving list of paradoxes included a number of ideas: that God's plan might have to allow for bad events; that God has a plan versus that individual actions matter (fate versus free will); that time is cyclical versus changeable; that time is cyclical as opposed to teleological or subject to a notion of progress; that there is an eternal nation or monarch versus a "history" of monarchy; whether history can ever be written or represented in a meaningful way; whether any given narrative or theatrical form can correspond to the actual form of history (if, indeed, history has a form); the idea that art and poetry can present the world "as it should be" versus the idea that a preordered foreordained world will always be "as it should be"; whether the lessons of history (if it is didactic) will always lead toward a positive moral; whether historical or prophetic truth can come from "evil" sources

(*Macbeth* was a touchstone pseudohistory play for us); whether violence is part of history or an interruption of it; the question of why the various prophetic moments we encountered are so obscure; why dreams require interpretation versus the idea that history is didactic; the history of a nation as a history of fighting versus rulers versus people versus geography versus spirituality.

These questions took the vibrancy of historiographic practice and used it as a tool to figure out what critiques the plays might be making.

The History Plays

Our reading of *Henry VIII* near the end of the course provides a clear example of the reading strategies we employed. In my brief introduction I mentioned that this play has been considered Shakespeare's only Jacobean history play. The students immediately recognized that it was substantially different in plot, character development, focus, tone, and possibly even genre from Shakespeare's earlier history plays. The students suggested that, until the final few moments of this play, there is no overriding historical narrative. Elizabeth's birth could bring an end to the chaos, but, as my students noticed, the ending seems contrived and somewhat insincere. My students then asked, given all our study of historiography and Shakespeare's familiarity with historiographic discourses, why his final "history" play would insert this sort of chaos in place of the careful patterns of the earlier history plays. In pursuit of this answer, the students researched statements Elizabeth and James made about the nature of history and the monarchy, thinking, perhaps, that Shakespeare's attitude toward history had changed because of the change in the monarchy. Our semester ended as we began to explore this rich possibility.

What Is a History Play?

We did not reach a singular, firm conclusion about what constitutes a history play. Some left class convinced there was no unified genre and that "history" was only incidentally the subject of these plays. Some decided that the best history plays critiqued historiographic practice but that most were just straightforward (often simplistic) dramatizations of historical events. Several of us, myself included, became convinced that there was a shift in historiographic practice from Elizabethan to Jacobean England and that something in this shift precipitated the end of the history play as a genre. This conclusion remained incomplete and led to several conference papers and an independent study where we pursued differences in concepts of monarchy under Elizabeth and James. Six years after the completion of the course, I still receive e-mails from students who have new ideas related to the class content. For our class, Shakespeare's history plays remain a tantalizing mystery to be revisited and re-explored, and therein lies their beauty and their pedagogical value.

Why Blind Arthur?
Writing about *King John* Using Shakespeare's Sources

M. G. Aune

Shakespeare's plays present students with a number of narrative and performative questions and inconsistencies. How many children had Lady Macbeth? How do Hamlet and Laertes *"change rapiers"* (5.2.244)? *King John* has its own share of such questions, in particular involving the deaths of Arthur and John. Why are we given multiple accounts of their deaths? My framing of these matters to undergraduates in an introductory Shakespeare course leads to an assignment that asks students to answer these questions by investigating Shakespeare's own sources, reading the play closely and constructing an essay with what they learn.[1]

The difficulties begin in 3.3 when King John abruptly becomes a much more complex character, behaving more like Macbeth or Richard III than the compromising, insecure monarch of the first two acts. Having captured his nephew Arthur, whose claim to the English throne has caused John and his mother anxiety (1.1.39–43), John plans the boy's death. With words of flattery, he extracts a pledge of fealty from the newly introduced Hubert and then turns the subject to murder:

> KING JOHN. . . . Good Hubert, Hubert, Hubert, throw thine eye
>   On yon young boy: I'll tell thee what, my friend,
>   He is a very serpent in my way. . . .
> HUBERT. And I'll keep him so
>   That he shall not offend your majesty.
> KING JOHN. Death.
> HUBERT.   My lord?
> KING JOHN.   A grave.
> HUBERT.   He shall not live.
> KING JOHN.   Enough.   (3.3.59–66)

Though surprised by the instructions, Hubert agrees to murder the young prince.

Following through on his promise, Hubert enters in 4.1 with two executioners carrying irons, a brazier, and a rope. He holds a document stating that he "must . . . with hot irons burn out both [Arthur's] eyes" (39). Arthur dissuades Hubert through appeals to his better nature and the intimacy of their relationship. Relieved that he will not have Arthur's blood on his hands, Hubert sets his young charge free. But two scenes later, in a moment of almost comic irony, Arthur kills himself when attempting to escape by jumping from the castle walls.

When read carefully, the narrative of Arthur's incarceration, near-blinding and -execution, and death raises several questions. In 3.3 Hubert was instructed to kill Arthur. In 4.1 he has a warrant to blind Arthur. In the following scene, Pembroke claims the warrant was for execution (4.2.70), which is confirmed later (216). Were hot irons in the boy's eyes to be the means of execution? If so, why such a horrible method? If not, why did John change his mind? Finally, does Arthur really believe that he can leap down from the castle walls and "not break [his] limbs" (4.3.7)?

John's death is only moderately clearer. In 5.3, he complains of "[t]his fever that hath troubled me so long" (3–4) and asks to be carried in a litter to Swineshead. Three scenes later, Hubert updates the king's condition: "The King, I fear, is poisoned by a monk" (5.6.24). When he expires in the next scene, the cause seems to be poison. Was the fever of 5.3 just a passing malady, or does Shakespeare give us two different explanations for John's death?

The text provides no good resolution to these inconsistencies. When discussing them, scholars invariably refer to Shakespeare's primary sources: Holinshed's *Chronicles* and Foxe's *Acts and Monuments*.[2] Like Shakespeare, these books provide multiple versions of both deaths, as Holinshed himself confesses: "But now touching the maner in verie deed of the end of this Arthur, writers make sundrie reports" (165). Thus as A. R. Braunmuller suggests in his edition of the play, Shakespeare appears to have either intentionally included inconsistent material or engaged in "incomplete revision or slipshod craftsmanship" (46). But Braunmuller is being hyperbolic here. In an earlier essay, he concedes that the play is confusing but argues that the confusion can be explained by Holinshed's and Shakespeare's desire to "obscure John's responsibility . . . and avoid partisanship . . . or censorship" (317–18). Shakespeare was concerned not so much about misleading his audience as about assuring that his play would not run afoul of the censors.

Though I did not find this argument completely compelling, it led me to consider Shakespeare's, Holinshed's, and Foxe's treatment of the two deaths as an opportunity for students to explore Shakespeare's sources and think critically about his strategies for using them. I developed a writing assignment that asks students to read the relevant scenes closely; locate, read, and evaluate Shakespeare's sources; and then pose an argument as to how Shakespeare's selective use of Holinshed and Foxe shapes his characters and the play.

I typically use the assignment in an undergraduate introduction to Shakespeare course, though it could be modified for more advanced students. It falls at the end of a section of history plays. I begin the first day with a brief account of the historical King John, the characters, and the geography relevant to the play. Although we have discussed Holinshed and Foxe as sources for other plays, I reintroduce them here. We read and discuss the play, attending to characterization and themes of legitimacy, right, and commodity along with tropes related to eyes, to seeing, and to writing.[3] During these discussions I do not explicitly address the inconsistencies about Arthur's and John's deaths. If a student asks, I briefly frame an answer in terms of Shakespeare's use of sources and promise to return to it.

Once we have finished with *King John*, I return to Arthur's death and ask students to account for the inconsistency. The most common explanation is that they assumed Hubert had intended to kill Arthur with the irons. I press them, asking why John, who seems quick to distance himself from the deed, would choose such a brutal means of execution. He is deeply concerned about his legitimacy and knows that most people assumed he would kill Arthur. Wouldn't he try to be as secretive about it as possible?

Because Arthur's death seems straightforward, students often find the questions about it less compelling. He dies jumping off the wall. But again, why would Shakespeare have him die by what seems to be coincidental means? We spend part of a class going through additional hypotheses. I try to give every idea consideration, as nearly any possible explanation could lead to a viable paper.

I then pass out printed pages from *The Holinshed Project* and *John Foxe's* The Acts and Monuments *Online* featuring the account of Arthur's death and ask students to highlight the relevant passages. As they do this, I circulate through the class helping with the orthography and other questions. If the students seem to have particular difficulty reading these excerpts, I have them work in pairs.

Again, I avoid saying anything definitive about the material, only that we know Shakespeare looked at and chose to use some of the same words as we are while ignoring the rest. Foxe writes, I point out, that Arthur speaks to John "stoutly & with great indignation" (273), and Holinshed has a similar exchange, but Shakespeare has no such moment. Indeed, after Arthur's capture, he and John share only one scene and never exchange words. Why wouldn't Shakespeare include a confrontation between the two if Foxe and Holinshed both describe it? The students discover that Foxe provides a shorter account than Holinshed and does not even mention the blinding. Holinshed does mention the blinding and that "Hubert de Burgh did preserue him from that iniurie" (164), suspecting that John had ordered it out of anger and would be grateful that Hubert did not hurt Arthur.

This account conforms closely to Shakespeare's version, but when Holinshed writes about Arthur's death, the ambiguities return. Holinshed writes that "[s]ome have written" that he tried to escape and drown in the Seine, that he died of "natural sicknesse," or that John "secretlie caused him to be murthered" (6: 165). Holinshed is not sure what really happened, but Shakespeare decides on one of the possibilities. Why? How does it shape the characters and events of the play?

Holinshed's and Foxe's accounts are the only ones I use in class discussion, hoping that some students will investigate other materials on their own. In practice, students tend to write about the material we have discussed in class. To

address this habit, I also include the material on John's death, sometimes dividing the class in half and giving each half a different set of materials to read,
discuss, and report on. The Protestant propaganda that suffuses Foxe's account
of John's death is sometimes confusing to students. The language of Holinshed
is less challenging, but he provides many more explanations of John's death. At
this point I distribute the actual assignment:

> *King John* Primary Sources Paper
>
> Like his peers, Shakespeare was not concerned with what we might
> consider factual history when he wrote his history plays. He used the
> same sources for nearly all of them: Raphael Holinshed's *Chronicles* and
> John Foxe's *Acts and Monuments*. These sources, however, do not always
> agree with each other or with themselves. They sometimes give multiple
> versions of events—forcing Shakespeare to choose which version he pre-
> ferred or to make up his own version.
>
> For this paper, you will examine an event in *King John* (either the death
> of Arthur or the death of John), locate Shakespeare's sources for the scene,
> and present an argument as to why he wrote the scene the way he did.
> Did his version of events emphasize a particular theme in *King John*? Did
> it emphasize or deemphasize a particular character? In simplest terms,
> your goal in this paper is to help your reader understand why Shakespeare
> made a particular choice. The paper will be a researched, argumentative
> paper.
>
> The paper will be five to six pages long and use quotations and para-
> phrases from the play and its sources to support its thesis. Links to the
> sources may be found below.
>
> John Foxe. *The Acts and Monuments* (death of John), www.johnfoxe
> .org/index.php?realm=text&gototype=modern&edition=1583&page
> id=279
>
> Raphael Holinshed. *The Chronicles of England, Scotland and Ireland*
> (death of John), english.nsms.ox.ac.uk/holinshed/texts.php?text1=1587
> _2964
>
> John Foxe. *The Acts and Monuments* (death of Arthur), www.johnfoxe
> .org/index.php?realm=text&gototype=modern&edition=1583&pageid
> =273&anchor=Arthur#kw
>
> Raphael Holinshed. *The Chronicles of England, Scotland and Ireland*
> (death of Arthur), english.nsms.ox.ac.uk/holinshed/texts.php?text1=1587
> _2748

After having revised and reworked the assignment, I have found that students
regularly produce thoughtful papers exploring the relation between characterization and theme. They are able to trace Shakespeare's presentation of Arthur
as an innocent boy who is the victim of the ambitious adults who surround
him. Shakespeare's John is less ruthless than Holinshed's and does much less to

deserve the wrath of the church. Additionally, the students often enjoy reading Shakespeare's sources and having a glimpse into his research practice.

One of the challenges of this assignment is that students will often build their theses around an assumption of theatrical effectiveness. They will try to argue that Shakespeare had John order Arthur's blinding because it would be more dramatic or more entertaining. I urge them not to pursue such arguments as the arguments rely too heavily on subjective assumptions about what is dramatic or entertaining. I ask students instead to build theses that can be defended in terms of what they have learned about the play. In other words, the paper should demonstrate what they know about the play rather than what they claim to know about Shakespeare's audiences.

In earlier iterations of this assignment I sent students to the library to consult its venerable copy of Geoffrey Bullough's *Narrative and Dramatic Sources of Shakespeare*. I liked that this instruction required students to use print books, but as the library holds only one copy, bottlenecks inevitably occurred. In addition, as Bullough decontextualizes Shakespeare's sources, his book feels more like a reference work and detracts from the students' sense that they are consulting an original source. In another variation, I did not distribute the excerpts in class and instead gave students the main URL to each site, expecting them to find the relevant passages. This choice proved too much for most students. They had difficulty navigating the sites, using the correct editions of Holinshed and Foxe, and locating the relevant passages. I hope to return to this variation eventually, since the interfaces for both sites have been updated in the past few years and are now much easier to use.

Although this assignment was developed specifically for use with *King John*, it would be useful for other history plays. It is even tempting to try with *Macbeth*, as Holinshed does indeed answer the question of how many children had Lady Macbeth.

NOTES

[1] Thank you to the many students who completed this project and provided invaluable feedback both implicit and explicit.

[2] I bracket the relation of *The Troublesome Reign of John, King of England* to *King John* and allow students to assume that Shakespeare wrote *King John*, drawing directly on Holinshed and Foxe. To introduce *Troublesome Reign* as an intermediary text would make the assignment overly complex for an introductory course aimed at nonmajors.

[3] Caroline Spurgeon's chapter on imagery in *King John* is very helpful here (245–52).

Teaching *Richard II* and Its Sources: The Ancient Constitution in the Digital Archive

Peter C. Herman

Shakespeare's *Richard II* does not stand on its own. As many have documented, Shakespeare and his audience came to this play through its various treatments in Tudor historical writing, in particular Edward Hall's *The Union of the Two Illustre Families* (1548) and Holinshed's *Chronicles* (1577/1587; Bullough 4: 353–82). As many also have noted, Richard II's deposition by Henry Boling-broke, later Henry IV, deeply resonated in Shakespeare's time, with some inter-preting this event as the original sin that caused the Wars of the Roses (Daniel sig. C2v) while others argued that Richard deserved his fate thanks to his of-fenses against the ancient constitution, the unwritten rules limiting monarchic power and guaranteeing the liberties of the English subject (Hayward 113–17). However, despite the chronicle tradition's importance for understanding Shake-speare's history plays, the lack of easily available, readable editions once made bringing historical writing into the classroom difficult. Fortunately, that obstacle has been largely solved by the electronic edition of Holinshed's *Chronicles* and the digital facsimiles of Henry Ellis's 1809 edition Hall's *Union* on archive.org.[1]

While students find early modern prose hard, the advantages of teaching the sources alongside *Richard II* significantly outweigh the problems, especially given the capabilities of *The Holinshed Project*'s Web site.[2] Reading Hall and Holinshed allows my upper-division students to see Shakespeare's imagination in action, to watch Shakespeare transform Hall's dolorous Richard, whose ser-vants find him "withered, broken and in manner, half dead" (11), and the Rich-ard Holinshed describes as "so greatlie discomforted, that sorrowfullie lament-ing his miserable state, he utterlie despaired of his own safetie" (499 [1587]), into the poet-king who delivers Shakespeare's first great soliloquy ("No matter where—of comfort no man speak . . ." [3.2.144–77]). Using Hall and Holin-shed as a foundation for *Richard II* also helps clarify the drama's themes and illustrates the range of interpretations open to Shakespeare. By prying apart the three narratives—Hall and the two editions of the *Chronicles*—students see that the story of Richard II was hardly static, and that Shakespeare's changes are in dialogue with his sources just as his sources are in dialogue with themselves.

I begin by asking students to read "The Back-story of the Tudor Dynasty: From Richard II to Henry VII" (Herman 27–58) as preparation for a brief lecture on how the Tudors came to rule England. I also ask them to read Hall's treatment of Richard II and his chapter on Henry IV until Richard's death (end-ing on page 21) and the 1587 Holinshed's treatment of Richard, starting with the joust between Bolingbroke and Aumerle in the twenty-first regnal year 1397 to 1398 (I reserve the 1577 edition for class). I then ask the class to compare and contrast the two texts. How are they similar? How are they different? Students quickly figure out that Hall (despite his reputation for prolixity) provides a tight, focused narrative, whereas Holinshed seems to exclude nothing. He includes, for example, a list of "what writers of our English nation lived in his daies" (508 [1587]). Filling in the blanks, I tell the class that Holinshed does the same for every other English monarch. Hall, on the other hand, is not interested in which writers lived in Richard's days, and after clarifying Richard II's and Henry Bolingbroke's genealogy, he begins with the events immediately preceding the joust. At this point, I ask the class where Shakespeare begins his play, and again, they quickly note that *Richard II* starts at nearly the same time as Hall's narrative (Kastan, *Shakespeare and the Shapes* 48; Grene 25). What other parallels can they find? What about Ireland? Students then note that both Hall and Shakespeare do not give Richard's Irish wars much space. In a resonant phrase to which I will return, Hall says that Ireland lies outside the *Chronicles'* themes: "what he did there is no parte of my processe" (6). Holinshed, on the other hand, goes into considerable detail about Ireland (496–97 [1587]).

This initial comparison teaches students that while Hall may be just another source for Holinshed (Djordjevic 138), for Shakespeare, Hall constituted a separate and distinct narrative, one that Shakespeare draws on as much as he draws on the *Chronicles*. The point is important, because most editions of *Richard II* focus on Holinshed as the main source, with little attention paid to Hall.[3] Students also realize that the sources themselves exhibit very different perspectives. What, I ask, does Hall mean by his "processe" (6)? What story is he trying to tell? Why does this story not require detailing what the king did in Ireland? How does that story differ from Holinshed's?

To help answer that question, I turn to the question of providentialism. Earlier generations of critics, most notably Lily B. Campbell (119–25) and E. M. W. Tillyard (*Shakespeare's History Plays* 3–20), regarded Shakespeare's histories as exemplifying God's hand in English history, that the Lord punished the deposition of an anointed king with years of civil strife. After giving the class representative paragraphs from those works, I ask them how much of a role God plays in the events described by Hall and Holinshed. To their surprise (or so it seems), the answer is much less than they expected. God is notably absent in Hall, who will expound on the mutability of fortune ("What trust is in the worlde, what suretie man hath of his life, and what constancie is in the mutable commonalty, all men maie apparently perceive by the ruyne of this noble prince" [20]) but at no point uses the term "anointed king" or asserts that God would punish Richard's deposition with a century of "intestine division" (1).

Holinshed, however, gives us a more complex picture, one that shows students the value of comparing the two editions of the *Chronicles* using the parallel text function on *The Holinshed Project* Web site. The 1577 edition incorporates Hall nearly verbatim (which also raises interesting questions about plagiarism and Holinshed's relationship to Hall):

And this thing is worthy to be noted with a whitestone, of al princes rulers and men set in auctoritee and rule, that this Duke Henry of Lancastre shoulde be thus called to the kingdome and have the healpe and
assistence of all most of all the whole realme, whiche perchaunce never
thereof once thoughte or yet dreamed, and that kyng Richard shuld thys
be lefte desolate void and despareate of all hope and comforte, in whom
if there were anie offense, it ought rather to be imputed to the frailtie of
wanton youth, than to the malice of his hart: but such is the deceivable
iudgement of man, which not regarding things present with due consideration, thinketh ever that things to come shall have good successe, with a
pleasant & delitefull end.   (Hall 8)

Thys surelye is a very notable example, and not unworthye of all Princes to
bee well wayed, and diligently marked, that this Henry Duke of Lancaster
shoulde be thus called to the kingdome, and have the helpe and assisance
(almost) of all the whole realme, which perchaunce never thereof thought
or yet dreamed, and that king Richard should thus be left desolate, voide,
and in despaire of all hope and comfort, in whom if there were anye offence, it ought rather to bee imputed to the frayletie of wanton youth,
than to the malice of his hart: but such is the deceivable judgement of
man, whiche not regarding thyngs present with due consideration, thinketh ever that things to come, shall have good successe, and a pleasante
delectable ende.   (Holinshed 1108)

I then click on the "compare 1587" button, and the relevant passage instantly
appears on the screen next to the 1577 column. Students quickly see that someone added this commentary:[4]

But in this dejecting of the one, & advancing of the other, the providence
of God is to be respected, & his secret will to be woondered at. For as in
his hands standeth the donation of kingdoms, so likewise the disposing of
them consisteth in his pleasure, which the verie pagans understood right
well; otherwise, one of them would neuer haue said,
    Regum timendorum in proprios greges,
    Reges in ipsos   Hor. lib. car. 3. ode. 1
    imperium est Jovis
    Cuncta supercilio moventis.[5]

It's not that religion is entirely absent from the 1577 edition (Henry VII's marriage is "authorized by God" [763]), but the 1587 edition significantly amplifies
what is a minor strain in the original (Walsham 431).

Comparing the two passages reveals an even more significant shift in the assessment of what caused the "unquiet" reign of Henry IV and his progeny. For
this point, I switch from discussion to lecture: going to the 1587 edition, I draw

the class's attention to the passage explaining how Henry "and his lineall race were scourged afterwards, as a due punishment *unto* rebellious subjects" (508; my emphasis). I then click on the "compare" button, and students can see for themselves that the 1577 version has a slight yet significant difference: Henry and his progeny "were scourged afterwardes, as a due punishment *with* rebellious subjects" (1117; my emphasis). In 1577, Henry's lack of "moderation and loyaltie in hys doings" results in his being punished "with" nonstop rebellions; but the 1587 edition implies ("unto") that the act of rebellion itself, along with Henry's lack of loyalty and moderation, causes the subsequent problems. The 1577 *Chronicles* implies that if Henry IV had a little more personal integrity, he might have gotten away with it. It's only in the 1587 edition that rebellion itself is condemned. As for Hall, silence in this case speaks volumes: he says nothing about divine retribution.

If Hall and Holinshed (1577) do not necessarily interpret Richard's deposition and murder in fundamentally religious terms and the Wars of the Roses as evidence of divine punishment for rebellion, how do they interpret these events? To return to Hall's provocative word, what is the "processe" of both these texts that is amended in the 1587 *Chronicles* to include religion?

The answer to that question, students quickly realize, is that Hall and Holinshed both regard Richard's deposition as a legal matter (I introduce the ancient constitution when I give a lecture at the start of the class on Shakespeare's world); his removal is a matter of law, not a coup d'état. Hall records that the nobles considered seizure of Bolingbroke's inheritance as "unlawful, unjust, and ungodly" (5) and includes a transcript of the thirty-five articles against Richard. For example: "[Richard] said that the laws of the realm were in his head, and sometime in his breast, by reason of which fantastical opinion he destroyed noble men and impoverished the poor commons" (10). Hall mentions that there are additional "instruments" for Richard's deposition, but does not go into detail. Turning to Holinshed, students first notice that he revises Hall by attributing the nobility's general sense of Richard's lawlessness to Edmund, Duke of York, who perceived that "neither law, justice nor equitie could take place, where the kings wilfull will was bent upon any wrongfull purpose" (496 [1587]). But students also notice that Holinshed, like Hall, sees Richard's deposition in legal terms (Patterson, *Reading* xii, 154–83). Like Hall, Holinshed includes the articles detailing Richard's offenses against the ancient constitution, and indeed, he credits Hall as his source. Here, Holinshed writes, are the "33 solemne articles, heinous to the eares of all men, and to some almost incredible, the verie effect of which articles here insue, according to the copie which I haue séene, and is abridged by maister **Hall** as followeth" (502 [1587]). But where Hall merely alludes to further documents, Holinshed reproduces them, such as "the instrument whereby King Richard resigneth the crowne" (503). Turning to Shakespeare, I ask the class how *Richard II* both continues and differs from the sources. What does Shakespeare use? What does he add?

The class usually finds continuities in the play's emphasis—now much more obvious because of the previous discussion of the sources—on constitutional issues. First, Shakespeare follows Holinshed by turning York into the spokesman for the ancient constitution, although he speaks about them in cosmic terms: "Take Hereford's rights away, and take from Time / His charters and his customary rights" (2.1.195–96). Even so, the basis of York's complaints, like those in the chronicles, is firmly rooted in the same English legal culture that produced the Magna Carta (1215) and, in the fifteenth century, John Fortescue's frequently reprinted *De laudibus legum Angliae* (*In Praise of the Laws of England*), both of which explicitly forbid the monarch's seizing the subject's goods without justification. The English monarch (unlike the ones in France) cannot "change the laws without the assent of his subjects nor to burden an unwilling people with strange impositions" (17). For Hall, the notion that the laws of England reside in Richard's "head" and are changeable at will is utterly preposterous, "very heinous to the eares of men, and to some almost uncredible" (9).

But inevitably a student will ask, what about absolutism, the belief that the monarch is accountable only to God, not to men and their laws? Doesn't Richard say that "The breath of worldly men cannot depose / The deputy anointed by the Lord" (3.2.56–57), and doesn't John of Gaunt refuse to avenge his brother's murder because "I may never lift / An angry arm against His minister" (1.2.40–41)? I then point out that such beliefs were certainly current in 1596, and that Shakespeare likely has in mind the "Homily against Disobedience and Wylful Rebellion" (1570), which asserts that "infinite places [in the Bible prove that kings] reign by God's ordinance and that subjects are bound to obey them . . . [and] God defends them against their enemies and destroys their enemies horribly" (95–96). But this view of monarchy as divinely sanctioned and above the reach of human law is not in Shakespeare's sources. According to the chronicles, Richard offends against the ancient constitution because he (mistakenly) thinks he has the political power to do so, not because he thinks that he is accountable only to God.

The question for the class (and an excellent source of writing assignments) is why Shakespeare would adjust his sources by adding this element. Is he endorsing absolutism? Or is he turning the story of Richard's deposition into an explicit conflict between two contrary political ideologies: the ancient constitution, in which the monarch is subject to the law, and absolutism, in which the monarch is above the law?

But often, students are less interested in politics than in personalities. And for those students, I have another lesson on Richard's psychology. First, I ask the class if Hall and Holinshed are consistent in their view of Richard, and (with a little prompting) they usually discover that both chroniclers are oddly contradictory. While both clearly consider Richard an incompetent monarch, Hall also writes that Richard's faults should be "imputed to the frailtee of his wanton youth then to the malice of his heart" (8), and after Richard's demise, he mourns the death of this "noble prince, whiche beeyng an undubitate kyng . . . obeyed and worshipped of the comon people, was sodainly disceived by theim which he moste trusted" (20–21). Holinshed incorporates Hall's sense that youth, not malice, caused Richard's bad behavior (499 [1587]). But Holinshed then takes Hall one step further by pointedly declaring that Richard was as much a victim of gross ingratitude as of his own missteps: "But if I may boldlie saie what I thinke: he was a prince the most unthankfullie used of his subjects. . . . But such was their ingratitude towards their bountifull & loving sovereigne, that those whom he had chéeflie advanced, were readiest to controll him" (507).

I then ask my students if there is anything analogous in Shakespeare's play, which offers the class an opportunity to explore the various means by which Shakespeare invites the audience to sympathize with Richard. What is the effect, I ask, of putting such spectacular poetry in the mouth of a politically irresponsible king? Why does Bolingbroke, who after all has the ancient constitution on his side, seem so leaden, so unappealing? Finally, I invite the class to speculate on Shakespeare's focus at the play's end on Richard's confusion over his identity ("Thus play I in one person many people, / And none contented" [5.5.31–32]). Why, I ask, should we care? After all, Richard is no longer king, and besides, he was a terrible monarch. Why does Shakespeare go out of his way to make Richard so compelling? Finally, I ask: did Shakespeare take Holinshed's stopping his narration to boldly say what he thinks as inspiration for focusing on Richard's subjectivity just before Richard is murdered? What does Shakespeare think?

Teaching *Richard II* using online resources has the extraordinary advantage of showing students how the Web can facilitate study of Shakespeare. The online versions of Hall allow students to read a text previously all but inaccessible to the classroom, and *The Holinshed Project* not only does the same but allows teachers and students to compare and contrast the two editions of Holinshed's *Chronicles*. Students can then see what Shakespeare draws from all three texts. The result is a dynamic class on a play students often find static and dull. They can actually see the arguments about Richard taking place in front of their eyes, and (with a little professorial help) get a sense of what is at stake and why Shakespeare's play can be so compelling.

NOTES

[1]There are several versions of Hall's *Union* available from archive.org. The digital facsimile from the University of Toronto library skips two crucial pages (4–5), but the ones from the Boston Public Library and Cornell are complete.

[2]While the *Chronicles* are typically ascribed to Raphael Holinshed, "they were in fact a corporate achievement, produced by men of varying origins and upbringings" (Kewes et al., "Making"). It remains uncertain who wrote the chapters on Richard II; however, for ease of reference, I will follow convention and refer to the author as "Holinshed." All

quotations of the *Chronicles* are taken from *The Holinshed Project*. The Web site provides the page numbers for the 1577 and 1587 editions, and so I cite both edition year and page number. I have silently adopted contemporary usage of i/j, u/v, and s/ſ.

[3] Many critics ignore Shakespeare's reliance on Hall (Bullough 362; Bolam 142). On Holinshed and Hall, see Goy-Blanquet; Lucas.

[4] Heal and Summerson identify Abraham Fleming as the author (14–15).

[5] "The power of dread kings over their peoples, / is the power Jove has over those kings themselves, / famed for his defeat of the Giants, / controlling all with a nod of his head" (Horace 3.1).

Authority and Legitimacy
in the History Plays

William A. Oram and Howard Nenner

Many Shakespeare courses teach only a single history play, and so it was a great pleasure for us when we began to teach the whole of the second tetralogy and *Richard III* (as well as *King Lear* and More's *Richard III* and *Utopia*) in a course at Smith College that we called Authority and Legitimacy in the Age of More and Shakespeare. The course grounds the plays in sixteenth-century history and political theory and reads them as thought experiments by two early modern writers about the nature of legitimate rule. Its premise is that Shakespeare's history plays gain in meaning from being taught together and from being studied in the context of other Renaissance works dealing with similar issues. Undergraduates tend to come to the history plays without much history and political theory and with limited skill in reading plays. Courses thus need to provide their own backgrounds—and we believe that students learn more by reading and discussing the words of, say, Machiavelli's *Prince* than by hearing a background lecture.

We created the course because we come out of different disciplines (Bill Oram from English and Howard Nenner from history) and felt that foregrounding our different approaches to the plays would benefit both ourselves and our students. Our thinking developed in 1982 when we went to a conference at the Folger Shakespeare Library on England in the late 1590s, which spanned both literature and history. We decided to focus on Shakespeare's treatment of legitimacy in the major history plays and added More to the mix because his *Richard III* and *Utopia* also examine the nature of rule, the latter from a strikingly radical perspective. All these texts concern themselves with legitimate rule—with the nature of legitimacy, the attempts to claim legitimacy, and the questioning of received truths about legitimacy.

The course falls into three parts: an initial two weeks on Renaissance political philosophy, a central seven and a half weeks on Shakespeare's second tetralogy and *Richard III*, and a final three weeks on the two most problematic texts, *Utopia* and *King Lear*. The class meets for two hours twice a week over thirteen weeks. In the opening class we ask the students to distinguish between authority and legitimacy in order to consider the difference between the power to command on the one hand and a legal sense of entitlement on the other. This distinction stresses more fully the new-historicist treatment of power, which is often a blunt instrument for understanding particular issues in the plays. We connect legitimacy with its root meaning in law and alert students to the course's ongoing attempt to understand the relation between authority and legitimacy. In that introductory session we also suggest that, while Shakespeare dramatizes historical figures who lived at least a century before he did, he is working out issues central to his own late-sixteenth- and early-seventeenth-century political context. We mention that his thinking is informed by the political climate of the 1590s, during mounting uncertainty about who would succeed Elizabeth and by what right.

The class then spends four two-hour sessions on three representative works of political theory. The first—the *Trew Law of Free Monarchies* by James VI and I—develops the divine-right argument as well as several others for the king's absolute authority. (Students consider early what a "free" monarchy in James's tract means, coming to recognize that the freedom is the king's, not the subject's.) They read parts of the second text, the *De Jure Regni apud Scotos* by James's former tutor George Buchanan, for an early modern version of the contrary argument—that subjects ought to revolt against an unjust king. The third text, Machiavelli's *Prince* (on which they spend a week), redefines the nature of legitimacy, since the author is less concerned with monarchs who have inherited their principalities than with rulers who establish and maintain themselves by their own *virtù*. Throughout these discussions students consider not only how each writer defines the nature of the prince's authority but how he argues—the evidence, for instance, that James uses (from the Bible, from analogy with the body, from a putative original conquest) differs from that which Machiavelli cites (largely from history or the Bible treated as secular historical narrative). Students also consider the audiences and the purposes of these texts. Writing the *Trew Law* in 1598, James was indulging in something more than an exercise in divine right theory. He wanted to establish his hereditary right to the English throne, a right he asserted was indefeasible. Machiavelli, by contrast, writes his book at least partly hoping to gain employment with Giuliano de Medici, to whom the text was first dedicated. This part of the course provides the students with ideas and language to make sense of the Shakespearean plays that follow.

Thus they can see that the struggle between Richard and Bolingbroke in *Richard II* echoes the opposition of James I on the one hand and a combination of Buchanan and Machiavelli on the other.

The class then reads through the second tetralogy, following it with More's *Richard III* (available in Sylvester's edition from Yale) and Shakespeare's *Richard III*. (We use Signet editions of the play because they're cheap and print excerpts from Shakespeare's sources.) This is the heart of the course. Students concern themselves, throughout their reading of the plays, with how Shakespeare dramatizes his characters' embeddedness in their historical moment as they attempt to deal from the start of each play with the consequences of earlier events and in turn create problems for future generations. When a play ends with seeming closure (e.g., *Henry V* or *Richard III*), that becomes a matter for remark and inquiry.

There are certain constants in the questions we ask as students move from play to play:

1. We ask students to consider the characters' differing assumptions about the nature of kingship. York and Richard disagree in *Richard II* act 2, scene 1 about the king's right to his subjects' property, and Shakespeare sets Richard's vision of his kingship as divinely sanctioned in act 3, scene 2 (reinforced by the Bishop of Carlysle in the abdication scene) against the practical actions that Bolingbroke (aided by Northumberland) takes to claim the throne.

2. From the beginning of *Richard II* on, we ask students to describe how characters present themselves to others in order to foreground the importance of characters' awareness that they are acting parts. In *Richard II* this leads to a discussion of Richard's theatricality, which is set against Bolingbroke's canny manipulation of his audiences and his capacity to forward his plans by deeds. In *1 Henry IV* the opposition between acting and action is complicated by the trio of Hotspur, Hal, and Falstaff.

3. In dealing with the tetralogy students consider how passages within plays and between plays recall one another. The garden scene (3.5) in *Richard II* echoes the vision of England as garden in Gaunt's dying speech (2.1) and his nostalgia for an idealized active kingship. The start of act 4, scene 1 recalls act 1, scene 1: in both cases opponents accuse one another of treason for Gloucester's death, but in act 4, scene 1 the ceremonious chivalric ritual has become in the "new world" (69) of Henry's dominance a kind of mobbing in which Aumerle runs out of gauntlets and must borrow more. The common analogy between the king and the sun receives a weirdly literal treatment by Richard in act 3, scene 2 but appears very differently in *1 Henry IV* when Hal uses it in describing his plans to dismiss Falstaff and his fellows. It continues to arise later in the tetralogy—most strikingly in the Chorus's idealizing description of Henry V visiting his soldiers in act 4 of *Henry V*—and each time provides an opportunity for students to locate a particular moment in relation to earlier ones. What Harry Berger calls the "echo chamber" of

the second tetralogy lends itself to discussion, and students gradually build up a sense of the problems of kingship as it registers in the language of the four plays.

4. Students return to the nature of history as understood by Renaissance writers. More's initial account of Richard in his *Richard III* includes the rumors about his birth, which enables students to question their assumption that Renaissance historians are primarily concerned with factual accuracy. We can then ask students what *is* primary for More, an inquiry that prepares students to explore what Shakespeare in turn takes and what he changes. His importing old Queen Margaret and her prophecies into the play as an embodiment of the revenge ethos of the Wars of the Roses, and his focus on the repeated false oaths of the characters, gives his account of Richard an ironically providential cast very different from More's psychologically inflected narrative.

As instructors, we have stressed, half-consciously at first and then with increasing insistence, the differences between our disciplinary approaches. In considering Bolingbroke's usurpation of the crown in *Richard II*, the history teacher emphasized the legal arguments for Bolingbroke's legitimacy that were made at the time and echoed in the play, while the English teacher stressed the guilt articulated by Henry in the plays in which he appears. Each of us tended to feel the other's views were mildly off-base, and the disagreement between our emphases made the students aware of how the disciplines we came from inflected our interpretations. One pleasing result was the increased freedom students felt to work out their own interpretations. The teacher's view became "the teachers' views," and students argued with us and with one another over the evidence. There are disadvantages to team-teaching a course—both of us felt on occasion that discussions slighted matters dear to our hearts—but students became both more sophisticated and more energetic in framing their own arguments.

Most students came to notice the peculiar reticence of Shakespeare's second tetralogy. Unlike *Richard III*, the Henriad tends to limit access to the minds of its leading characters, allowing no soliloquy at all in *Richard II* until the deposed king speaks from prison and (with the exception of Falstaff) few soliloquies thereafter. Shakespeare thus withholds, for instance, our knowledge of Bolingbroke's intentions in *Richard II*, and when in *Henry V* he furnishes us with a chorus, that figure gives an idealizing picture sometimes at odds with what we see (as in act 4).

The third section of the course considers *Utopia* and *King Lear*. Here the students explore each author's most radical thought experiment. The class reads *Utopia* in the probable order of its composition, with book 2 coming first, in order to establish the nature of the Utopian polity before considering the effect of prefacing it with the dialogue between More and Hythloday. Discussion of book 2 begins with questions about the effects of eliminating private property in the imagined commonwealth—its effects on class, ethics, values, architecture—and the extraordinary freedoms that elimination generates. The class then considers the limits on utopian freedoms and the reasons for those constraints. When eventually we come to book 1 we start with the differences between the books and the effects of placing the dialogue of the first book before the description of the second. Students then discuss opposition of Hythloday and More as persons and as citizens. A final class on More considers William Roper's *Life of Sir Thomas More* as another kind of biography—and hence, history—which the students consider in relation to More's life of Richard III.

The discussion of *Lear* focuses on Shakespeare's skeptical treatment of legitimacy in the play, and it benefits from being read against the background of the more limited thought experiments in the history plays. Here Richard Strier's classic essay on servants and service informs the discussions, and Lear's sense of his entitlement as king is better understood when set against that of Richard II. The students compare Richard's loss of his sense of self when deprived of his kingship with Lear's even more drastic loss. In *Lear* the stakes are higher, since the play concerns itself with the justice of the cosmos as well as the future of the English throne.

The course proceeds largely by discussion. We give the students reading questions, which prepare them for many of the issues of the play, and they come primed to talk. At the start of each class, one of us begins with a mini-lecture of ten or fifteen minutes about backgrounds that students need to know—the Italian political situation out of which Machiavelli writes, the nature of the English stage, the Welsh and northern marches, and so on—and we introduce each play with a capsule account of the historical issues with which the characters are grappling (students also buy Saccio's *Shakespeare's English Kings*, reading the relevant chapter before beginning the play). Then for the rest of the two hours the class discusses the text and its implications. While the mini-lectures increase the clarity and perceptiveness of the subsequent discussions, there is a limit to what lectures can do. We can imagine the course taught in a series of lectures, but we feel that it would likely lose its distinctive, student-generated energy.

We screen films of each of the plays. We use the 1980s BBC versions of *Richard II* and *1* and *2 Henry IV*, but for *Henry V* we screen both the Laurence Olivier and Kenneth Branagh versions, and the last class on *Henry V* discusses the different readings that the two films provide. With the exception of *Henry V* we don't require attendance at the films, but a good percentage of the class shows up, and we feel that seeing and hearing performances fixes the plays, as nothing else can, in students' imaginations.

From the start the course has involved two formal class debates about the historical issues dramatized by the plays. In each case half the students (the class is normally limited to twenty-five) serves as spectators and judges, while the other divides itself into opposing teams. The first, which comes after the discussion of *1 Henry IV*, debates the proposition, "resolved, that Henry IV is a legitimate monarch." (Among other things, this gives the student groups a chance to work with the various ways in which legitimacy has been defined.) The second, which succeeds the discussion of *Richard III*, concerns Richard's responsibility for the deaths of the princes in the tower. For both of these, students often read outside the class texts. We've encouraged the debaters to dress in costume, and they often do—costumes can have the useful effect of moving them beyond their ordinary selves. Students generally love the debates, which enable them to work in teams, although occasionally some of the quieter members of the class have felt a bit anxious.

There are two ten-to-fifteen-page papers. The first, on the interpretation of a Shakespearian scene, has the students read one of several possible episodes from *Richard II* and *1 Henry IV* (*Richard II* 4.2 or 5.2–3; *1 Henry IV* 1.3 or 5.3–4) against the historical accounts available to Shakespeare. (The Signet classic editions of the plays include excerpts from the sources, and we also make available online the relevant portions of Bullough's *Narrative and Dramatic Sources of Shakespeare*.) The assignment enables students to look over Shakespeare's shoulder as he is creating the play, to think about what he does with his sources—adding this, suppressing that, reorganizing something else to give it a new emphasis. We give specific directions for structuring the paper, suggesting that students start with the history as Shakespeare inherited it and then detail his alterations and their effects. The second is a "historical" paper, which asks the students to take a position as to whether the actual Richard III was a legitimate king. It encourages them to look at the texts for the course (More, Shakespeare, and Saccio, to which we add Walpole's classic defense of Richard III) with a historian's skeptical eye, considering what in each of them is to be trusted and why. The formal papers punctuate the first two-thirds of the course, and we give a take-home exam on *Utopia* and *King Lear* at the end. (On the final day of the course, however, when we give back the second essay, we announce that only those students caught between two grades, for whom the final might raise their grade—usually about a third of the class—need to take it.)

The limitation of team-teaching is that there is no time to do full justice to each discipline—at least not so long as this remains a discussion course. Its great advantages are the way that students see how the two approaches to a text illuminate different facets of it and the subsequent increased sophistication of their own arguments. We believe that the course might be taught by a single teacher, but that in that case it would lose an important strength.

Teaching Political Rhetoric
in Shakespeare's History Plays

Jonathan Hart

Teaching rhetoric in Shakespeare often begins with the opposing speeches that Brutus and Antony speak in memory of Caesar after the assassination. In the English history plays, Henry V appears to be the paramount orator, persuading his men to heroics, but rhetoric—the art of persuasion or the relation between speaker and audience—in the name of politics is much more nuanced than that and has a wide spectrum in the English history plays. There are vying rhetorics of political advantage, high and low, king and rebel, English and other, male and female, old and young. In the contention over kingship, for instance, Richard II and Bolingbroke use language to achieve different political ends. All the English kings share a field of political rhetoric, but with a difference, especially surrounding the theme of legitimacy. Henry IV, Hal, Falstaff, and Hotspur contend over honor as a way to understand political and personal rhetorics. Joan de Pucelle, Lady Grey, Queen Margaret, Queen Elizabeth, Anne, Queen Isabella, and the Duchess of York all express tensions between private and public speech that have political implications. Machiavellian and saintly rhetorics vie in the speech of Richard III and Henry V (Hal in *1* and *2 Henry IV*). The public rhetoric of King John and Cardinal Wolsey round off the political language of the ten English history plays. Teaching this rhetoric involves teaching students the basics of rhetoric (schemes, tropes, strategies) and how language takes into account the audience and the means of persuasion. Such language shows the tension between the personal and the political, whether in soliloquies that contribute to dramatic irony or in speeches that are more overtly public and appeal to an audience within an audience. Shakespeare gives the epic life of England an appropriate, invigorating, and wide-ranging political rhetoric.

Thus a rhetoric of politics in the history plays is important to understanding the plays, particularly with respect to the intersection between politics and theatricality. Teaching this aspect of the plays has practical benefits for students because Shakespeare, a master of rhetoric and poetics in nondramatic and dramatic works, probably attended the petty and grammar schools, where pupils studied language closely and came to master the literary, grammatical, and rhetorical arts (T. W. Baldwin, *William Shakespere's Petty School* and *William Shakespere's Small Latin*). Students today learn from Shakespeare, who, as a student, learned rhetoric in school. Shakespeare's rhetoric is a topic much traveled, but scholarly work continues and has implications for teaching and communications, even if some of it can be at a theoretical and critical level more focused on research than teaching (Atkins; Joseph; Streuver; Wills; Lyne; Enterline; Mann; Christiansen; Palfrey). Although in previous work I have discussed rhetoric and political theater in Shakespeare's history plays, especially in the second tetralogy, and have explored the history plays and the politics of Shakespeare's drama more generally, I wish here to concentrate on the relation between rhetoric and political and public theater in terms that help the teaching of the history plays (Hart, *Theater, Columbus, Shakespeare: Poetry, Shakespeare and His Contemporaries,* and *From Shakespeare*).

Though I lecture, teach undergraduate and graduate seminars, and give supervisions, and have done so on both sides of the Atlantic for a long time, I keep changing approaches to teaching. In lectures, one can structure the handouts and technical matters concerning rhetoric in Shakespeare's histories and read a passage or speech in some detail; in one-on-one or small-group supervisions or tutorials, the students can perform a reading together and build the interpretation as a group. This technique can also happen in seminars, which tend to be a little smaller. We take rhetoric, with its schemes and tropes, and see how it is used in a speech and how it relates to the art of persuasion in the private and public worlds of Shakespeare's histories. I tend to workshop writing on rhetoric, so that in-class discussions or small essays can be reworked into longer essays, and midterm or in-class essays of test length can lead to related work on the final examination (in regular or lecture classes). Thus, technical skills become part of close reading and an understanding of themes. This approach gives the students a chance to improve and correct without a feeling of finality.

When teaching the rhetorical modes to students, I discuss their place in late medieval and Renaissance pedagogy and their role in the education of a prince and of Shakespeare. The medieval pedagogical focus on grammar, logic, and rhetoric—the trivium—persisted as central subjects in the curriculum of the Renaissance and would have been keys to Shakespeare's education, formal and informal. Rhetoric informs how Shakespeare and his contemporaries were educated and how "history"—that is, stories about the past—was written and read. The connection between rhetoric and history happened past and present, so that Shakespeare's contemporary audience and we, in our viewing or reading of his work, experience a rhetorical bond. Shakespeare and much of his audience would have shared the study of rhetoric at school or university. A point worth repeating is that rhetoric is the art of persuasion, as Aristotle defined it in the *Art of Rhetoric*, or the relation between speaker and audience, writer and reader—an inherently political act.

The education of gentlemen and princes also involved an emphasis on rhetoric. Rhetoric was about the spoken word and about oratory, which prepared gentlemen for political speeches, as well as about style, schemes, and tropes. Theater, the written word of the playwright delivered orally, likewise included writing and speaking. Shakespeare's political theater involved many places of power, including the court, and in Shakespeare's time, courtesy books, rhetorics, and other texts of education were influential in courtly circles. In one such text, the *Institutio Principis Christiani,* or *The Education of a Christian Prince* (1516), Erasmus relates the king to the father and the state to the family, and in the English history plays, Shakespeare connects public rhetoric to private language, so that he represents the king, warrior, and courtier in the sphere of state and family (Erasmus 17, 25, 33–37, 45, 59, 66; Pierce 3). Moreover, Thomas Hoby's translation of Baldassarre Castiglione's *Libro del cortegiano*, entitled *The Courtyer of Count Baldessar Castilio* (1561), gives an important place to oratory, including the relation between writing and speaking, in the education of the gentleman. For Castiglione, rhetoric in oratory should make the words appear to be delivered with ease. But rhetoric could serve another purpose besides educating the gentleman orator. Shakespeare shows the education of Hal partly through the foolish rhetoric of Falstaff. Erasmus, Rabelais, and Shakespeare all create characters who praise folly, and Falstaff in *1* and *2 Henry IV* is the one that exemplifies this encomium to foolishness, a comic and satiric use of language to complicate the dramatic representation of history (Kaiser). Falstaff parodies religious and political rhetoric, especially in his verbal play and agon with Prince Hal in the tavern scenes of both plays. Falstaff is part of the education of a prince, Hal, who becomes king, Henry V. Falstaff, a master of language, acts out the father-son relation, which becomes part of coming to terms with the roles in family and state. Falstaff plays the fool to this future king. The performance of rhetoric in the private sphere of the tavern helps to hone the skills that will make Hal–Henry V a skilled speaker of political rhetoric.

One of my strategies in teaching the histories is to use comparison and contrast, so that private and public speech define each other. I stress different aspects of political rhetoric and the rhetoric of the nonpolitical or apparently private. Gender is one such element in Shakespeare's histories. Do women have a political voice? In *1 Henry VI*, Joan of Arc dresses as a man, challenges gender roles, and has a strong voice that is both religious and political. This exists in contrast to the female characters in the second tetralogy, who have private voices and who try to egg on the male characters to political action, as the Duchess of Gloucester does in trying to persuade Gaunt to avenge the death of her husband (*R2* 1.2.9–36). When the speech of the family is the speech of the royal family, private utterance also has political implications, and female characters are seldom given scope to speak as public political authorities. Hoby's translation of Castiglione may distinguish between male and female, but it also includes the courtier manipulating his prince, the kind of persuasion the duchess may be trying to use with Gaunt. Sometimes the rhetoric of the women in the second tetralogy shows an ineffectiveness in persuading a male who will not listen, as with Gaunt's ignoring the words of the Duchess, Richard's those of Queen Isabel, Hotspur those of Kate. The language of politics, I emphasize with students, is not always an overtly public or political rhetoric. This relation between private and public rhetoric is something that allows students to debate the nature of politics in Shakespeare's history and the implications then and now. We also discuss a question about why women seem to have more public rhetoric and play more of a political role in the first tetralogy (*1H6, 2H6, 3H6, R3*) than the female characters in the second tetralogy.

Two plays that are less taught, *King John* and *Henry VIII*, are also good to teach in terms of political rhetoric. Both plays mix the rhetoric of religion with the rhetoric of politics. King John defies Pandulph, a cardinal from Milan, who accuses the king of interfering with the Archbishop of Canterbury, something with which the king of France cannot agree, that is in defiance of the pope. King John uses a rhetoric of the sacredness of kingship to defy papal control of England and belittles the pope: "no Italian priest / Shall tithe or toll in our dominions" (3.1.147–60). In Shakespeare, and especially in the history plays, the rightful authority or king and the usurper are a common political theme, and in this speech, students get to see the making of content through the poetic and rhetorical form. From the middle of the play to the beginning of act 5, John shifts his rhetoric according to his strength or weakness in his political position (5.1.1–2). The periphrasis becomes an epithet for the crown that he hands to Pandulph, who hands it back, now that John has recognized the papal authority in crowning him, a reversal from the rhetoric of defiance and the divine right of kings to the language of obeisance and obedience to the pope. The students would reflect on how this rhetoric might be similar or different from the language that surrounds them and how the rhetoric of religion and politics mingle, something that has not left our world. The sacredness of the crown and the rightful king and the ambition of the usurper are something quite visual and verbal in the deposition scene in *Richard II* (4.1), when Bolingbroke and Richard both have their hands on the crown. Authority and usurpation as well as the nature of kingship are keys to Shakespeare's political rhetoric.

As in the choruses to *Henry V*, the prologue to *Henry VIII* addresses the audience directly. This type of address creates atmosphere and gives information to frame the acts or plays, a kind of dramatic narrative voice, but the prologue also makes history and politics present by asking the audience to use their imaginations (25–27, 29–30). The prologue uses a kind of rhetorical and poetic sleight of hand to make the audience think they see the elements presented. This appeal to thought, imagination, and invention is a way of persuading the audience that the author includes them in the making of the play and its meaning, in the performance of its historical and political rhetoric (25, 27, 29). Moreover, the performance of language dramatizes the politics and history and involves a rhetorical and theatrical contract between author and audience that functions through the words of the characters. The characters are rhetorical constructions, but they are also actors and people pretending to be other people who, in the history plays, once lived. Acting and performance are part of politics and history and, in Shakespeare, the language is the centerpiece.

The rise and fall of the great, especially but not exclusively of kings, is one of the main themes of Shakespeare's history plays, a *De casibus* view found in Boccaccio or the wheel of fortune in Chaucer's The Monk's Tale, a kind of tragic fall. Kings have "conscience" that is "a tender place," as Henry VIII says to Wolsey about his personal and political decision regarding his wife, Queen Katherine (2.2.142–43). Wolsey himself, like Katherine, ends up falling from power and being on the wrong side of Henry. To Henry, Wolsey had said of Katherine that scholars are "allow'd freely to argue for her" (112). Argument is a matter of rhetoric as well as logic, and so there is a kind of metalanguage about persuasion and argumentation, a kind of self-reflexivity, in the rhetoric of the typology of the personal and the political that, as we have seen, overlaps in the royal household and court. In the history plays, Shakespeare often uses prophecy, which has religious precedents in the Bible—biblical typology has something in the Old Testament prefigure or prophesy something in the New Testament—to predict something that has already passed in English history, so the prediction of the future is a recounting of a representation of the past. Comparing the prophecies of Gaunt and Cranmer shows the temporal and historical arc of Shakespeare's history plays, at least from *Richard II* to *Henry VIII*, although the composition of the histories seems to have begun with *1 Henry VI*. The comparison of these two prophecies allows students to discuss the mixed nature of the political rhetoric, how it mingles with religion and personal concerns, and its role in the representation of temporality, of past and present in the history plays. Gaunt's dystopian political rhetoric represents a sick England while Cranmer's shows a happy England, so that Elizabeth I helps to redeem the fall of Richard, and England is made whole again, a unified polity with people glad to have such a monarch. The education of the "prince" and the role of that ruler are keys to the political rhetoric of all the history plays.

Shakespeare's histories use political language less directly than the way Richard, Duke of Gloucester, the future king, opens *Richard III*: "Now is the winter of our discontent." This soliloquy gives background to the audience that "I am determined to prove a villain" and his Machiavellian determination (1.1.1, 30). His personal and political rhetoric, as privately conveyed to the audience, can be different from the speeches of his political theater as he deceives others, including his own family, in his quest for the crown. Political rhetoric in Henry V's speech appeals to bonds, not simply of dominion, as King John did in defying Pandulph, but of brotherhood, the army, or the state as a family: "We few, we happy few, we band of brothers" (4.3.60). Henry gives his speech on Saint Crispin's Day, a religious day to mark the early Christian martyrs Crispin and Crispinian, and here the religious moment or religious language marked on such a day reinforces and mixes with political and martial intent.

Political rhetoric in Shakespeare's history has many dimensions. Shakespeare and his audience, as well as princes, were educated in rhetoric. I discuss the various aspects of that political rhetoric with my students, such as the language of theatricality, the education and roles of princes, the relation between private and public, the linguistic sphere of gender, and the concerns of religion, kingship, and prophecy. Students get to see how Shakespeare performs the politics of history through language. As a future audience, they also learn that they perform the drama of meaning in understanding Shakespeare's political rhetoric. Understanding this rhetoric is a key element in comprehending the history plays, which are the representation of a lived politics even if they exist through the theater. The world of the theater and the theater of the world interact: political theater and the theatrical nature of politics are the two faces of Janus, a typology or a diptych, something students consider and take away.

"It Is a Reeling World Indeed":
Teaching *Richard III* as a Skeptical Text through Montaigne

Mary Janell Metzger

Though the problem of English kingship as sanctified political authority figures in all the history plays, it reaches a tipping point in *Richard III*—which a quick overview of the ancestry of Tudor princes lays bare. Explanation of the argument for divine right and the source of Tudor kingship quickly engages even the most resistant student with the problem of political mythology in *Richard III*.[1] Students ask, the infamous Tudors descend from an upstart servant and the French widow of the nationalist hero Henry V? Even without knowledge of Richard II's regicide, the Wars of the Roses, or the the censorious eye of the master of the revels, students quickly grasp the challenge Shakespeare faced in creating a tragic hero in Richard while affirming Elizabeth I's divine kingship.[2]

Such a pedagogical hook is, however, just the beginning of teaching *Richard III* in a way that engages questions of literary form, early modern politics, and the relation of Shakespeare to the history of ideas.[3] As Ayanna Thompson has argued, "[D]estabiliz[ing] Shakespeare does not mean to destroy, vilify or denigrate; rather, it means to shift the foundation so that new angles, vantages and perspectives are created" (18). Teaching *Richard III* through Montaigne and the crisis of belief that led to the emergence of modern skepticism reveals the formal and historical context that weakens belief in philosophical certainty —even as it appeals, as both Montaigne and Shakespeare do in the end, to a priori belief in divine order as a form of political refuge. In the process, the history of ideas that often culminates today in an undifferentiated mix of skepticism, cynicism, and idealism becomes clearer to students, as does the imaginative and philosophical power of *Richard III*.

Montaigne and Shakespeare

> He does not reason, he insinuates, charms and influences, or if he reasons, you must be prepared for his having some other design upon you than to convince you of his argument.   (Eliot 157)

T. S. Eliot's description of Montaigne evinces not only the alignment of Montaigne's work with Shakespeare's but Montaigne's correspondence with the gleefully plotting Richard. Like all provocative claims, Eliot's suggests essential questions about how we read Montaigne and, by extension, Shakespeare's representation of Richard.[4] For example, how do Shakespeare's malevolent Richard and Montaigne's inconstant self illuminate the compelling reason and rhetorical charm each uses to persuade us of their own unreliability? How does Montaigne's skepticism anticipate and clarify the contradictions of *Richard III*—a play that undermines the theatrical illusion and brute force of rhetorical and political power in order to culminate in a celebration of those "true succeeders" (5.8.30) who claim, much like those who precede them, to "reap the harvest of perpetual peace / By this one bloody trial of war" (5.2.14–15)?

These questions appeal to students' sense of the untrustworthy nature of politicians and media alike. But the claim that both writers solicit an ideal world and skepticism about its credibility suggests a compelling line of inquiry. As students often assert, today we are wary of claims not only of absolute truth but also of knowledge itself as a means of interpreting the world or navigating its conflicts. Questions of how we can know anything, and the utility of skepticism in pursuit of such knowledge, present challenges that they, like Montaigne, in their pursuit of understanding find sustaining.

Thus, in discussing Montaigne's "To the Reader" and essays such as "On Lying," "On Constancy," and "To Philosophize Is to Learn How to Die," we identify patterns and tensions useful in interpreting *Richard III*: Montaigne's desire for knowledge of himself and human nature, his insistent reliance on the natural world and the proverbial wisdom of classical writers for understanding and historical example, his preference for religious and political tradition as a guard against extremism, and his distrust of his own perception and social convention, even as he relies on observation and experience to make his arguments. Through facilitated close reading and periodic student presentations on historical contexts,[5] we wrestle with the social and political crises of belief and knowledge that Montaigne's *Essays* reveal. For example, we consider the following passage from "On the Power of the Imagination," in which Montaigne addresses the veracity of his own claims:

> [W]hen I borrow *exempla* I commit them to the consciences of those I took them from. The discursive reflexions are my own and depend on rational proof not on experience; everyone can add his own examples; if anyone has none of his own he should stop believing that such *exempla* exist, given the number and variety of occurrences. If my *exempla* do not fit, supply your own for me. In the study I am making of our manners and motives, fabulous testimonies—provided they remain possible—can do service as well as true ones. Whether it happened or not, to Peter or John, in Rome or in Paris, it still remains within the compass of what human beings are capable of; it tells me something useful about that.   (119)

Montaigne's equivocation provides students a formal and philosophical introduction to the ambiguities of Shakespeare's work. On the surface, he attempts to defend himself against accusations of abjuring truth for fiction and thus deluding his readers. Anticipating the disjunction between historical event and historical writing that Shakespeare capitalizes on in *Richard III* (and the history plays in general), Montaigne's defense relies on both skepticism and belief. He believes in the power of human stories as propositions—"provided they remain possible"—while rejecting the necessity of truth. Showing students Shakespeare's indebtedness to Thomas More's fictive Richard III, a figure marred by nature and hence incapable of goodness, clarifies how Shakespeare realizes Montaigne's collapse of truth and fiction in an argument for utility in his highly entertaining but profoundly political and ultimately providential play.

"Whether it happened or not," Montaigne insists, such stories remain "useful" (119). The loose allusion to Aristotle's defense of the credible impossible (*Poetics* 75) in literature is hardened and undermined by the equally Aristotelian allusion to the superiority of poetic fiction over historical fact: "there are some authors whose aim is to relate what happened; mine (if I could manage it) would be to relate what can happen" (119). If not representing factual truth, Montaigne insists on his reason and aspirational fidelity to the story itself and the likelihood, given human nature and the utility of story suis generis, of any tale to convey something essential about our life—even if that something reveals the transiency of meaning itself.

The problem such passages illuminate for students of *Richard III* is how to understand the early modern challenge to traditional and unquestioned forms of knowledge long authorized by the church fathers—what Richard Popkin calls "the criterion of truth" (1). Reading Montaigne's essays, students begin to grasp the formal nature of contingent testimony that undermines such a tradition. Like Shakespeare's persistently confessional Richard and the play itself, Montaigne contradicts himself from sentence to sentence and over the span of the essays themselves. Like Richard in his exuberant and shifting performance of political ambition, Montaigne's doing so does not weaken but strengthens his (and Shakespeare's) case for the value of studying not "being but becoming" (908). Yet, again, like Shakespeare in his final resort to Providence in his act 5 sanctification of Henry VII, Montaigne's appeal to faith in a mysterious God brings students back to questions of the relation between story, form, and utility: is Shakespeare's conclusion, like Montaigne's, an evasion or an assertion of his power as a story teller? Is it a weak or keen philosophical response to the impossibility of human knowledge?

Teaching **Richard III**

Initiated into the philosophical and historical context of early modern culture and *Richard III*, students begin to engage the problem in Shakespeare's seemingly contradictory representation in the Machiavellian and retributive world of the play of human knowledge's unreliability and the extrahistorical force of divinity that resolves narrative and political conflict. As the conversation between Catesby and Lord Hastings about Richard's aim to possess the crown makes explicit, political loyalty as a commitment to "true descent" (3.2.50) finds an ironic counterpart in a world of rampant and quid pro quo political patronage and the ability to enforce one's desire with charges of treason: "It is a reeling world indeed" (35). In such an age, innocence as the absence of skepticism, even in the young, is a dangerous quality. In Shakespeare's world, as in Montaigne's and our own, students soon argue, it is better to have "a sharp and prodigal wit" (3.1.132) and the capacity to act on it, for where power beckons "sin will pluck on sin" (4.2.66).

The understanding of the formal, political, and philosophical tensions in Montaigne developed through regular close reading, and the directed historical research that students undertake, prepare them to grapple with the political crisis of Tudor kingship that *Richard III* metaphorizes. Thus when we begin our discussion of the play with a close reading of Richard's opening soliloquy in act 1, the shifting nature of his claims and references reveals both particular and general meanings. A celebration of peace in a context of unending war, Richard's initial lines, students recognize, appeal to competing notions of enduring and affirmative nature and its concurrent and inevitable transience. Figured as seasons, a past "winter of discontent" and present "glorious summer" (1.1.1–2), Richard's metaphors mark sharp antitheses, revealing a pattern of implicit irony that increases to the point of violence as it is repeated throughout the act and the play. Thus the conventional image of seasonal beauty gives way to sexual corruption, and his anaphoric depiction of "our" combat points up the weak "he" who "capers nimbly in a lady's chamber / To the lascivious pleasing of a lute" (1.1.12–13). Noting the shifting echo of the opening "now" in Richard's later redirectional phrase "And now," students quickly recognize Richard's mix of opposition and conflation in his suggestion that the realm's masculine "mounting of barbed steeds / To fright the fearful adversary" (1.1.10–11) has given way to a diminished "he" who capers in the feminine realm of "a lady's chamber."

Primed by their study of the Reformation's challenge to universal religious truth, and the problem of Tudor kingship in the declining, childless years of Queen Elizabeth, students quickly grasp Shakespeare's interrogation of what little we have to rely on as a form of knowledge in the play. Are we to value peace and its historical if feminine and hence unreliable staying power or masculine war and its resurgent political glories? Should we value history writ large as the story a crown tells, or the local "now" that reveals the insecurity of any one "chronicle"? The rhetorical power of Richard's "But I am not made for sportive tricks," his appeal to tales of his own monstrosity,[6] and the theatrical effect of his false equivalence that "since [he] cannot prove a lover [he is] determined to prove a villain" (1.1.28, 30), clarifies the conflation of political, philosophical, and theatrical forms that Shakespeare presents.

Like his best villains, Shakespeare's Richard compels with his brutal clarity. Yet, as students note, like his contemporary Frank Underwood of *House of Cards*, the accumulating bodies he leaves in his wake give pause. But with Montaigne's skepticism at hand, Richard's Machiavellian villainy thickens, unlike Underwood's, to philosophical theater. Indeed, Richard's opening soliloquy heightens the significance of an unquestioned "criterion of truth" in a play appealing to the divine truth of Tudor kingship. Evil, yet profoundly entertaining in his transparent villainy, Richard offers students a focused argument for skepticism of human truths as an argument "[d]evised to keep the strong in awe" (5.6.40). The gleeful power of his "wooing" of Lady Anne in act 1, scene 2; his witty diminution of Queen Elizabeth and her entourage in act 1, scene 3; and his icily effective plot to murder his brother George, Duke of Clarence, all by the fourth scene of act 1, illustrate the weakness of political power that is reliant on idealized forms of human story. Whether through the skepticism of Richard's speeches, Anne's equivocation, Clarence's fearful dream and weak legalisms, or the murderers' antithetical views of judgment, act 1 proves invaluable as interpretive practice for students' interpretation of the appeal to divine truth as familial, civic, and national story—and the utility of women in making it[7]—represented throughout the play but with pointed finality in act 5.

Given the Elizabethan context and the absence of women (barring Anne's presence in Richard's dream) in the play's final act, the question of the literal and figurative role of women in Shakespeare's juxtaposition of philosophical skepticism and political nationalism is crucial. Certainly, their final erasure, some students argue, is explicable given the martial nature of the closing scenes. But given Richard's misogyny, others will point out, the queens' poignant if inadequate countervailing force and the role of the princess Elizabeth as the authorizing and negotiable body of political continuity, their elision raises questions about the shifting nature of political fidelity in the play and the credibility of the providential nationalism with which it ends.

In considering these, women's politically useful but inherently unreliable status figured in Anne's assertion that "to take is not to give" (1.2.190), following Richard's placement of his ring on her finger, looms large. Students respond energetically to Anne's submission to Richard and easily discern that, while her claim is patently true, her distinction signals her weakness following her earlier relenting wish: "I would I knew thy heart" (1.2.130).

When compared with Margaret's appeals to the transcendent truth of familial love as a torch of political vengeance in act 1, scene 3, Anne's sentimental idealism in the face of Richard's unflinching violence illuminates the power of the Lancastrian queen's idealized narrative of political factionalism in act 4, scene 1. There the echo of Margaret's prophecy of loss confronts students with the inefficacy of the York women's appeal to individual virtue as a form of political resistance. When Margaret appears again in act 4, scene 4 as the voice of the apocalypse embodied by Richard's bloody reign, and the queens admit that their only recourse is theatrical hyperbole, students confront Shakespeare's skepticism in presenting such alternatives. "Bett'ring thy loss makes the bad cause worse" (4.4.122) advises Margaret, in a less explicit equivalent of Richard's plan to "seem a saint when most I play the devil" (1.3.336).

Following such comparative analysis, students read act 5 with a heightened sense of the skepticism Shakespeare exercises in the play and the difficulty of appealing to certain truths and the idealized stories the Tudors—and our own age—use to illustrate them. Like Montaigne's elusive self, Shakespeare's Richard, students note, defies political and even theatrical fixity. He insists even in the face of a chorus of victims that, though conscience has "a thousand several tongues" (5.5.147), it "is but a word that cowards use" (5.6.39).

Like Montaigne, Shakespeare leaves us with a figure of great political and psychological ambiguity: a split subject who addresses himself in the form of a liar's paradox—"I am a villain. Yet I lie: I am not" (5.5.145). Aspiring to knowledge, Montaigne weakened our sense of its guarantees. Similarly, Shakespeare, in a form seemingly aimed at authorizing the story of divine kingship, reveals the ground of its historical and philosophical crisis.

Significantly, students' interpretation of *Richard III* in the light of Montaigne heightens rather than weakens the meaning of the final juxtaposition between the upstart Henry and the royal Richard. By offering a figure of early modern skeptical and theatrical power along with Henry's appeal to divine sanction— "God say Amen!" (5.8.41)—Shakespeare allows us—students and teachers alike—a means of engaging not only the formal problem of an early modern tragic "history play" but also the philosophical skepticism of both Shakespeare's age and our own.

NOTES

[1]This source lies in the marriage of Elizabeth of York, Edward IV's daughter, to the Earl of Richmond, the grandson of Henry V's widow queen and her Welsh servant.

[2]Elizabeth descended from Henry, Earl of Richmond, a mere major domo's grandson.

[3]Here I address major survey and seminar courses but in larger general university courses a modified approach using excerpts from Montaigne and Popkin and minilectures on the religious wars and English history have worked as well.

[4]Essential questions are those critical to disciplinary study and which offer no definitive answers; they are those that sustain our inquiry and our relation to what we study in both the general and particular sense. See Metzger 108–10.

[5]Groups of students, in consultation with me, develop class presentations on topics such as Reformation sects; religious wars and political succession in France and England; sex, class, and power in early modern culture; historical event and historical writing in sixteenth-century England; and the place of the public state in early modern culture. Such presentations enhance student research and presentation skills and develop student background knowledge.

[6]Reference to More's account of Richard as "little of stature, ill featured of limbs, crooked-backed, his left shoulder much higher than his right, [and] hard-favored in appearance" (More, *History* [Logan] 5) plays well here with students, as may the alleged recent discovery of his scoliotic and murdered body beneath an English car park.

[7]See Rackin for more on this approach.

Teaching Religion and Character
in *Richard III* and *Henry V*

Matthew J. Smith

In the past I have attempted to broach the topic of religion with students in Shakespeare courses by assigning encapsulating primary works of historical theology. One was Martin Luther's *A Commentary on St. Paul's Epistle to the Galatians*. My intention was to introduce Luther's foundational accounts of doctrines such as salvation by grace alone, salvation by faith alone, law and gospel, and the bondage of the will. In this instance, I faced two main problems. One was that most students did not understand much beyond the crude distinction between salvation by faith and salvation by works, and the other was the way this approach disconnected religion from Shakespeare's plays. When I attempted to lead students into a discussion connecting Luther's Protestant notions of sin and spiritual identity to Richard II's concession speech—"Ay, no; no, ay; for I must nothing be" (4.1.190)—it was clear that the realms of religion and drama were separated by a categorical divide that needed to be addressed more deliberately. A better approach, I have found, is to use assignments and reading exercises that encourage students to understand religion not as a potential context from which Shakespeare sometimes draws but, rather, as a world of ideas, institutional forces, and symbols that represent parallel engagements of the topics that Shakespeare addresses in his own work.

In many ways, students' lack of theological literacy, especially as pertains to historical Protestantism, is useful insofar as we recognize that most early modern audiences also would not have a summary understanding of the imagined tenets of Reformational theology. Or, at least, many early moderns' arguably robust religious lives were grounded in cultural practices that often but not always corresponded to creedal and state-sponsored theology. Thus, while my students tend to enjoy exploring the plays' Christian figures and allegorical moments, I would suggest that the most student-accessible and propelling issues of religion in Shakespeare's history plays center on the big questions of character motive, identity, and divine intervention. In short, I recommend querying problems of interpretation—how Shakespeare represents characters of great national reputation as vulnerable to the cosmic yet lonely quandaries of God and belief. In this essay I will discuss ways to accomplish this task around character formation and in scenes of soliloquy in Shakespeare's histories. I adopt Shakespeare's *Henry V* and *Richard III* as my primary examples because of their relatively overt engagements of religion.

When students read the opening soliloquy of *Richard III*, what religious contexts should come to mind? In Shakespeare's history plays, the fifteenth-century dynastic wars run parallel to the religious upheaval of the Tudor monarchs, and both are manifestly religious in nature. Other cultural products emerged in the brief respite from religious change under Elizabeth I, including popular books like Foxe's *Acts and Monuments* and devotional manuals; seventeenth-century sermons; major religious controversies, headlined by theater polemics, emerging puritanism, and the increasing visibility of "stranger" religions such as Judaism and Islam; and, of course, the re-fashioned relationship between state and religion, propagandized in pamphlets and new laws, where the threat of Catholicism was synonymous with the threat of Spain. It can be useful to outline these concerns in lecture in order to demonstrate that religion was neither wholly public nor wholly personal, as students might understand it today. I remind students that whereas some extreme Christian denominations in the United States blame secular society for disaster, early moderns would have blamed the church—its radicals, holdouts, or lax morals.

A good way to show students what popular dissemination of religious thought looked like is through popular religious literature and ballads in particular. Prophecy ballads often present faith as a matter of being attentive, identifying threats, and reforming the church. "England's New Bell-Man" and "The Distressed Pilgrim," both available on *English Broadside Ballad Archive* (*EBBA*), convey this perspective. On the important transition from the Catholic Mary to the Protestant Elizabeth, I have assigned the short and relatively accessible *Marian Injunctions* (1554) alongside the *Act of Supremacy* (1559) and Elizabeth's own *Injunctions* (1559) (G. Bray 315–17, 318–28, 329–34). These texts have direct relevance to the history plays' treatments of the divine right of kings, as expressed by Gaunt in act 1 of *Richard II* or, in an antagonistic way, by Bates and Williams in *Henry V*. Following class lecture or discussion, I ask students to write on one of the following prompts: How do historical texts diverge in their public presentations of the monarch? What is the monarch's relation to the church or to the spiritual well-being of her subjects? Alternatively, I have students focus on the opening scenes of *Henry V* and the interactions between the king and the clergy and to compose a close reading of the scene in the light of the Elizabethan documents.

The point here is to isolate the individual in Shakespeare's histories. Can Christian religion, broadly speaking, be counted on to guide one through the pressures of war, ambition, betrayal, and doubt? To explore this question further, I sometimes ask students to diagram Richard's opening soliloquy. I instruct them to divide it into three or four main sections according to his flow of thought. Students are often surprised at the theological logic of the soliloquy and its interrogation of God, nature, and human responsibility. The aim is to theologically contextualize Richard's biological determinism, which would have resounded with emerging Calvinistic notions of predestination (1.1.28). By extension, Richard is saying that he is "rudely stamped" and thus designed to flourish in wartime contexts that may have been analogous to the violence, heresy trials, and iconoclasms of Henry, Edward, and Mary (16).

My students have made a conclusion in the diagramming exercise that Richard's spiritual crisis—insofar as there is one—is largely about the interpretation of phenomena and events—that is, the problem of teleology. Richard notes his own physical anomalies, observes his felt disadvantage in romance during peacetime, and concludes that circumstances direct his will toward villainy and ambition. We discuss whether Richard thinks he is defying God or simply acting in accordance with his created nature.

To contextualize Richard's logic, I offer students two contrasting yet influential Christian interpretations of physical disproportion or ugliness. The first is from the sixteenth-century French barber-surgeon Ambroise Paré's work on monsters and marvels. Its opening pages provocatively list possible "causes" of deformity: "The first is the glory of God. / The second, his wrath," and so on, including what today we would call genetic explanations (3). Which of his causes aligns with Richard's account? Are there certain causes that Richard conspicuously neglects to consider? Given Paré's categories, what view of God's intervention in human matters does Richard reflect? Paré's list of causes is succeeded by elaborations on each cause. Students might discuss in groups the explanations of God's glory and God's wrath, as these explanations provide competing reasons for the existence of physical deformity—to tutor subjects to conversion versus to warn them of God's displeasure toward certain behavior. I reconvene class by having students discuss Richard's explanation of monstrosity. Parenthetically, Paré also provides many conversation-starting illustrations of his monsters.

The second source I use for discussing the religious logic of Richard's soliloquy is Augustine's famous "Late have I loved thee" monologue from *The Confessions*. The monologue expresses Augustine's view—influential on Reformational thought—that the ugliness of the soul allows beautiful things to lead people to vice: "upon the shapely things you have made I rushed headlong, / I, misshapen. / You were with me, but I was not with you" (262). Having instructed students to read this passage to themselves and to write notes on its applicability to the soliloquy, I then ask: does Richard blame himself, the world, God, or some combination of the above? There is a philosophy of sin in Richard's soliloquy, prominent in the Renaissance, that students can explore by looking at the ways Richard uses "shapely" things—such as romance in his courting of various women, or kingly symbolism and magnanimity, or even rhetoric. In groups during class or as a homework assignment students compose a close reading of another scene of their choosing with the religious complications of the opening soliloquy in mind. Does the scene show the strength or weakness of Richard's position, and what defines such strength? Then together we turn to the final peripeteia. Do the views about self-identity expressed in the soliloquy fall apart in Richard's moment of anagnorisis—perhaps a turn to God—at the end?

Henry V dramatizes similar tensions between divine action and individual identity, particularly in King Henry's pivotal soliloquy in act 4. Ceremony can be a productive religious concept to discuss with students because it shares aspects of mediation and spectacle with theater (M. Smith). The king, like the church and the theater, mediates authority and meaning through ceremony.

Students will wonder what Henry means by ceremony. To introduce the general concept, we look at the allegory of Ceremony in Marlowe and Chapman's *Hero and Leander*, a passage that requires minimal context to be meaningful (50–51). Here "memory" is one of Ceremony's "shadow[s]": how does memory also characterize early modern Christian devotion, through sacrament, liturgy, reform, and spiritual exercise? To introduce the religious context of ceremony, I print and distribute copies of the morning prayer office from the 1559 *Book of Common Prayer* and have students list the titles of each prayer and reading in order (Church of England 41). We discuss how there is relatively little space provided for extemporaneous prayer and how the authority of God and of the church are reinforced by the office's structure—not unlike Henry's description of monarchical symbolism.

Alternatively, I have assigned Richard Mulcaster's *The Queen's Majesty's Passage*, especially its first pageant, "The Uniting of the Two Houses of York and Lancaster," where ceremony and pageantry are used to celebrate Elizabeth but also to project public expectations (Warkentin 79). In smaller classes, I have had students graphically illustrate the pageant on the board in groups in order to explain its symbolism through their own visual illustrations. Where do religion and royalty intersect? I then ask them what remains ambiguous about the pageant, especially in the relationship between its texts and images. I have had success following this exercise with an in-class dramatic reading of Henry V's soliloquy in act 4 (or showing it on film, in larger classes). I ask students to consider the ambiguous relation between the topic of the speech—ceremony—and its soliloquy form. Does Henry break out of the trappings of "idol ceremony" here, or does a performance of the scene reveal that he is as trapped as ever? Is ceremony a usefully lens through which to think about the soliloquy form?

I sometimes repurpose the diagramming exercise for Richard's soliloquy to Henry's, but the religious subtext of Henry's soliloquy can also be discovered through a translation exercise (beginning at 4.1.212). After students (potentially in groups) translate the soliloquy into modern language, and after we clarify major discrepancies, I have them summarize the main argument and then discuss the difficulties of paraphrasing a speech that comes from such a deeply divided character. I also ask students which images seem difficult or too foreign to translate into modern idiom; students often point to the invectives surrounding the complaint against "idol ceremony" and the penitential practices mentioned in the prayer to the "God of battles" (222, 271). My students have responded with shock at the cultural sensationalism surrounding religious reform and iconoclasm, which I sometimes demonstrate by showing early modern woodcuts of zealots pulling down religious statues, defacing altars, and mocking popery. Moreover, the 1559 Prayer Book is amended in the beginning with a didactic section titled "Of Ceremonies: Why Some Be Abolished, and Some Retayned." This passage provides students a sort of middle opinion on the issue and suggests a useful historical vocabulary: on the one hand, it conveys a subject's Christian "discipline" and "duetie" to the state, and on the other hand, it describes ceremony's positive effort "to styrre up the dull minde of manne" (19).

A natural place to turn after dwelling on Henry's act 4 soliloquy is the Saint Crispin's Day Speech, and, in fact, my students typically register different responses to the speech when we have spent significant time on the soliloquy. In writing or in groups, students analyze the speech in the light of the soliloquy. What problems of selfhood and religion introduced in the soliloquy, if any, does Henry address in the Crispin's speech?

One point I try to make with this speech is that Shakespeare's use of ceremonial authority and public address not only represent an institution but, more importantly, create depth of individual character—and in the history plays religion is often at the heart of this character-building strategy. To get at this strategy in the Crispin's speech I have begun by displaying a broadside ballad published in 1603, the notable year of King James's accession, called "A Mournefull Dittie, Entituled Elizabeths Losse" (available on *EBBA*). The ballad laments the death of Queen Elizabeth and projects the speaker's praises of Elizabeth onto James as expectations. I read selections of this ballad and ask students to note that the monarch has spiritual authority over her subjects, now a foreign concept. An even more direct approach would be to look at "The Ballad upon King Henry 5th's Victory over the French at the Battle of Agincourt." Its verse reads: "Our King went forth to Normandy, with Grace and Might of Chivalry. There God for him wrought marvelously, Wherefore Englonde may call and cry, deo gratis [etc.]." *EBBA* provides the tune and a recording of a related ballad, "The Battell of Agen-Court," and my classes have had fun singing the ballad together. All these balladic examples help students to understand that Henry's paternalistic religious persona would not have been out of the ordinary and perhaps was generally celebrated.

At the same time, the Crispin's speech is ideal for discussing the symbolic power of religious imagery. Maurice Hunt has outlined the speech's Christian imagery, noting especially its eucharistic language (36). My approach to the religious valences of the speech has been to surround it with paratexts that disclose to students the historical religious contexts from which Henry draws. On the subject of the brotherhood of the faithful in this speech, I sometimes provide copies of the 1559 Communion consecration prayer ("Almighty God our heavenly father") and the Prayer of Humble Access ("We do not presume to come to this thy table"), both depicting the salvation of souls as a kind of cohabitation with God and as a community of believers: "that we may evermore dwell in him, and he in us" (102–03). Another salient text is Cranmer's "Preface" to the Great Bible (1540). It is famous for its articulation of *sola scriptura* but also provides high-profile theological context for Henry's class-mixing egalitarian language (G. Bray 239).

In response to contextual readings, I encourage students to entertain opposing viewpoints in the Crispin's speech. First, I give them time to write an argument contending that Henry's egalitarianism is genuinely Protestant. A follow-up question is to consider how this position reflects a Protestant audience's potential response: is Shakespeare then using religious imagery to inspire his audience in support of the king? Next, I ask them to take the opposite position of Henry as a rhetorical pragmatist and to consider this follow-up question: is it Henry, rather than Shakespeare, that is using religion for ulterior purposes? Norman Rabkin's well-known rabbit-duck analogy—wherein Henry always appears both as an earnest Protestant champion and as a Machiavel—makes terrific homework reading by providing a memorable visual image for the character problem with which the students have wrestled.

Additionally, such questions of character motive, religion, and rhetoric lend themselves fruitfully to a longer-form word study essay. A prompt I have used instructs students, "Choose a word/concept from the St. Crispin's speech that strikes you as evocatively embedded in questions of religion, politics, and personal motive; trace this word through the play (or through multiple plays in the Henriad), and suggest what that term's usages reveal about Shakespeare's engagement of religion."

My overall approach to teaching religion in Shakespeare's histories is to prompt students to articulate the logic and rhetorical meanings of religion in various scenes—through class discussion, group work, diagramming, singing, translation, performance, and writing. I have observed that many students understand religion—and particularly historical religion—in terms of images and euphemisms. Many students' grasp of ideas like iconoclasm, salvation by faith, the divine right of kings, conscience, and confession are only by association, as it were. Thus, much of the payoff I have experienced in teaching religious themes has come through activities that encourage students to explain basic religious concepts: read this prayer liturgy and restate its logic of confession. Synthesis with the plays often naturally follows this sort of simple exercise. When teaching Shakespeare's history plays in particular—rich with ceremonial religious symbolism and with the language of the divine right of kings—making connections to religion in the plays is often easily facilitated by familiarizing students with individual Reformational practices and doctrines.

I want to offer a final example of this strategy in action in the classroom, but this time through the absence of religion—that is, through godlessness. Richard III provides an ideal instance of a character who becomes more complex and more affective by comparison to the Christian devotion and rhetoric that surrounds him, even though he rejects it. I begin this class exercise by asking students if there are any characters in *Richard III* that appear notably devout, earnest, or conscience driven. Clarence is a common answer but others work as well. We discuss whether that religious identification makes the character more or less sympathetic and if it adds character depth or if it appears derivative. Next, we read the visitation of the ghosts and Richard's subsequent soliloquy in act 5, scene 3, which I set up by comparing it to uses of devils and spirits in mystery drama, where the visitations of spirits typically represent a dichotomy of heaven and hell, salvation and damnation. The repartee between the Good Angel and the Bad Angel in Marlowe's *Doctor Faustus* can serve as an illustration and, by contrast, can help students understand the ghosts that visit Richard as cognitive and spiritual embodiments of sorts. I direct students to the lines, "All several sins, all used in each degree, / Throng to the bar, crying all, 'Guilty! guilty!'" (5.5.152–53) and tell them to imagine the scene dramaturgically. In a theater in the round, do the ghosts appear from a trapdoor, from the space "above," or perhaps from various stage doors? My intention is to tease out the relation between overt signals of the spiritual (the ghosts) and character psychology. The importance of the ghosts' presence for the scene's portrayal of Richard's interiority can be relayed by showing the scene as produced in the 1911 silent film by Frank Benson and in the 1995 film, in Ian McKellen's performance. In the latter, the ghosts are replaced by disembodied dream voices. As a side note, the silent version tends to awaken students' awareness of the power of visual representations for character psychology in theater.

Having read the soliloquy and viewed both film versions, I lead students to unfold how religion and spiritual dimensions generally contribute to the phenomenon of dramatic character. I do this by drawing back from the play and considering the relation between religion, conscience, and character in visual art. I've found particular success showing illustrations of Judas's betrayal of Christ. Three images that work well are Caravaggio's *The Betrayal of Christ* (1603), Nikolai Ge's *The Last Supper* (1863), and Ge's evocatively titled *Conscience, Judas* (1891). Together, these works reveal a range of characterizations, or humanizations, of Judas. On the one end is *The Last Supper*, which shows a barely visible, shadowed monster departing from the onlooking yet confused assembly of Christ and disciples. On the other end is *Conscience, Judas*, where Judas himself is the well-lit onlooker, facing the barely visible crowd walking down the road with the detained Christ. *The Betrayal of Christ* lies somewhere in the middle; Christ and Judas appear pressed amid a crowd of soldiers. Judas resolvedly attempts the fatal kiss, while Jesus leans away in a tentative posture. In groups, students answer a series of questions about each painting:

1. Through what does religion appear in this painting?
2. What separates Judas and Christ—in setting, action, technique, history, symbolism, and story?
3. What connects Judas and Christ—in setting, action, technique, history, symbolism, and story?

Loneliness always surfaces as a quality of Judas across the paintings, separating him from Christ. Yet the connections between Judas and Christ—despite the fact that the scene is a betrayal, essentially a breaking apart—are often most productive in conversation.

The last exercise in this sequence is to apply the same rubric of questions to Richard's soliloquy. There is ambiguity behind what represents religion in this scene and in the play as a whole. In the past, I have substituted "Christ" variously with "conscience," "innocence," and "the spiritual realm." Placing them in groups of three, I ask students to take turns reading the soliloquy aloud, answering one question on each rotation:

1. Through what does conscience appear?
2. What separates Richard and his conscience—in setting, action, technique, history, symbolism, and story?
3. What connects Richard and his conscience—in setting, action, technique, history, symbolism, and story?

The exercise on visual art typically leads students to locate Richard in the same range in which they found Judas: Richard as human or monstrous, or, more theatrically, Richard as personal or depersonalized. I conclude the exercise by making the point (if students have not already) that each painting's version of Judas appears also in Richard. In this soliloquy Shakespeare builds character depth through his dynamic movements to and away from religion. How is Richard's identity—"I am I"—built around the religion and conscience that he rejects, and, indeed, how is it built around the very act of rejecting them? In instances when I also taught *Hamlet*, I have followed this exercise with a homework assignment asking students to compare Richard's soliloquy to Claudius's attempted confession and to focus on the role of godlessness in character building.

I hope that these exercises show the variety of angles from which instructors can approach religion in Shakespeare's histories. There is, of course, the directly historical angle, making connections to topical religious events. But, perhaps more compellingly, there are also characterological, dramaturgical, and philosophical angles. Often these latter approaches, which ask students to repeat the logic and imagery of religion in their own words, allow students the best access to the plays and characters.

Teaching Perspective in *1 Henry IV*

Kathleen Kalpin Smith

The tavern scenes in *1 Henry IV* stage several moments of trickery, disguise, and performance of roles. After Falstaff has been tricked by Hal, cowardly surrendering his ill-gotten loot, Falstaff denies all, proclaiming, "By the lord, I knew ye as well as he that made ye" (2.5.246).[1] The audience knows, though, that Falstaff's claim to have known the real Hal behind the disguise and deceit is false. Falstaff's claim highlights a topic that recurs in the play: the difficulty of knowing a person's true identity, especially when characters attempt to manipulate the way that others view them. These questions of identity and recognition run throughout both the main and subplots of the play and relate to the play's investigation of political theory and historical mythmaking.

My Shakespeare survey course includes as wide a range of plays and genres as possible. The course often has only one history play; that play then both introduces students to the genre and is its sole representative example. Thus, course lectures and discussions need to illustrate what sort of work history plays can do while also attending to the specific topics engaged in our given play. When teaching *1 Henry IV*, I find that students are quite interested in the introduction to early modern debates over the dominant ideologies of kingly succession. In this essay, I describe a series of class lessons and activities that together highlight the interconnected issues of early modern political theory and concepts of performance. In a multiple-day lesson plan, we move from (1) close reading of the play's passages that discuss visual perspective (including Hal's "imitate the sun" speech and Henry's "but like a comet I was wondered at" speech) to (2) discussing the play's employment of characters as foils for one another, which emphasizes the ways that comparison can affect perspective and to (3) analyzing the moments when characters step into and out of character on stage (especially the fake deposition scene, which we read together and also watch on the screen). Together, these lessons enable us to examine the play's engagement with kingly succession, which culminates in a discussion of the play's critique of the history-making process.

Day 1: Ideologies of Succession, Close Reading of Passages

I introduce the class to the play by explaining early moderns' interest in history and then transition to a more specific summary of divine kingly succession. I begin, simply, with a discussion of the value of studying history. In answer to the question, "Why do we study the past?" students' responses are often limited to some version of the idea that "we study history so that we don't repeat the mistakes of the past." When I quote Barbara Hodgdon's claim that Philip Henslow's diary suggests the play enjoyed what she calls "immense popularity" (*The First*

Part 6) during Shakespeare's lifetime, students are interested in finding out why that might be. Phyllis Rackin's *Stages of History* and Derek Cohen's "History and the Nation in *Richard II* and *Henry IV*" provide sources for this early lecture. Rackin argues that "[f]or subjects as well as sovereigns, the emergent nation-state made the study of English history a matter of pride and interest as well as an essential source of self-definition. Living in a time of rapid social, economic, and political change, Renaissance readers looked to the past for the roots that would stabilize and legitimate their new identities" (4). I also use this text to prepare the class for our discussion of the ways history and historiography can be more complicated than we might guess, focusing on Rackin's assertion that "[d]espite the widespread interest in history and the overwhelming chorus of praise for the benefits its study could confer, there was no clear consensus about its nature and purpose; for this was a period of transition, when radically different conceptions of history and historiography were endorsed, often by the same writer" (5). Similarly, Cohen prepares the class for an engagement with historiographical questions: "The king, in his lifetime, while making his history, is feeding the maw of his posterity—the successors and descendants who will remember him, will praise or blame him, and the writers who will reinvent him for their time" (297). I then introduce two competing ideologies of kingly succession: one in which authority begins with God and resides with the king as his representative on earth and the other in which power originates from the people who then allow the king to rule them. In discussing divine kingly succession, questions emerge for the class, including the following: Can one ever depose a king? What does it mean for the future succession when one does depose a king? How can you tell if the king truly was chosen by God? The play engages with this last question in a variety of provocative ways, I suggest to the class, through its emphasis on perspective. As we move into the play, from lecture to discussion, I ask the students to work through a close reading of Hal's "imitate the sun" speech from act 1, scene 2. In groups, they are to paraphrase the speech and draw as literally as possible one image invoked in it. This activity falls on or near the day that they receive their first essay assignment, an explication of a passage; thus this class activity will also demonstrate the level of attention required for their writing assignment. Students share their paraphrases and illustrations with other small groups and then we discuss as a whole class.

Typically we move through the speech in three sections. Hal's opening image is the easiest for the students to interpret:

> Yet herein will I imitate the sun,
> Who doth permit the base contagious clouds
> To smother up his beauty from the world,
> That when he please again to be himself,
> Being wanted he may be more wondered at
> By breaking through the foul and ugly mists
> Of vapours that did seem to strangle him.   (1.2.175–81)

Students are able to understand the comparison Hal makes between himself and the sun, and many choose this image of the sun breaking through clouds to illustrate for the assignment. As a class, we label the parts of the illustration in order to make clear that Hal is the sun and the clouds are his current compatriots (as well as his own loose behavior and the gossip or rumor that surrounds his actions). Similarly, students need little assistance understanding the reference to the rarity of "playing holidays" (1.2.182). We end with Hal's reference to himself as a metal glittering on the ground:

> And like bright metal on a sullen ground,
> My reformation, glitt'ring o'er my fault,
> Shall show more goodly and attract more eyes
> Than that which hath no foil to set it off.   (1.2.190–93)

After discussing this image, we are able to move into a broader discussion of perspective that will occupy us for several days: Hal argues that perspective can be manipulated, shaped, by presentation. This argument connects directly to our questions about the divine right of kings (how do individuals know they are witnessing the true representative of God on Earth?). The ways that our perception can be shaped, especially in the case of the heir apparent, raises questions about this ideology of kingly succession altogether. This first day brings this issue to the fore and sets up our next two days, in which we will focus on foils and comparisons as well as performing roles.

Day 2: Literary Foils

Hal's speech explicitly mentions the use of foils to enhance or shape perspective. Students are accustomed to identifying literary foils and will have little difficulty naming foils in the play. They have less experience moving the discussion beyond identifying foils to arguing for the effect of the comparisons on the audience's reception of the characters or for their contribution to the overall themes of the play.

The king begins the play by admitting that comparing his son to Hotspur leaves him envious and ashamed:

> Yea, there thou mak'st me sad, and mak'st me sin
> In envy that my lord Northumberland
> Should be the father to so blest a son—
> A son who is the theme of honour's tongue,
> Amongst a grove the very straightest plant,
> Who is sweet Fortune's minion and her pride;
> Whilst I, by looking on the praise of him,
> See riot and dishonor stain the brow
> Of my young Harry.   (1.1.77–85)

Students identify Hotspur and Hal as foils easily, and they are able to identify Hotspur as a foil for Falstaff, as the two display opposing views of bravery and honor. For this comparison, we begin with Hotspur, eagerly anticipating his confrontation with Hal:

> Come, let me taste my horse,
> Who is to bear me like a thunderbolt
> Against the bosom of the Prince of Wales.
> Harry to Harry shall, hot horse to horse,
> Meet and ne'er part till one drop down a corpse.   (4.1.120–24)

This quotation, along with Hotspur's exclamation before battle, "Doomsday is near: die all, die merrily" (4.1.135), stands in opposition to Falstaff's position on honor and bravery: "Can honour set-to a leg? No. Or an arm? No. Honour hath no skill in surgery, then? No. What is honour? A word. What is in that word 'honour'? What is that 'honour'? Air. A trim reckoning! Who hath it? He that died o'Wednesday. Doth he feel it? No. Doth he hear it? No. 'Tis insensible then? Yea, to the dead" (5.1.130–36). Comparing these character foils and their positions adds to our understanding of honor, bravery, and masculinity more broadly. Specifically in the example above, we note that both Falstaff's and Hotspur's perspectives offer the audience competing, yet ultimately unsatisfactory, positions on the idea of bravery in battle being a prerequisite for an adult masculine identity. Students argue that Hotspur's eager desire to die in battle is indeed futile as Falstaff suggests, but at the same time, Falstaff's lack of any honor toward his role in battle is not satisfactory. The foils in this play, then, are not just a literary device but have thematic importance, for they demonstrate that how we view something affects our interpretation of it.

Day 3: Performing Roles

Hal's "imitate the sun" speech also draws our attention to the ways that he acts out a part for a desired goal. In a third day on the play, we examine the role of performance in the play and then compare Hal's fake exchange with Falstaff to his actual exchange with his father. Throughout the semester, we identify and discuss metatheatrical references, examining what these moments bring to the plays in which they are located as well as comparing these types of scenes and references across different plays and genres. Specifically in *1 Henry IV*, we discuss how performance issues in the play draw our attention yet again to the fact that perception can be manipulated, using as our examples two moments from a tavern scene: Bardolph and Peto's explanation of Falstaff's faked attack and Hal and Falstaff's alternating roles of father and son, both in act 2, scene 5. This day begins with the question, what do we learn from the scenes in which we see characters act?

Hal's examination of Peto and Bardolph reveals their use of theatrical devices, including makeup and props, to fake their story of their attack. Hal examines Peto and Bardolph about their disguises, asking, "how came Falstaff's sword so hacked?" (2.5.279–80). Peto explains, "Why, he hacked it with his dagger, and said he would swear truth out of England but he would make you believe it was done in fight, and persuaded us to do the like" (281–83). Bardolph adds a description of their makeup: "Yea, and to tickle our noses with speargrass, to make them bleed; and then to beslubber our garments with it, and swear it was the blood of true men. I did that I did not this seven year before—I blushed to hear his monstrous devices" (284–87). Falstaff's "monstrous devices" are the tools of the theater; they help to alter reality for the audience in attendance. In this exchange, acting is both manipulating perspective as well as lying, monstrously. Our discussion of this scene prepares the class for the mock deposition scene. Later in act 2, scene 5, Hal and Falstaff play the roles of Hal and the King so that Hal can "practise an answer" (341). Falstaff begins playing the king, then he and Hal switch roles. Alison Findlay has argued that this "idle ceremony . . . subverts the early modern fragile notion of 'idol ceremony' and painted pomp" (89). In addition, this scene then contrasts with the real encounter between Hal and his father in act 3, scene 2. After watching the two scenes from the 1979 BBC filmed version of the play, students close read the exchanges while volunteers perform the scenes in class, focusing on Bolingbroke's advice for his son.

After seeing two characters "act" like a king, we see in contrast how a real king looks and acts in act 3, scene 2. We discover that even the "real" king distorts perspective in order to look like a king to others and to gather their approval. Bolingbroke advises his son:

Had I so lavish of my presence been,
So common-hackneyed in the eyes of men,
So stale and cheap to vulgar company,
Opinion, that did help me to the crown,
Had still kept loyal to possession,
And left me in reputeless banishment.   (39–44)

Students are able to see that the father's advice is already very similar to the son's plan and that the imagery even suggests similarities, replacing the sun/cloud image with that of a comet: "By being seldom seen, I could not stir / But, like a comet I was wondered at" (46–47). Henry IV explains how his control of his public persona facilitated his rise to the throne:

Thus did I keep my person fresh and new,
My presence, like a robe pontifical,
Ne'er seen but wondered at—and so my state,
Seldom but sumptuous, show'd like a feast
And won by rareness such solemnity.   (55–59)

The practice exchange between Falstaff and Hal offers a contrast to the real exchange between father and son, and in each we see men performing the role of king: first Falstaff as Henry IV, then Hal as his father, and then Henry IV revealing the extent to which he has performed a role, manipulating the perspective of the masses so that he appears more kingly. Hal assures his father that he will be more himself from then on: "I shall hereafter, my thrice-gracious lord, / Be more myself" (92–93).

What does it mean for Hal to be more himself? The class discusses what this might entail, engaging the question of which Hal is the real Hal. At the end of the discussion, if it has not already been suggested in other terms by a student, I propose Stephen Greenblatt's assessment that Hal "clearly does not reject all theatrical masks but rather replaces one with another. . . . 'To be oneself' here means to perform one's part in the scheme of power rather than to manifest one's natural disposition" (*Renaissance Self-Fashioning* 46). Classes typically engage enthusiastically with this theory.

By the end of these three days on *1 Henry IV*, the class is prepared to discuss the play's commentary on how one's perception shapes reality and in turn to consider the play's position on the historical enterprise, for the play provides a historiographical critique by reminding the audience that what is true about history depends on whose perspective is used to tell the tale. A similar approach may be used in the instruction of other history plays as well. For example, Hal's "imitate the sun" speech could be compared to the Bastard's "A foot of honour" speech in *King John*, in which the Bastard reveals to the audience his plan to control outward appearances as a step to his "rising" (1.1.182–216). Both men are aware that their outward performances affect others' perceptions of their character and abilities. The discussion of acting within *1 Henry IV* also links to discussions of being and seeming that will recur in different contexts throughout the semester. Here, acting within the play reminds the audience that the king and prince act—they fulfill a role, something staged—creating an ambivalent commentary about acting. Indeed, the play ends with a contradictory note as we see Hal, appearing kingly after his actions in battle, exclaim on discovering that Falstaff has only been playing dead: "thou art not what thou seem'st" (5.4.133). Overall, this approach to the play pairs well with a course that will eventually end with *The Tempest*, at which point we circle back from *The Tempest*'s epilogue to *1 Henry IV*'s debates over the nature of authority and the theatrical enterprise's role in it.

NOTE

[1] I cite from the second edition of the Norton Shakespeare; in other editions, including the third Norton edition, this scene is act 2, scene 4.

The Forgotten Map:
Teaching Britain in Shakespeare's History Plays

David J. Baker

Start with a map. This is what Shakespeare and the Lord Chamberlain's Men did when, in *1 Henry IV*, they had to give their own audiences a sense of Britain. It's the first scene of the third act, and we find ourselves in Wales, where a diverse crew of rebels has gathered to plot against the English king, Henry Bolingbroke. They are, at first, stymied. Hotspur, a Northumbrian, tells them that he has "forgot" the map. Suddenly, Glyndŵr, a Welshman, finds it to hand ("No, here it is" [5–6]). Now they can see (and divide) their prize. Hotspur will take all the land to the north of the river Trent, up to the border with Scotland, Glyndŵr what lies to the south and west of its course, including Wales. Mortimer, an Englishman with his own claims to the throne, will be the lord of "England from Trent and Severn hitherto"—here, he gestures at the map—"By south and east" (71–72). But if the map lends a certain clarity to their proceedings, it also promotes dissension. Just because the men can see the map, they can also see what each has to lose or gain. Why, look here, says Hotspur, "how this river comes me cranking in, / And cuts me from the best of all my land." He'll have it dammed and redirected. No, he won't, retorts Glyndŵr, who prefers the existing topography: "I'll not have it altered" (95–96, 112). Despite its tangibility, the map shows them not so much Britain as it is but Britain as they want it to be. Right in front of us, they are carving it up and putting it back together in new ways. Of course, the Britain that their wrangling conjures up is in no sense a stable polity. In this scene, we do not see the emergence of a formal political union (indeed, the words "Britain" or "British" are not uttered). But some potential entity is emerging here, as former foes ally with one another, as the obstreperous north links up with the belligerent southwest, and as this array of contingent allegiances threatens to collapse in on an English "center" of power that, it seems, might not hold. Britain here is a land of these rebels' own conflicting (and deeply self-interested) imaginings.

If today, some four centuries after the first performances of *1 Henry IV*, it is still useful to use a map when teaching the "matter of Britain," this is because the challenges faced in the classroom are not unlike those that Shakespeare and his colleagues faced at the Globe. First, how to convey Britain as an interlocking ensemble of kingdoms (or better, perhaps, regions), each of which has been defined by its interactions with the others over the course of many centuries? Second, how to convey some sense of the cultural specificity of each of those regions, of Wales and Welshness, for instance, as in this scene? Third, and most important, how to make the history of those interacting kingdoms dynamic and vivid, not incidental to the history of the plays but integral? It's one thing to talk about the history of the British Isles, about how and when the English, Welsh, Scots, and Irish came together (sometimes violently) to influence one another. It's quite another to show that the history of this sustained mutuality *is* the history of Shakespeare's history plays, that we don't understand them (or their characters) very well if we don't see how British they truly are. Of these three goals, it's the third that teachers will care about most, and that's the one on which most class time will be spent. But, to get to the third, you first need to go some way toward meeting the first two.

So, start with a map. Students will need some coaching in the historical basics. What we know as Britain early in the twenty-first century is somewhat (though only somewhat) more defined than any British polity would have been in the late-sixteenth. Today, the term is usually shorthand for Great Britain, comprising the kingdoms of England, Scotland, and Wales, which, together with Northern Ireland, make up the United Kingdom. But that agglomeration did not take its present form until 1922, and in Shakespeare's day the disposition of the British kingdoms had changed and would soon change again. In 1597, when Glyndŵr first brandished his map, Scotland was a distinct kingdom from England, though it would not be so for long. In 1603, James VI of Scotland would become James I of England and declare a "union of crowns," bringing both under his personal rule. Wales was not legally a distinct kingdom, having been annexed by Henry VIII through a series of legislative acts between 1535 and 1542, when he also declared himself the head of the kingdom of Ireland. Nonetheless, both Wales and Ireland remained culturally and linguistically distinct, as contemporaries often remarked. And, needless to say, legal incorporation did not in and of itself create a cohesive Britain, even politically speaking. (Much of Ireland, for instance, did not recognize itself under this, or any English, rubric.) As *1 Henry IV* was first performed, "Britain" was a political term of art, but it was taking on greater and greater cultural resonance as well. Historians, jurists, poets, and political theorists of the time, most of them English or Welsh, were beginning to think about what such an entity might be and to write and rewrite its history. Often, they did this with the encouragement of the royal house of Tudor, which traced its own origins to Wales, and still further back to the alleged founder of Britain, Brutus of the legend of Troy. In Shakespeare's time, "Britain" named a project, one with political, historical, and cultural features.

This still-emerging Britain is not particularly easy to teach. That Glyndŵr and his fellow conspirators cannot make up their minds about the polity they mean to rule is just the point, and it requires a real effort of geopolitical imagination to keep up with their cartographic quarrels. To convey this Britain *in potentia*, you will need, in effect, to devise a map of your own. Here the class can get involved, because teaching the geography of early modern Britain means asking your students to become, if not mapmakers, then map readers. Early modern maps themselves are a useful place to start, but not, surprisingly, because they are especially good at conveying the complexities of "Britishness." Take John Speed's map of the "Kingdome of Great Britaine and Ireland" from *The Theatre of the Empire of Great Britaine* (1612). This is included in *The Norton Shakespeare* (3296) and, as Jean E. Howard points out in her helpful essay "Early

Modern Map Culture," it reflects the ambitions of James I for a unified realm (*Norton Shakespeare* 3292). It's a visually arresting map and well worth studying as an ideological artifact. But, just because it conforms so closely to official topography, it makes Britain seem much more static and defined than it was. Perhaps for this reason, the collection's editors have also included a map titled "Ireland, Scotland, Wales, England, and Western France: Places Important to Shakespeare's Plays" (3293). Here, we can see the boundary between Scotland and England and locate several key sites (Birnam Wood, and so on). Its cartography is schematic, as it is on similar maps you can find online. Of "Britaine," what we see, mostly, is an outline.

This sort of map, which is essentially a Britain-shaped tabula rasa with place names push-pinned into it, is ideal for teaching purposes, and precisely because it allows students to fill in the blanks. To encourage this, you will want to pose questions about Shakespeare's history plays to which the answer is necessarily cartographic. First, inquire about the contours of Britain and its constituent parts. (I send such questions out before we talk about each play in class. I also direct students to the map in *The Norton Shakespeare*, provide them with the URLs for several online maps, and ask them to locate borders, regions, and so on.) Second, put the map in motion by asking students to trace movements across the terrain that they have begun to reconstruct. At the beginning of *1 Henry IV*, for instance, the king is clearly in a predicament and is assailed on all sides. But what, exactly, are those "sides"? He is told, in rapid sequence, that "A post from Wales, loaden with heavy news," brings word of the "irregular and wild Glyndŵr," that atrocities have been committed on the corpses of English soldiers, and then that the Scots have been engaged on the northern border by "Young Harry Percy" and many taken prisoner (1.1.37, 40, 53). Henry IV's precarious strategic situation at the start of the play leads students in two directions: down to the south and west past the Severn River where the barely assimilated and rebellious Welsh threaten to break into the English midland, and then up north to the Scottish border where the Percies have been holding back the "giddy neighbor" that, as Hal will remember in *Henry V*, has oft come "pouring like the tide into a breach / With ample and brim fullness of his force / Galling the gleanèd land with hot assays" (1.2.145, 149–51). To finish off the sequence, you will want to relate, when and where you can, the conflicted geography of the history plays to the conflicts among the plays' dramatis personae. The contrast between Hotspur and Hal, which will soon be so marked in *1 Henry IV*, is a contrast between their bravery on a British landscape and their range across it. Hal might be the prince of Wales, but so far he has campaigned mostly in London's taverns. Hotspur, it seems, has been more engaged. He has "discomfited" the earl of Douglas and captured his son, "an honourable spoil, / A gallant prize" (1.1.67, 74–75). Soon, however, he will address this same earl, now his coconspirator, as "my noble Scot." No man, he will declare, has a "braver place / In my heart's love" (4.1.1.7–8). Neither Hal nor Hotspur is the king that Britain needs, at least not yet.

Now eventually, as we know, Hal will become this king. As many critics have remarked, there is an overall arc to the story that Shakespeare tells in the Henriad. Early modern Britain, as Shakespeare portrays it, is a terrain of shifting demarcations, lines of attack, and contested zones—a jumble, really, of intersecting narratives and counternarratives that don't add up to a stable entity. But he was not content with that jumble or, at least, he seems to have felt that his audiences would not be. In the Henriad, and most especially in *Henry V*, he puts forward a version of Britain antithetical to the polity that Glyndŵr and his cohort imagine when they meet in Wales. Theirs is a plastic Britain, and, just as important for them, it is also multicentric. Wales and Scotland will be their own domains, not subordinated to the England that Mortimer will rule. But the Britain that Shakespeare upholds in *Henry V* is rigorously Anglocentric. The Henriad traces the rise of an ideal English king, from reprobate Hal to Henry V. A key aspect of his kingship is that it is English in its authority and British in its sway. He might be the usurper Henry Bolingbroke's son, but his famous victory at Agincourt establishes him as "This star of England" (epilogue 6). If there are moral ambiguities to his ascent, they are his with which to wrestle. Other destinies, and particularly other British destinies, are subordinated to his. The point has often been made: the army that Henry V assembles is conspicuously made up of characters who represent the various peoples on the British Isles: Gower (for instance) the Englishman, Fluellen the Welshman, MacMorris the Irishman, Jamy the Scotsman, and all of them serving under the just lordship of England's great king. This roster is ahistorical, but in a way that's the point. Evidently, we should number Shakespeare among those English poets who, at the turn of the seventeenth century, turned to Britain as a political trope and found in it a power worth celebrating. This Britain is bound to emerge in the classroom, where Henry V, the nature of his kingship, the extent of his domain, and his qualifications to rule are inevitable topics. Whatever else you may want to do with the "matter of Britain" in Shakespeare's history plays, you have to acknowledge at least this: the most plausible, coherent, and visible Britain in them is the one that puts England at the center and the top, and puts other "nations" more or less outside of it and close to the bottom. The Britain that most of the characters in Shakespeare's history plays inhabit—heterogeneous, never fully coherent—is the Britain that Henry V transcends.

If he never quite manages to obliterate this emergent Britain, though, it is because its tensions are intrinsic to it, as they are to so many of Shakespeare's British characters. Glyndŵr, for example, is a Welsh rebel. He is, in fact, the most persistent and successful Welsh rebel ever to have threatened English sovereignty. "Three times hath Henry Bolingbroke made head / Against my power," he says, and "thrice from the banks of Wye / And sandy-bottomed Severn have I sent him / Bootless home and weather-beaten back." But, as he reminds Hotspur, "I can speak English, lord, as well as you; / For I was trained up in the English court" (3.1.61–64, 118–19). Then there is Fluellen in *Henry V*, who switches his Bs for Ps, as the Welsh were said to do ("Alexander the Pig" [4.7.10]), who has all of the grandiloquence and pomposity that the English attributed to the Welsh (traits he shares with Glyndŵr), and who expatiates, often tediously, on his Welsh heritage. Despite that, he is unreservedly loyal to his English king, Henry V, and even serves as an instrument of correction for Pistol, a cowardly Englishman ("You thought, because he could not speak English in the native garb, he could not therefore handle an English cudgel. You find it otherwise" [5.1.67–69]). Or the pugnacious MacMorris, also in the army of Henry V, who famously asks the questions, "What ish my nation? Who talks of my nation?" as if they had obvious answers, when, just as famously, they have none (3.3.62–63). MacMorris is either an entirely dutiful Irishman taking his place under English command or an avatar of Irish ferocity and rebellion ("And there is throats to be cut . . ." [51–52]). There is also the Kentish rebel, Cade, in *2 Henry VI*, whom York chooses as his simulacrum for Mortimer. Why? Because, says York, he has seen Cade "In Ireland . . . / Oppose himself against a troop of kerns" till he is "like a wild Morisco, / Shaking [with] bloody darts" (3.1.360–61, 365–66):

> Full often like a shag-haired crafty kern
> Hath he conversèd with the enemy
> And, undiscovered, come to me again
> And given me notice of their villainies.   (367–70)

These characters are cultural doubles. They are partly compounded by Shakespeare out of the traits that he and his audiences associated with Welshness (or Irishness, or Scottishness, or Englishness), but they are not fully resolvable down to those traits. Cade the Kentishman is uncannily like an Irishman (which allows him to play a role in English politics). Conversely, Fluellen and MacMorris are, in some ways, uncannily like their English counterparts in Henry V's army (which allows them to play loyal parts in it). Such characters are compelling because they are intrinsically contradictory. And just because of those contradictions, they also imply the uneasy coexistence of the many British kingdoms and cultures. When you teach the British history in Shakespeare's history plays, this, most likely, is where such history will come in, with these contradictions. Why is the Welshman, Fluellen, so preoccupied with his kingdom's history, so insistent about it ("the Welshmen did good service in a garden where leeks did grow" [4.7.90–91]), and yet so touchy about it too? Perhaps because, in Shakespeare's day, British history was often Welsh history, and the Welsh were seen as its (semi-loyal?) expositors. Why is Ireland and why are Irish characters so fraught with sometimes ambiguous menace in the history plays? Because Ireland *was* fraught with menace for the English in this period. *Henry V* is a wartime play. It asks its audiences to imagine the joy they would feel if, "As in good time he may," the "General," the earl of Essex, were to return "from Ireland . . . / Bringing rebellion broachèd on his sword" (5.0.30–32). MacMorris's "nation" is a savage one. Might it be rendered civil, even somewhat so, any time soon? That remained, like MacMorris's famous queries, an open question. "Where is he living, clipped in with the sea / That chides the banks of England, Scotland, Wales," Glyndŵr demands to know, "Which calls me pupil or hath read to me?" (3.1.42–44).

Which Britain to teach: the Britain that seems to be assembling itself, as in these lines, out of the rebels' quarrelsome negotiations, or the more tightly interlocking Britain over which Henry V comes to preside? Ideally, I would say, both. Shakespeare's Britain is an inchoate domain of contested cultural identities, and then it is also an overarching political construct. In his history plays, each of these implies the other. To teach the "matter of Britain" in these dramas is to trace their ongoing interplay. You start with a map, and you move on from there.

Global Consciousness, English Histories

Barbara Sebek

To begin this discussion of teaching the histories from a global perspective, I turn to a moment from a less canonical, less frequently taught, generically mixed, and likely coauthored English history play. In the opening scene of *Henry VIII*, the Duke of Norfolk gushes to the Duke of Buckingham about the "view of earthly glory" (1.1.14) that he beheld during what came to be known as the Field of the Cloth of Gold—a series of competitive, lavish displays over the course of three weeks of meetings between the French and English kings and their retinues:

> Today the French
> All clinquant all in gold, like heathen gods
> Shone down the English; and tomorrow they
> Made Britain India. Every man that stood
> Showed like a mine.   (1.1.18–23)

I cite Norfolk's account because it effectively encapsulates the comparative,[1] competitive, and global mindset through which Shakespeare often dramatized English history. Although this passage doesn't mention the key role of the Holy Roman Empire in this chapter of geopolitical maneuvering during Henry VIII's reign, it advances its characterization of Anglo-French rivalry by emphasizing the centrality of the Indies in marking and even constituting the stature and wealth of Britain. Norfolk's lines also illustrate how Shakespeare subtly mobilizes multiple and simultaneous temporal frames: it was and is "tomorrow" when the English "made Britain India." Norfolk's anticipatory image of Indian wealth already incorporated into and constituting Britain and its individual subjects ("every man") simultaneously acknowledges and denies the belatedness of the English—even still at the beginning of the seventeenth century—in embarking on and establishing strong trade networks in the Indies and in Spanish dominions across the globe. Although Norfolk initially speaks with unqualified enthusiasm for the glorious displays that he witnessed, his use of "clinquant" is interesting, both because this English word is borrowed from French—working against the strict national opposition that the passage at first seems to advance—and because its partial sense of mere surface glitter hints at the consternation that the play evinces about grand expenditure as political strategy. ("Clinquant" is also interesting because this distinctive bit of diction suggests the hand of John Fletcher, who uses it in a different play.[2]) Norfolk's phrase, "they made Britain India," equates the making of Britain with its transformation into and incorporation of the Indies. Like global consciousness itself, the phrase posits not simple oppositions but intricate interconnections between here and there, internal and external, local and far-flung. These conceptual blurs, elements of competitive and comparative thinking, multitemporality, and attunement to the constitutive role of trade in establishing English eminence together comprise some of the key features of global consciousness in Shakespeare's era. My goal in this essay is to offer a brief glimpse of how I globalize the English histories.

I have infused a variety of courses on early modern English literature, women writers, colonial and postcolonial literature, as well as Shakespeare with critical questions about global consciousness and multiple categories of difference that complicate a teleological understanding of the consolidation of national identity. In addition to elaborating on some key premises informing the global that I invite students to take up and test in our discussions of the plays, this essay describes a few practical teaching materials and strategies that I have used or that I assembled in the process of this writing. The teaching examples I offer here mostly come from two upper-division undergraduate courses in my department's curriculum devoted to Shakespeare's works.[3] My teaching of particular plays and poems is not nearly as coherent or programmatic as writing about them might make it appear. Indeed, my pedagogy in general is pointedly eclectic. Such eclecticism allows more openness to diverse learning styles and empowers students' observations and questions to unsettle my own critical axioms when they start to harden into dogmatic "givens" rather than avenues of inquiry.

Conceptualizing the Global

To stimulate a discussion of what counts as global and how geographical knowledge was reconfigured in Shakespeare's period, I have started using the BBC Radio 4 podcast "England Goes Global," an episode in British Museum curator Neil MacGregor's series *Shakespeare's Restless World*. Addressing Francis Drake's circumnavigation, various cultural artifacts commemorating it, and the impact of these representations on the English cultural imagination, the fourteen-minute podcast serves as an accessible introduction to the globalizing forces in the period.[4] In a lecture after assigning this podcast, or after listening to it together in class, I address how a variety of developments in the late sixteenth and early seventeenth centuries reconfigured how many English men and women understood their place in the world and how they conceptualized the contours of the global itself: Francis Drake's circumnavigation of the globe as addressed by MacGregor; new technologies of mapping and navigation; the establishment of organized long-distance trading companies and expanding trade networks; English incursions into the waters and territories of rival and more established colonial and economic powers; and the growth of London—a port town with a large shipbuilding industry—as an economic, political, and cultural center where seafaring and global trade were emphatically local and topical matters. As Daniel Vitkus puts it:

> Once we begin to think globally, even the most domestic-seeming texts and local issues are found to have transcultural elements. After all, no culture is sealed off, pure or static, and if we look at early modern England,

we find a textile-exporting and luxury-importing island with a rapidly developing maritime culture. London, the site of so much literary and theatrical activity, was a commercial port directly connected by the Thames River estuary to the open sea and thus to the world. (34)[5]

I situate Shakespeare in these historical developments by noting that his professional theatrical company—organized according to principles not unlike those of the long-distance trading companies—took to the stages of the Theatre, the Curtain, the Globe, and the Blackfriars at the historical moment when these developments were transforming the cultural imagination. Readings that I have assigned in conjunction with this lecture include Andrew Gurr's essay on the stage in the *Norton Shakespeare*, various selections from the *Norton Shakespeare* "General Introduction," an excerpt from Jean Howard and Phyllis Rackin's *Engendering a Nation*, and most recently, the aforementioned audio podcast "England Goes Global."[6]

The artifacts MacGregor discusses in this episode include terrestrial globes first produced in London in 1592, a world map from the second edition of Richard Hakluyt's *Principal Navigations* (1599), and two commemorative renderings of the route of Drake's circumnavigation in 1578 to 1580—a pocket-sized silver medal and a splendid wall map displayed in Whitehall. Through its treatment of these objects and an opening analogy between Drake's circumnavigation and the moon landing, the podcast invites students to consider global consciousness as a newly enlarged spatial perspective, a patriotic exercise in asserting English claims to far-flung territories, and a newly elaborated notion that the whole world can be viewed at a glance and can be represented in a small place. MacGregor notes that *theater* is the same term used by Abraham Ortelius in his *Theatrum orbis terrarum* (*Theater of the Lands of the World*), what MacGregor characterizes as "the first atlas as we would recognize it" (14). MacGregor emphasizes the pointed topicality of the name of the Globe Theatre. For a more sustained critical treatment of the conceptual overlay between theaters and maps, I borrow from John Gillies's "Theatres of the World," a chapter in his *Shakespeare and the Geography of Difference*, from which I have assigned other excerpts or to which I refer in my early lecture. In calling Drake's circumnavigation and the discourse and artifacts commemorating it "the sixteenth-century equivalent of the 'space-race,'" the podcast encourages students to see continuities between Shakespeare's era and our own. (Future secondary school teachers, a substantial portion of our majors, are particularly keen on this idea, as they are wrestling with their future responsibility to make Shakespeare "relevant" to high school students.) What the "space-race" analogy also does—and what is just one among several ways to frame global engagements in the period—is assume the dominance of bilateral rivalry between the English and Spanish. MacGregor presents a clip from the map librarian at the British Library, who notes the anachronistic inclusion of the Virginia colony on the silver medal, which was not yet founded when Drake returned from his voyage. MacGregor includes this tidbit as part of his reading of the patriotic and propagandistic work that the medal performs, noting that the silver out of which the medal was made might have been procured from one of Drake's raids on Spanish ships.

Globalizing the English Histories

When we get to the Henry IV plays, replete with references to Spanish sack wine, I recall the podcast's suggestion of straightforward Anglo-Spanish rivalry and then complicate its assumption of a simple, bilateral, Eurocentric model of transglobal competition. Either as a guided reading question assigned in advance or as a small group activity during class, I ask the students to track references to the substances that Falstaff consumes. I might ask them just to list instances or to consider the diction, imagery, and dramatic situations in which particular foods and beverages appear. (This activity can work whether one includes both Henry IV plays, which I usually do in our Shakespeare I course, or if one assigns the first of the two plays, which is probably the norm.) The students' first responses typically understand the pervasiveness of wine references as evidence of Falstaff's irresponsibility, self-indulgence, or his bad influence on the prince. At some point in the discussion, I bring in tidbits from my research on factors in global commerce, whose conflicts with the merchants they served outweighed their conflicts with foreigners abroad. Hal makes a pointed and intricate reference to this occupational category when he promises his father that he will redeem himself by trouncing Hotspur:

> Percy is but my factor, good my lord,
> To engross up glorious deeds on my behalf;
> And I will call him to so strict account
> That he shall render every glory up . . .
> Or I will tear the reckoning from his heart.   (2.3.147–52)

Hal's conceit demonstrates intricate familiarity with particular accounting duties of overseas factors—duties that they were frequently accused of shirking. These occupational details were not arcane knowledge in the period but would have been familiar to segments of Shakespeare's audience. Factors were "on the sea" and "on the ground" participants in the complex situation of Anglo-Spanish wine trade during the period when the second tetralogy was written and first performed. Likening his rival to a factor, Hal's conceit—in conjunction with the proliferation of sack references throughout the Henry IV plays—allows us to see how global consciousness entails a complicated picture of global trade networks, transnational alliances, and intra-English tensions that MacGregor's simple notion of English patriotism covers over.

If students are interested in trade details, I might offer some context on the longstanding ventures of English traders in the Canary Islands, one of the Spanish dominions where sack was produced and procured, even when England was officially at war with Spain. The wine that is on the lips of the Prince in his very first utterance in *1 Henry IV* (1.2.2), like the sugar in Poins's "sack-and-sugar" (1.2.100) epithet, is part of a vast system of transglobal trade networks stretching from the Mediterranean across the Atlantic. "This intolerable deal of sack" (2.5.493) that the Prince notes in Falstaff's receipts is not unique to this character, nor to Shakespeare's fictional Eastcheap tavern world. This increasingly popular beverage helped to enmesh the English in trade networks abroad and patterns of consumption back home, and it came to carry a range of cultural, religious, and political codes in literary culture. In the second tetralogy, this Spanish wine is a pointed anachronism, not unlike Norfolk's account of the sumptuous displays at the Field of the Cloth of Gold that "made Britain India." Shakespeare fills the late-fourteenth- and early-fifteenth-century world of his plays with a decidedly sixteenth-century wine. (The Spanish brought the grape that came to be cultivated on the Canaries after the Canarian sugar trade lost to competition from sugar production in Brazil and the West Indies.) By attending to material trade practices and the way that objects of trade circulate discursively, we can keep multiple temporal frameworks in view. Instead of assuming a uniform consensus about the "black legend of Spain," and generalizing about animosity toward Spain or toward that nonexistent group, the "non-English," considering sack's material history turns our attention to networks of relations and encounters, especially trade-generated ones. Trade-based relations can be exploitative and violent, but they can also be cooperative, forging alliances that cut against national affiliations and that undercut generalizations about patriotism.[7] Intense antagonisms emerged among the English, whether rival aristocratic factions, conflicting classes, or local competition over access to the lucrative trade, particularly after the 1604 peace treaty with Spain opened the floodgates to what had been a clandestine but flourishing trade.

When Poins and the prince read Falstaff's letter requesting a loan in *2 Henry IV*, sack wine becomes a vehicle not for expressing anti-Spanish sentiment but for venting animosity and fantasizing physical violence against the indebted knight. Poins says: "My lord, I'll steep this letter in sack and make him eat it" (2.2.115), as he and the prince plan one last trick on Falstaff, disguising themselves as tavern drawers and catching him badmouthing the prince. In order to concretize abstract ideas of how wine as material object functions both in global trade and on stage to complicate the binary of English versus non-English, I sometimes spend an extended session on the staging of that prank in act 2, scene 4 of *2 Henry IV*. The violent antagonisms and spirited verbal exchanges between Falstaff, Doll Tearsheet, Pistol, and Mistress Quickly that precede the arrival of disguised Poins and Hal are fun to read aloud or imagine blocking on stage. In addition, workshopping this scene vividly enacts how we find not a simple binary between English and non-English but rather an energetic depiction of differences in the category of Englishness itself, with wine (especially though not only Spanish wine) serving to both arouse animosity and allay it. Mistress Quickly remarks on an early insult exchange between Falstaff and Doll Tearsheet, "You two never meet but you fall to some discord," urging Doll to relent since she is "the weaker vessel, as they say, the emptier vessel" (2.4.48, 51–52). Despite having "drunk too much canaries" (21), Doll wittily retorts that Falstaff is the vessel, "a huge full hogshead" who carries "a whole merchant's venture of Bordeaux stuff in him; you have not seen a hulk better stuffed in the hold" (53–56). Falstaff greets the swaggering Pistol with a "cup of sack" (96). Doll rebuffs Pistol's advances, brandishing a knife and swearing "by this wine" that she will stab him if he accosts her (108). As their skirmish unfolds, Pistol accompanies a momentary offer to lay down his sword with repeated demands that Quickly "give's some sack" (156, 159). Of course, the prince and Poins enter the scene disguised as drawers who serve the stuff. As Norfolk's account with which I opened this essay revealed, imagining English-ness is always already enmeshed in a variety of global trade networks, alliances, and conflicts. By reading the scene aloud and trying different options for block-ing movements and action, students can render concretely the abstract concep-tual moves entailed in situating the histories globally, loosening the grip of the "nation" and even "English" as a primary or always-already emergent category of identity. At the very least, enacting the wine-fueled antagonisms and uneasy, wine-enabled alliances between Doll, Pistol, Mistress Quickly, Falstaff, and the prince reinforces how unstable the notion of national identity and belonging was. In the 1590s—as now—the notion was precarious and variously defined. Positing the crown as the centerpiece of the nation was hotly contested, just as claims to the crown and concepts of kingship themselves were contested.[8]

There are good reasons for studying how Shakespeare's history plays register the uneven emergence of constructions such as the nation and Englishness, but I've tried to suggest here that there might be even better reasons for loos-ening the hold of these concepts. Globalizing the plays helps disrupt binaries such as native/foreign and English/non-English, as well as uncritical notions of patriotic sentiment that these binaries can fuel. The impulse to question the exclusionary and top-down operations of patriotic nationalism emerged in a controversy that happened to be unfolding while I was teaching Henry V (and finishing this essay) during the fall of 2014. Our study of the play coincided with several weeks of public school student protests, teacher sick-outs, and in-ternational media attention catalyzed by a school board proposal to change the advanced placement history curriculum in a large public school district near Denver, down the road from my university. In its initial proposal, subsequently edited in response to public controversy, the recently elected conservative school board enjoined, "Materials should promote citizenship, patriotism, es-sentials and benefits of the free enterprise system, respect for authority and respect for individual rights. Materials should not encourage or condone civil disorder, social strife or disregard of the law."[9] Complexly enmeshed in a range of ongoing national debates about educational reform; partisan politics; and secondary teacher pay, evaluation, and self-governance, the widespread student protests to the controversial proposal not only enacted resistance to the imposition from above of a "more patriotic" version of United States national history, they also illustrated the ongoing, continual negotiation and struggle that constitutes history in general. I believe that globalizing our pedagogy of Shakespeare could fruitfully follow their cue.

NOTES

[1] As Colin Burrow notes, addressing a passage in *Henry V* when Fluellen compares Henry V and Alexander the Great (4.7.9–45), "Cross-cultural comparison was a deep part of both history and literary history in the sixteenth century" (204).

[2] The *OED* cites a line from Fletcher and Rowley's *The Maid in the Mill*, a play with a Spanish setting that was performed by the King's Men in 1623. Loosening the grip of Shakespeare on our curricula might be an important step in teaching history globally, but that line of inquiry does not belong here.

[3] The courses are divided chronologically into Shakespeare I and Shakespeare II. About half of our English majors are required to take one of these two courses. The typical section of forty students includes thirty to thirty-five English majors.

[4] MacGregor has produced a book based on the podcasts. The text in the book varies somewhat from the audio content. I use a document camera to project images that are mentioned in the podcast and that appear in the book. Some are available on the BBC 4 Web site as well.

[5] Vitkus offers a good bibliography and captures the animating interests of global systems theory accessibly and helpfully in this essay. Historical work in a global vein that has crucially shaped how I teach and write about early modern literature and history also includes Ogborn; Wallerstein; and A. Smith. A number of other essays in Singh's *Companion* discuss the interpenetrations of local and global, internal and external, and macro and micro. See, for example, Bartolovich; Morrow; and Smyth.

[6] The section that I target from Howard and Rackin appears in the chapter "The History Play in Shakespeare's Time" (11–16). The *Norton Shakespeare* sections "Henry VIII and His Children," "A Female Monarch in a Male World," "The Kingdom in Danger," and "The English and Otherness" are the most pertinent to the topic of the global. For a discussion of ways that I try to complicate simplistic self-other binaries that the "English and Otherness" section sometimes fosters in students, see my "Different Shakespeares: Global Consciousness in an Early Modern Literature Course." There is a large body of recent literary scholarship to which I'm indebted but don't necessarily assign to undergraduates. Some key sources are Helgerson, *Forms*; Gillies; Brotton; Harris, *Sick Economies*; and Singh. Also see the readings I discuss in "Different Shakespeares."

[7] I discuss these dynamics in "Morose's Turban."

[8] William Carroll offers an accessible discussion of competing modes of understanding kingship. In the scene in question, Falstaff alerts us to these debates as he calls for more sack and the prince and Poins unmask their wine drawer disguise. By jestingly referring to Harry as "a bastard son of the King's" (2.4.256), Falstaff jabs at the precariousness of Hal's legitimacy by associating him with an inferior Spanish wine.

[9] The proposal is quoted in two *Guardian* articles covering the story: Jessica Glenza's "Colorado Teachers Stage Mass Sick-out to Protest US History Curriculum Changes" and Nicky Woolf's "US 'Little Rebels' Protest against Changes to History Curriculum."

Historicism "By Stealth": History, Politics, and Power in *Richard II* and *Henry IV*

Neema Parvini

When I first started lecturing I was very keen to introduce students to theoretical approaches to *Richard II* and *Henry IV*. I would teach them Louis Althusser and Michel Foucault directly, and then talk them through the central tenets of the work of Stephen Greenblatt, Alan Sinfield, and Jonathan Dollimore. In time, I stopped doing this because I found that students would, rather disappointingly, simply reproduce the new-historicist and cultural-materialist approaches they had been taught—or, worse, they would simply echo my own critiques of them. Instead, I have developed a way of approaching the plays that encourages students to develop historicist approaches to texts while maintaining independence of critical thought. This approach is anchored in my view that students learn best through reaching their own conclusions rather than through replicating someone else's; it is the difference between passive and active learning.

In this essay, I will outline my approach to teaching history, politics, and power in *Richard II* and the two parts of *Henry IV*. I will begin by summarizing the necessary contextual groundwork that I establish before approaching the plays. Next, I will explain how I develop an ideologically informed critical understanding of the plays, emphasizing key questions of power as manifest in strategies of kingship and of whether history is driven by human beings or by divine Providence.

Teaching Shakespeare's history plays to undergraduates presents a peculiar set of challenges. In order to comprehend fully what is happening in them, the student must appreciate three things. First, the plays are based on real historical events of which students should have a working knowledge, namely the Wars of the Roses, which we cannot assume that students already possess. Second, the eight plays—from the *Henry VI* trilogy to *Henry V*—form a sequence, with recurring characters and action that carries on from one play to the next. This fact presents a challenge because it is unlikely that a class will read the whole sequence. For example, in my own undergraduate teaching, I only cover *Richard II* and the *Henry IV* plays. Third, an understanding of the broader theoretical contexts in which Shakespeare himself was writing is important in developing informed critical views of the plays and what they do ideologically and politically. One challenge is the temptation to teach the plays through the lens of influential cultural-materialist or new-historicist readings, whether it is the older "Tudor myth" view of E. M. W. Tillyard or the readings by Greenblatt, Graham Holderness, Phyllis Rackin, and others (see, e.g., Greenblatt's "Invisible Bullets"). In my case, as the author of a recent book-length study of the histories, *Shakespeare History Plays: Rethinking Historicism*, another temptation might be to teach them my own reading. The danger here is that students may take over existing historicist approaches to the plays verbatim, which discourages critical thinking. It is a challenge to find a balance between making students aware of these readings and compromising the independence of their own thought. Accordingly, I prefer to provide them with all the raw materials needed to make their own readings. My approach is to build this knowledge from the ground up. This is a form of knowledge transfer that is best covered in lectures. Even if some students have existing knowledge of these contexts, it is important for the whole group to be on the same footing. This is the necessary groundwork for active learning to take place.

These raw materials can be grouped in four main areas:

1. Early modern Christian beliefs inherited from the medieval period, indeed the very period that Shakespeare is writing about in the history plays
2. The structure of feudal and semifeudal society
3. Emergent humanist ideas about history and politics imported from Renaissance Italy, especially those of Machiavelli
4. The key events of the Wars of the Roses and the corresponding key plot points of Shakespeare's two tetralogies

The first two of these areas can be tackled together. For this purpose, Tillyard's *The Elizabethan World Picture*, for all its problems, still provides a useful and succinct overview of the official doctrines. Using this, I introduce the students to the great chain of being, the five kingdoms and their rankings including those of the animal kingdom, the astrological ranks, the four elements, and the four humors. In addition, I stress the importance placed on the divine right of kings and explain the providential view of history as outlined by Tillyard. Students must understand that this is a hierarchical, static view of the universe with fixed ranks. It is a conservative doctrine that does not tolerate challenges to the status quo because to challenge that is to challenge God and God's plan.

Once the general concept of the great chain of being is understood, the structure of feudal and semifeudal society is fairly straightforward to explain since this merely constitutes the ranking of human beings, who sit atop the animal kingdom and just below the spiritual one. However, there are some crucial and often overlooked aspects of it that are of real benefit to students reading Shakespeare's plays, or indeed, early modern literature more generally:

> The human ranks from king to peasant. It is important for students to understand that dukes are ranked above earls who are ranked above barons, for example. It is important for them to know that when a duke is speaking in a Shakespeare play he wields significant power. It is also worth noting the special status of knights, who as beneficiaries of honorary titles are neither peasants nor part of the aristocracy.
>
> The concept of vassalage and what characters mean when they use the word "liege." I often explain this by telling them that one's liege is "like a boss for life."
>
> The concept of homage, namely the taxes and military support that vassals would pay to their lieges.
>
> Once these concepts are understood, it is possible to explain how the power of the monarch was kept in check by the aristocracy: since England had no standing army, the king relied on the support of his vassals to provide money and troops. If he was seen as tyrannical, this support could be withheld.
>
> Finally, it is important to understand how noble titles work in two respects: first, that they were governed by male-preference cognatic primogeniture, and second, that once ordained it was incredibly difficult for the monarch to strip nobles of their landed titles. Students need to understand that stripping such titles (which amounts to the seizure of land and assets)—as we see Richard II do to Bolingbroke shortly after John of Gaunt's death—was seen as tyrannical and would have been deeply unpopular.

Once the students have absorbed Tillyard, I introduce them to the central tenets of Machiavelli's *The Prince*. I emphasize Machiavelli's radical departure from previous "mirrors for princes"–style manuals in his cynical insistence on viewing men as they are, not as they ought to be. I outline his consequentialist doctrine of the ends justifying the means. Finally I introduce them to his humanist view that history is driven by the self-interested actions of men rather than by God—this is the early modern shift from "first cause" (of God) to the "second causes" (of mankind) outlined by Rackin in *Stages of History*, what she calls "the gradual separation of history from theology" (6).

If students can understand the fundamentals of both Tillyard and Machiavelli before reading the history plays, they will be well placed to start thinking seriously about their ideological alignments. I have found this sequence to be much more effective than having them directly encounter new-historicist or cultural-materialist readings that position Shakespeare firmly either as conservative or radical. It is best for students to make their own connections and to draw their own conclusions, not least because it widens the scope for energetic in-class debate.

Finally, turning to the stretch of history that the plays cover, I use the royal family tree to explain the key events from 1397 to 1485. It is important to show the students how and why the Wars of the Roses came about after Henry IV's usurpation of Richard II's crown and how they culminate in Richard III's defeat at Bosworth by Henry Tudor. I note how Thomas of Woodstock led the Lords Appellant (who were composed of Richard FitzAlan, Thomas de Beauchamp, Henry Bolingbroke, and Thomas de Mowbray) in a successful armed rebellion against Richard II in 1397. I also note Richard II's role in the imprisonment and murder of Woodstock, which is an important pretext to the argument between Bolingbroke and Mowbray in the first act of *Richard II*. I point out that the claim of the Mortimers is superior to the claim of the Lancasters. I also provide a detailed general outline of the plot of the first tetralogy—of all of the history plays, the *Henry VI* plays are likely to be the ones with which students are least familiar. Finally, I draw students' attention to the Bishop of Carlisle's prophecy (*R2* 4.1.125–40) and the weight given to it by critics who insist that Shakespeare wished to portray the Wars of the Roses as divine punishment for Bolingbroke's transgression against God's plan. I also mention that critics point to similar prophecies spoken by Henry VI in the *Henry VI* plays and by Margaret in *Richard III*. However, I end by insisting that students must make up their own minds when watching and reading these plays.

Students need to be au fait with the entire narrative arc of the eight plays in order to make informed judgments on whether or not Shakespeare takes sides in the conflicts he depicts, whether or not he has an agenda to propagate the Tudor myth as Tillyard argues, and finally, whether he subscribes to the providential view of history or to the Machiavellian view of it. In the first seminar on *Richard II*, I focus students' attention on Richard's handling of the dispute between Bolingbroke and Mowbray in the first act. This is a close reading exercise designed to help students understand the various subtexts at play. Mowbray and Bolingbroke were once allied in rebellion against Richard as members of the Lords Appellant. Having been humiliated by them before, Richard's position is precarious: he cannot afford for these two lords to be reconciled and risk a future rebellion. His twin aims in this first act are to distance himself from Mowbray and from complicity in the murder of Thomas of Woodstock while limiting the power and influence of the increasingly popular Bolingbroke. Therefore, Richard cannot afford to let the proposed trial by combat take place, as a victory by either lord puts him in an undesired position: Mowbray's victory would risk Richard's complicity in Woodstock's murder and Bolingbroke's victory would increase Bolingbroke's popularity. Richard is also militarily weak and so does not want to set a precedent in which matters are decided by the sword, since he must rely on the "soft power" of language.

In order to maximize time in the seminar, I organize the class into four groups, asking them to focus on act 1, scene 1 and act 1, scene 3. Each group must analyze the scenes and come up with some conclusions about how Richard handles this delicate situation. In addition, I give each group one key question to consider:

> Group 1: Do you think Shakespeare takes sides in this conflict? How? Do any characters come off better than any others?
>
> Group 2: What does Richard's power in these scenes rest on? What does he rely on to get his own way?
>
> Group 3: When exactly do you think Richard makes the decision to end the duel at Coventry?
>
> Group 4: Has Richard opened himself up to any unnecessary risks?

Once each group reports back to the rest of the class, some stimulating discussion usually ensues. There is often disagreement over the question of when Richard makes the decision to halt the combat. Some students think that this was his plan all along and a shrewd calculation designed to display his power in a setting of heightened pomp and ritual; others think that Richard is a much more insecure, indecisive, and impulsive character who makes the decision on the spur of the moment. There is also disagreement over whether or not the decision to banish both characters is politically prudent. Typically, there is more agreement on the fact that Richard rests on the ideology of kingship, as manifest in language, to rule over his subjects. Students mostly agree that Shakespeare appears to be neutral during the dispute, although some have argued that Bolingbroke seems like a more honorable character than Mowbray or the king. Every so often, a student might argue that Mowbray seems like the most honest character and that Bolingbroke is depicted as a Machiavellian schemer. This session is designed to get students used to looking at texts in a different way: they are actually performing a kind of Foucauldian power analysis or new-historicist reading. But this is done by stealth—that is, without my telling them that this is happening. It is more effective for students to come to their own conclusions and then expose them to the prevailing new-historicist or cultural-materialist views than vice versa, because they will be much more likely to defend their position and develop counterarguments once their own view has formed.

In the second seminar, the focus is much wider. The first half of this class takes the form of a broad comparison between the reigns of Richard II and Henry IV. I ask students to identify each monarch's overall strategy of governing the country to consider what each did well and what each did poorly. Students are adept at recognizing that Richard mostly relies on the ideological strategies of soft power, while Henry is a man of action who often enforces his rule through physical violence. They also recognize that while Henry is ostensibly the more successful king, his kingdom is fractious and under almost constant threat of rebellion. They tend to reach a consensus that a successful king would need a mixture of both strategies of power. This is a version of the reading I offer myself in *Shakespeare's History Plays* (174–214)—although again, the students' conclusion is arrived at mostly by stealth.

In the second half of this session, I turn to the ultimate political and ideological questions at stake in these plays:

> Does Shakespeare make it appear that the causes of history are driven by men or by God? How?
>
> Does Shakespeare's vision of history conform to the great chain of being or is it more realist and Machiavellian? How?
>
> Does Shakespeare appear to have greater sympathy with Richard II or with Henry IV? How?

All three of these questions get at the same thing in different ways, and I usually expect a range of answers from students. Again, by stealth, they will likely retrace critical debates that took place between Tillyard and the liberal humanists of the 1960s and 1970s (e.g., Prior or Sanders) or between new historicists who see Shakespeare as primarily a conservative royalist playwright, especially Greenblatt and Rackin, and more recent studies, such as those by Nicolas Grene or myself, that seek to overturn that view. Works by these critics should be on the recommended reading list for those students wishing to write on the histories in their assessed essays.

Using the approach I have outlined, I have been able to take a historically informed approach to *Richard II* and *Henry IV* while fostering independent critical thinking in my students without reproducing the dominant orthodoxies. By the end, they should be able to produce nuanced analyses of the history, politics, and power in these plays.

Richard II:
Presentism, Pedagogy, Ecocriticism

Lynne Bruckner

This essay focuses on how *Richard II* can engage students in considerations of land use, political power, and ecological stewardship in both early modern and contemporary culture. Ecocriticism and presentism complement each other. In his "An Ecocritic's *Macbeth*," Richard Kerridge writes, "The sense of emergency with which ecocritics must read belongs peculiarly to our own time. . . . To read ecocritically is therefore to read from an extremely specific present" (193–94). And the short answer to Sharon O'Dair's self-posed question, "Is It Shakespearean Ecocriticism If It Isn't Presentist?" is a resounding "no" (71). In my course Shakespeare: Ecocriticism,[1] I work with students to dismantle the presentist-historicist dichotomy, following Cary DiPietro and Hugh Grady's view that "the act of interpreting Shakespeare always involves multiple pasts and a changing, developing present" (45). Early in the semester, students research and deliver historically based presentations on topics ranging from early modern deforestation to pollution and the little ice age. Later they present on a twenty-first-century ecological issue sparked by a Shakespeare passage. Such work prepares students to read *Richard II* from a presentist and ecological stance.

Richard II was understood as a play about politics in the Elizabethan era, and it resonates politically for readers today. In the final week of the semester, we focus on Richard's profligate use of state funds, the expense of war, and the consequent need to treat the earth as an economic resource (rather than as a resource to be protected). As the play underscores, a good leader should be a good steward of nation and nonhuman nature, though caring for nature in the sixteenth century is far from synonymous with current notions of ecological stewardship. In this century, ecological responsibilities include guarding against further losses in biodiversity; protecting nonhuman species, systems, and spaces; safeguarding aquifers, watersheds, and the global ocean; trimming our carbon emissions; checking our consumerist habits; and curbing the assumption that we deserve to live highly convenient lives. In the Renaissance, however, good environmental stewardship focused largely on trimming, checking, and curbing nature itself.

To give students some grounding in early modern notions of nonhuman nature, I assign key sections from Keith Thomas's *Man and the Natural World: Changing Attitudes in England, 1500–1800*. Thomas explains that for early moderns "a tamed, inhabited, and productive landscape *was* beautiful" (255). He notes, as well, that "agricultural improvement and exploitation were not just economically desirable; they were moral imperatives" (254). While certain kinds of "improvement" were controversial (enclosure and market-driven crop production), a cultivated, productive landscape was the aesthetic and cultural ideal.

Thomas's important book prepares students for their first presentations. I provide deliberately broad research topics (animals, gardens, weather), allowing students to select their particular focus. In the introduction to her first presentation, for example, Ris Jenkins wrote, "There were three reasons for hunting in the period—obtaining food, managing pests, and killing for pleasure. We will focus on the last." Drawing on multiple sources, Jenkins zeroed in on the privatization of royal forests, noting that through "the abuse of waste laws and subsequent enclosure of previously common land, the aristocracy was able to create more deer chases"—a point that allows us better to understand the abuse of land in *Richard II*.

Similarly, Sarah Hancock focused on formal gardens, explaining how the cultivated "landscape of the garden took precedence over the freedom of the natural landscape." The garden (central to *R2* 3.4) became a sustained interest for this student. Riffing off Polixenes's nature and art speech (*WT* 4.5), Sarah's contemporary eco-issue centered on an extreme sort of improvement—genetic engineering. Other presentist eco-issues ranged from hurricanes to green burials and alternatives to consumer culture.

Courtney Druzak concentrated on ecological degradation and the body (broadly construed). Drawing from Ken Hiltner for her early presentation, Druzak asserted that "similar to what we currently experience . . . in our encounters with pollution, inhabitants of Early Modern England found themselves '. . . unable to reconcile their need for coal with the dangers it wrought both on their health and on their glorious nation.'" Her eco-issue, sparked by Orlando's desire to "carve on every tree" (*AYL* 3.2.9), focused on "tree girdling." Students recognized that current and historic issues are distinct yet connected; Shakespeare's plays resonate with both.

While students give four presentations in this seminar (including a discussion lead and final paper proposal), I present on hydrofracturing (fracking) and *Richard II*. My goal is to identify for students the nexus between Richard's (and Elizabeth I's) exploitation of forests and the recent "management" of Pennsylvania's state forest system.[2]

Gas companies remind us that drilling for natural gas has been occurring in Pennsylvania's state forests for over fifty years. The older shallow wells are small, "about the size of a single gas pump, with a home air conditioning unit . . . next to it" (Detrow). Not so with hydraulic fracturing. A single well pad requires clear-cutting five to fifteen acres of forest; each pad requires a wastewater pool of three to five acres and approximately twenty feet in depth. The majority of shale wells are drilled to a depth of roughly 7,000 feet; from there the drilling runs horizontally for up to two miles. Up to seven million pressurized gallons of "slick water" (chemically laced water mixed with sand or other propellants) are injected into each well to release the gas. About one-third of that water will come to the surface; the "flowback" contains the proprietary chemicals and immensely briny (sometimes radioactive) foundation waters. In Pennsylvania alone unconventional gas wells "have produced 5.8 billion gallons of liquid waste" ("Well Watch").

Few people are aware that nearly 700,000 acres of Pennsylvania state forest have been leased to gas drilling companies; 140,000 of these acres—some in primitive forest—have been leased for Marcellus pads (Detrow). In April 2014, the Pennsylvania Department of Conservation and Natural Resources released the first *DCNR Shale-Gas Monitoring Report*. While it is too early to gauge long-term effects on state forests, concerns include forest fragmentation, increases in invasive species, and compressor noise in excess of state guidelines.

In upper-level courses, I share what I am working on—including the difficulties I encounter as a scholar. Students in Shakespeare: Ecocriticism (fall 2012) knew I was working on fracking in the region and in relation to *Richard II*. It is, I think, not a bad thing to share one's scholarly arguments, particularly when it is an argument about which one feels passionate. When *Richard II* arrives on our syllabus, students have already submitted their proposals for their term papers, have already found their own passionate arguments.

When talking about things ecocritical in *Richard II*, it seems best to start in the garden scene (3.4) and Gaunt's sceptered isle speech (2.1). Setting forth the ideals of good kingship, these scenes yoke responsible management of the natural world to responsible management of the nation. Scholars have long read the garden scene as an allegory of good government and an explicit critique of King Richard's failures of leadership.

Ecocritics tend to focus on materiality; from this perspective, the scene is about tending an early modern garden. In their ecofeminist reading of the Gardener's statement, "O, what pity is it / That he [Richard] had not so trimm'd and dressed his land / As we this garden!" (3.4.56–58), Rebecca Laroche and Jen Munroe find that "he calls to our attention not the fact that Richard . . . neglected imagining England in metaphoric terms as a garden but rather that Richard would have ruled the kingdom better had he taken a cue from those who work outside with the land" (43). This material focus also highlights that tending the land is predominantly a matter of positive discipline—tying back what has gone wild, pruning what grows too quickly, eradicating weeds, and killing caterpillars:

> GARDENER. Go, bind thou up yon dangling apricots,
> Which, like unruly children, make their sire
> Stoop with oppression of their prodigal weight.
> Give some supportance to the bending twigs.
> Go thou, and, like an executioner,
> Cut off the heads of too fast-growing sprays
> That look too lofty in our commonwealth.
> All must be even in our government.
> You thus employ'd, I will go root away

The noisome weeds which without profit suck
The soil's fertility from wholesome flowers.   (3.4.30–40)

While words like "executioner," "commonwealth," and "government" gesture toward allegory, the passage also underscores the physical actions of the Gardener and his men. The Gardener's directive to bind the "apricots," which are like "unruly children," fits neatly with a parallel drawn by Thomas: "it was widely held that most children would need to be beaten and repressed. Timber trees, correspondingly, were to be pollarded (i.e., beheaded), lopped or shredded" (220). While recent scholars have qualified Lawrence Stone's assumptions about the subhuman status of early modern children, such treatment was often viewed as good nurture and—according to Thomas—necessary to the stewardship of nonhuman nature.

Yoking materiality and allegory, the garden allows students to discuss the act of gardening and larger issues of land management and politics. The garden, as Heidi Scott notes, is "a microcosm of Richard's isle"—and for Shakespeare's audience, of Elizabeth's isle as well (267). The years between 1593 and 1597 were a time of extraordinarily poor harvests and famine, as the "1590s marked the beginnings of the apogee of the Little Ice Age" (Fagan 103). Making things worse, the parliament of 1593, due to the "great plenty and cheapness of grain," discontinued the statutes against the conversion of arable land to pasture, exacerbating the crop yield in the fall of 1594 (Thirsk, *Agrarian History* 228). Between 1593 and 1597, flour prices nearly tripled (Rappaport 136–67). Scarcity and want, moreover, were amplified in years of war: "the crown's armies and people competed for food or other consumables in the 1590s" (136). It is difficult not to believe that the original audience for *Richard II* (ca. 1595) connected the garden scene to failures of stewardship.

While Gaunt's "scepter'd isle" speech occurs earlier in the play, it accumulates meaning once students have grasped Elizabethan notions of stewardship. Inaugurating the play's ruminations over Richard's abuse of the land, Gaunt also presents the island as an ecological and geographical fantasy, constructing England as an untouched gem, inviolable by her enemies (war and disease). Although a critique of state corruption and Richard's profligate abuse of the land and national coffers, the speech describes England as a "precious stone set in the silver sea" (2.1.46). Gaunt's vision of the island is an ecological fantasy—a wish that the island is impenetrable, perfect, and whole. Claiming that the sea serves the island in "the office of a wall, / Or as a moat defensive to a house / Against the envy of less happier lands," Gaunt works to establish England as a chosen "other Eden" that cannot be defiled—at least not externally (2.1.47–49, 42). Gaunt's perspective on England's "natural" protection is (and was) a myth, not only in terms of the history of the British Isles, but also in terms of ecological realities; an island can no more be sealed off from biotic influence than can the human body (Bruckner, "Teaching" 223–24).

Early in the semester, students write ecologically inflected papers on one sonnet using close reading and the *OED*; word choice was a frequent preoccupation in our 2012 class. Gaunt, in this speech, rarely uses the word "land"; "land" is less lively than "earth," and it connotes use value ("arable land") or ownership. Tellingly, the one line in which Gaunt uses "land" (and twice) is as he transitions from his ideal of England to its degradation by Richard:

> This land of such dear souls, this dear dear land,
> Dear for her reputation through the world,
> Is now leased out—I die pronouncing it—
> Like to a tenement or pelting farm.   (2.1.57–60)

The pun on "dear" signals not only the land's status as beloved but also its economic value, that which makes it subject to abuse. Indeed, having lived too high on the courtly hog, Richard is forced to put the realm to farm in order to pay for the war in Ireland. Exploiting the earth for immediate cash in hand, Richard gives others (his favorites) the right to "to extort taxes on their own behalf" (Shakespeare, *R2* [Gurr] 93n45). As Gaunt underscores, Richard diminishes the earth, reducing it to a tenement or smallholding—a mere source of direct revenue.

When Richard enters the scene, Gaunt confronts him: "Thy deathbed is no lesser than thy land, / Wherein thou liest in reputation sick" (2.1.95–96), drawing a parallel between the body of the king and the waste of the land. The ailing Duke of Lancaster attempts to show Richard not only his error in judgment but also his misapprehension of the earth. Harping on the word "land," Gaunt insists to Richard that his wellbeing and that of the earth are one and the same: "Thy waste is no whit lesser than thy land" (103). As he makes this point, Gaunt's (Shakespeare's) linguistic choices indicate that to value the earth in purely economic terms is to reduce it to land. Such thinking has consequences:

> It were a shame to let this *land* by lease.
> But, for thy world, enjoying but this *land*,
> Is it not more than shame to shame it so?
> *Landlord* of England art thou now, not king.   (110–13; my emphasis)

Nowhere in this exchange with Richard does Gaunt refer to the earth or its fecundity; nowhere does he depict the king as anything other than ill. Richard's economic exploitation of the land would likely draw condemnation from the play's sixteenth-century audience. As William O. Scott finds, the very idea of leasing "might well have aroused controversial associations, quite apart from what Gaunt makes of it" (278–79).[3] While Gaunt's error is imagining a pristine England that never was, Richard's is far more destructive; he has reduced the living earth to a financial asset.

For not tending to England as does a careful gardener his plot of land, Richard has "suffered this disordered spring"; he is "the wasteful King" (3.4.49, 56), who in wasting the earth is wasting himself. The word "waste"—"uncultivated country"—is a signal term in the play for scholars of land law. Focusing on the "doctrine of waste," Dennis Klinck finds that Richard is both landlord and wasting tenant (24).[4] Waste can occur as a matter of action (felling Bolingbroke's timber to generate income) or neglect (failures of stewardship). Significantly, "seigniorial rights stemming from the land—rights associated with being king —did *not* mean the land was the king's 'own'" (Berg 228–29). In short, Richard has the right to collect fees from Bolingbroke's land, but not the use of the land itself.

The violation of Bolingbroke's property rights is one of Richard's most egregious acts. Richard abuses his royal privilege and sets in motion his own demise by denying Bolingbroke his lawful inheritance: "we seize into our hands / His plate, his goods, his money, and his lands" (2.1.210–11). The king's disregard for Bolingbroke's rights galvanizes the resistance against him; Ross expresses outrage that Richard "hath not money for these Irish wars / His burdenous taxations notwithstanding, / But by the robbing of the banished Duke" (260–62). Here, Richard violates the rights of his subjects and compromises natural resources in the service of a war he can't afford. It hardly needs to be said that the connection between environmental degradation and war is both longstanding and ongoing.

In the play, Richard's agents (Bushy and Green) compromise Bolingbroke's property. Unfolding "some causes" of their deaths, Bolingbroke states, "you have fed upon my signories, / Disparked my parks and felled my forest woods" (3.1.22–23). While not specified in *Richard II*, "disparking" would be using Bolingbroke's parks for activities other than protecting deer for the hunt. The charge of illicitly felled timber would be a sharp sting for early moderns, as deforestation was perceived as a severe problem. Not unlike Richard, Elizabeth "readily sold off timber from royal forests to finance military projects such as the Irish war" (Theis 52), and shortages in wood were felt acutely in "urban centers and . . . those regions where the iron and shipbuilding industries depended on an abundant supply of wood and timber" (Nardizzi 13). The ongoing debt under Elizabeth led to granting entrepreneurs "space in the forests in return for immediate cash" (Schama 155).

Throughout her reign and particularly during times of war, Elizabeth also sold extensive portions of crown land; such sales facilitated not only the move to agrarian capitalism but also "the enclosure of both common and demesne land" (W. Scott 279). Many must have resented the Crown's shift in use of early modern forests from royal hunting grounds, which allowed customary use, to a site of industry (Schama 152). The play connects war, national debt, faulty land management, deforestation, and displacement.

Reading through an ecocritical and presentist lens, students can locate the intersections not only between Richard's and Elizabeth's land and timber management but also between early modern land use and issues that pertain to Pennsylvania's state forests. Pennsylvania is central to the fracking boom more because of politics than the quality of its shale gas resources. As Bill McKibben writes, "The powers that be in Harrisburg have been remarkably congenial hosts to the new fracking industry, rolling out the red carpet" and offering up state forests as drill sites. We need only to follow the money to understand current decisions about Pennsylvania's state forests. Pre-shale-gas activity in state forest and parks (ca. 1947–2008) generated "a total income to the commonwealth of approximately $153,659,522" (*DCNR*); these funds went back into the state parks and forests for maintenance and improvements. With the advent of hydraulic fracturing, however, gas revenue was appropriated to the state, often to pay down debt. In recent years (2009–2012) shale drilling in Pennsylvania state forests yielded $582,250,644 (*DCNR*). The April 2014 *DCNR Shale-Gas Monitoring Report* states that "one of the bureau's most significant roles is to act, in the public trust, as steward of the commonwealth's 2.2-million-acre state forest system" (5)—a statement that is likely to incite student debate regarding the ever-blurring distinction between stewardship and exploitation.

NOTES

[1]Shakespeare: Ecocriticism is an upper-level seminar for undergraduates who have previously taken the Shakespeare survey and for MFA and MAT graduate students. Students cited in this essay are Chatham University undergraduates: my sincere gratitude to all students in the 2012 iteration of this course.

[2]For connections between *Richard II* and fracking in national parks, see Bruckner, "Consuming."

[3]Scott notes that landlords used a variety of methods to convert relatively secure copyholds to less secure leases, often leading to enclosure.

[4]In addition to Klinck and to W. Scott on land law, see Berg. On enclosure, see Siemon.

Teaching the Roles of Women in Shakespeare's English History Plays

Phyllis Rackin

Until quite recently, the roles of women in Shakespeare's history plays attracted little attention. The critical literature focused on the male protagonists and their struggles for power and legitimacy, and in performance the roles of women were frequently cut down or even eliminated. However, focusing on the roles of women offers unique opportunities to explore issues central to the dynamics of the plays and to the historical contexts in which the plays were first produced and subsequently reproduced.

An effective way to begin a class discussion of women's roles in these plays is to start with the statistical evidence for their relatively small size and number and ask students to consider possible explanations for these limitations.[1] To be sure, women's roles in all of Shakespeare's plays are generally smaller and less plentiful than men's, but women were most marginalized in the genre of the English history play. One explanation likely to come up is the unequal place of women in Shakespeare's historical sources. At this point, it is useful to explore the reasons Tudor history centered on the deeds of men. Until recently, most history did the same. What mattered to historians were the political and military conflicts that shaped the fates of nations, and since both these arenas were dominated by men, women were necessarily marginalized. In the specific case of Tudor history, however, it is also worth discussing the implications for women of the fact that claims of patrilineal succession legitimized political authority.[2] Still another reason worth exploring is the unequal status of women, not only in Shakespeare's historical sources and in his world but also in the times and places of the plays' subsequent reproductions. A brief survey of the plays' reception history raises provocative questions about the cultural contexts in which the popularity of different plays rose and fell. In our own time, for instance, their relative popularity, both among critics and scholars and in teaching and theatrical production, has been almost inversely proportional to the size of the female characters' roles.[3]

In a general survey of Shakespeare's plays, this introductory material can be followed by an examination of two plays—first, one of the less canonical plays, such as *1 Henry VI*, in which women's roles are most prominent and female characters most powerful, and second, one of the better known and more highly regarded plays, such as *1 Henry IV*, in which female characters are most marginalized.[4] In a course devoted entirely to women's roles in the history plays, the introductory material can be expanded to two or three weeks. After that, I find it useful to study the plays, not in the order in which the kings reigned and the plays were listed in the First Folio, but in the order in which the plays probably first appeared. The First Folio order implicitly designates the plays as dramatized history; the order of their theatrical production designates them as historical drama and also facilitates their analysis as products of their own time and place. In a course focused on women's roles, a further advantage of this organization is that students who have become accustomed to the relative prominence of the female characters in the first tetralogy and *King John* are likely to be struck by their marginal status in the more popular plays of the second tetralogy, an exclusion which they might otherwise take for granted as "normal." Once students have seen the difference, I ask them to explore the possible causes, effects, and implications of women's suppression in those later plays.

In *King John* and the plays of the first tetralogy—*Richard III* and the three parts of *Henry VI*—there are more female characters, they have more time on stage and more lines to speak, and they take active roles in the represented action. Students who have already read these plays are more likely to interrogate the circumscription of women's roles in the better known plays—*Richard II*, the two parts of *Henry IV*, and *Henry V*. One way to mark that diminution is, as I have said, simply to check the statistics. Another is to ask the students to note the locations in which female characters appear. In the two parts of *Henry IV*, for instance, no women appear on the fields of battle or in the royal court—the places where history is made. They can be found only in the plebeian and anachronistically modern place of the Boar's Head Tavern and at the homes of the rebels, located at the geographical margins of England. This marginalization is unlikely to seem noteworthy unless students have read the earlier history plays, where female characters have active roles in the court and battlefield scenes.

Another way the statistics can be fleshed out is by looking at the lines Shakespeare assigns to female characters. It is significant that the number of words spoken by female characters in the plays of the second tetralogy never reaches ten percent of the script. The quality of the female characters' speech is also worth noting. I always ask my undergraduate students to prepare for class by reading the plays aloud, taking parts; but even if you don't do this, you can show them in class that the women in those plays are often marked as defective speakers. In *1 Henry IV*, for instance, Lady Mortimer speaks no English at all, and Mistress Quickly's malapropisms make her the object of ridicule. Even Lady Percy, the only female character whose lines are written in Standard English, is subjected by her husband to a critique of her language (3.1.242–52).

A telling contrast to these women's verbal disempowerment can be provided by asking students to read aloud the exchange between Joan la Pucelle and Sir William Lucy in act 4, scene 7 of *1 Henry VI*. Not knowing that Talbot has died, Lucy looks for him on the battlefield. His speech is stiff and formal:

> But where's the great Alcides of the Field,
> Valiant Lord Talbot, Earl of Shrewsbury,
> Created, for his rare success in arms,
> Great Earl of Washford, Waterford, and Valence,
> Lord Talbot of Goodrig and Urchinfield,
> Lord Strange of Blackmere, Lord Verdun of Alton,
> Lord Cromwell of Wingfield, Lord Furnival of Sheffield,
> The thrice-victorious Lord of Falconbridge,
> Knight of the noble Order of Saint George,
> Worthy Saint Michael, and the Golden Fleece,
> Great marshal to Henry the Sixth
> Of all his wars within the realm of France?   (4.7.60–71)

It will be difficult to read these lines aloud with any expression except exaggerated pomposity—an interpretation that is quickly ratified by Joan's response:

> Here's a silly, stately style [i.e., list of titles] indeed.
> The Turk, that two-and-fifty kingdoms hath,
> Writes not so tedious a style as this.
> Him that thou magnifies with all these titles
> Stinking and fly-blown lies here at our feet.   (4.7.72–76)

Clearly, Joan has the best of this verbal encounter. While Lucy recites the titles that designate Talbot's patriarchal lineage and heroic military achievements, Joan relies on what she can see and smell to topple the formal monument Lucy has constructed with his tower of names and titles. Joan's vigorous, colloquial language has an obvious appeal for an audience.

Imagined in the context of the represented historical action, Joan is clearly demonized—a peasant French bastard, she is characterized in direct antithesis to the aristocratic English hero Talbot, with his noble lineage. But Joan's role is likely to be more fun for student actors to perform and for their audience to observe. If the noble English men are privileged in the represented action, it is the French peasant girl who is privileged in the theatrical representation. The contradiction between Joan's positive theatrical appeal and her negative role in the represented action provides an opportunity to discuss the importance of thinking about a play theatrically.[5] Reading the text silently, the temptation is to approach the characters as you would in real life or in a novel. Envisioning the play in theatrical terms involves thinking about the way it would look and sound in a playhouse and the responses it might elicit from other playgoers. The perfect example of the distinction is, of course, Richard III—the villain of the represented story but the most entertaining character on stage. In contrast to Richard's, Joan's part is relatively small, but like him she is arguably the most entertaining character on stage, not only because of her vivid language but also because of her physical energy. In her first appearance (1.3) she defeats the Dauphin in single combat, and a few scenes later (1.7) she fights Talbot to a draw. In act 3, scene 2, she enters the gates of Rouen disguised as a poor marketwoman. In the following scene she appears at the top of the city's wall holding a burning torch. In act 5, scene 3, she summons evil spirits to the stage, who appear accompanied by thunder.

Joan also provides a model for discussing the roles of the other female characters in the play—the Countess of Auvergne and Margaret of Anjou. Their roles are smaller and less developed than hers but, like her, they are French, and like her they threaten the English historical project of maintaining the legacy of Henry V. I ask for volunteers to read aloud the Countess's encounter with Talbot in act 2, scene 3, and then ask the class to speculate about the point of the Countess's insulting description of Talbot's physical presence as "a child . . . a . . . dwarf . . . a weak and writhled shrimp" (21–22). If the students are keeping in mind that they are reading a script designed for performance, one suggestion that should come up is that Talbot's part may have been written for a small actor. This, in turn, will invite useful speculation about whether the actor's small stature influenced the nature of the part Shakespeare wrote for him or if Shakespeare wrote the part for a small actor in order to emphasize the difference between Talbot's unimpressive physical presence and his heroic spirit. Another question that should emerge in discussion concerns the ways the Countess's contemptuous description anticipates Joan's later reduction of Talbot to a stinking, flyblown corpse that belies the glorious titles marking his heroic place in English history.

Many scholars believe that *1 Henry VI* was actually written later than parts 2 and 3, but whether it was written first or last, it is clearly designed as a prequel to the other plays, not only because it depicts the first part of Henry's reign but also—and more important in a class centering on women's roles—because Joan is depicted as a prototype for Margaret, the only character who appears in all four plays of the first tetralogy (and in fact the only character who appears in four of Shakespeare's plays). In a class that covers all the history plays, it is instructive to trace Margaret's role in the remaining plays of the first tetralogy.

The connection between Joan and Margaret can be demonstrated in class by asking the students what staging is implied by the directions at the end of act 5, scene 4 and the beginning of act 5, scene 5 in part 1. At the end of act 5, scene 4, Joan is led off the stage as York's captive. Immediately thereafter, at the beginning of scene 5, Margaret enters the scene, led onto the stage as Suffolk's captive. Margaret's characterization is minimal in *1 Henry VI* and her only obvious similarity to Joan is that both are French women; but in parts 2 and 3, she will emerge as the inheritor of Joan's legacy as a fierce warrior and a determined opponent to the English men who are the plays' protagonists. As a warrior, she usurps her husband's role on the battlefield; in court politics, she threatens his authority; but her most dangerous resemblance to Joan may be a distinctly female form of transgression embodied briefly in Joan's sexual promiscuity but greatly magnified in Margaret's adulterous passion for Suffolk, which threatens the purity of the royal succession. Margaret's marriage to the king of England will bring the subversive forces that both women represent to the heart of the English court.

In a class that covers only two plays, it is instructive to follow *1 Henry VI* with one of the better known plays of the second tetralogy because any of them will provide striking contrasts to the earlier play. I have already mentioned the marginalization of the female characters in the *Henry IV* plays, but although women's roles are more prominent in *Richard II*, those female characters, like the ones in *Richard III*, are cast in the traditional roles of suffering and bereaved wives and mothers. The Duchess of Gloucester pleads with Gaunt to avenge her murdered husband, but to no avail (1.3). The queen learns that her husband has been captured by Bolingbroke and will be deposed only when she overhears the Gardener and his helper discussing the news. The Duchess of York does manage to obtain an audience with the new king, but her son and husband are there before her, and once she enters the stage, the action of the scene descends to farce (5.3.77–78). In *Henry V*, the only English woman who appears is Mistress Quickly, still speaking in malapropisms, and the French princess is quite literally domesticated, taught to speak English in preparation for her destiny as a term in the peace treaty that will make her the bride of the English king.

In a class that examines women's places in all the plays, *Richard III* can be seen as a transition. Here, as in the earlier plays, women's roles are relatively prominent. Although female characters are assigned only a bit more than twenty-two percent of the words in the script, this is far more than in any of Shakespeare's other English histories. And although no female characters appear on the battlefield, their presence is felt in the conflicts of the English court. Nonetheless here, as in the second tetralogy, all the female characters—even Margaret—are reduced to helpless widows and bereaved mothers. And this play, like *Henry V*, reaches its triumphant conclusion in the announcement of a marriage in which the bride will be a prize won in battle to serve as a vehicle for dynastic succession.

The paradigms that emerge from these eight plays can also be used to study *Henry VIII* and *King John* even though *Henry VIII* was written much later, probably in collaboration with John Fletcher, and even though the history depicted in *King John* antedates the subjects of Shakespeare's other English histories by over a century. The central issue in both these plays, as in all the others, is dynastic succession, an issue that necessarily involves women and, since the privileged route of succession is patrilineal, necessarily requires their containment. In *Henry VIII*, for instance, neither Katherine of Aragon nor Anne Boleyn plays an active role in the court politics that constitute most of the action, and although the play concludes in the birth of the future Queen Elizabeth I, it drastically elides her role as a maker of English history. Elizabeth appears on stage only as a newborn infant, represented by a theatrical prop rather than a living actor, and although Cranmer greets the babe with an extravagant prophecy of her future glory, his speech further elides her history. I like to ask a student to read Cranmer's prophecy aloud and then invite the class to analyze the implications of its rapid passage from her birth to her death, his characterization of the future queen as "the maiden phoenix" (5.4.40), and the fact that his speech ends in a celebration of her male successor, James I (5.4.14–54).

NOTES

[1] Two good places for students to explore some of this evidence online are sites .google.com/a/shakespearelinecount.com/www/shakespeare-characters-line-count and www.theguardian.com/stage/interactive/2012/dec/10/shakespeare-women-interactive. A print source where all this evidence can be found is Spevack's *Complete and Systematic Concordance*.

[2] See chapter 4, "Patriarchal History and Female Subversion," in Rackin, pages 146–200.

[3] For a fuller discussion of this point, see Howard and Rackin 23–24. For statistical evidence supporting it, see 217–18.

[4] According to Spevack's *Complete and Systematic Concordance*, the percentage of words spoken by female characters in *Henry IV, Part 1* is 3.468, the lowest in any of Shakespeare's English history plays. In *Henry VI, Part 1*, by contrast, it is 12.497.

[5] Of course, Joan's role may also be more sympathetic for a generation that devoured the *Hunger Games* trilogy, as she is a kind of prototype for Katniss Everdeen.

Queering *Richard II*:
Teaching Love, Sex, and Gender Historically

Rebecca Ann Bach

One of the most interesting things about teaching issues of queer and LGBT identity in Shakespeare's history plays is how immediately queer social and sexual relations appear in those plays if they are looked at carefully. In these plays, men and women, men and men, and women and women simply do not relate to one another in ways that conform to normative sexual, love, and friendship behavior as we might see it today. For the purposes of this teaching essay, I am defining *queer* as nonnormative, as denoting both sexual and love relations not between a man and a woman and gender categories outside male and female. However, this queerness can be deceptive. Since people in the English Renaissance did not categorize people in ways that are familiar to people today, it is very easy to make mistakes about the queerness we see in the plays, to try and contain it by assigning characters identities that we understand today. As I, and many others, have shown, familiar sexuality categories such as heterosexuality, homosexuality, and bisexuality did not exist in the Renaissance, and gender categories, such as masculinity and femininity, could be defined so differently as to be unfamiliar to us. In this essay, I would like to make a case for teaching close reading and also for challenging the assumption that we can easily fit what we see into modern categories. Although it might be comforting for us and our students to see themselves reflected in Shakespeare's works, I would argue that, paradoxically, seeing that reflection may work to their (and our) disadvantage. If things have always been the same, if same-sex love relations were always minoritized and persecuted, and if views of gender remain unchanged, then it is harder to conceive of gender, love, and sex ever being treated completely differently.

Attitudes and laws related to queer and LGBT issues are changing fast, hopefully in the direction of fairness and equality. Also, attitudes and laws are currently different depending on where in the country or world one is. Regardless of location, I think it is very important when teaching about these issues to run a safe classroom. When I am running a discussion class or section, I like to have an opening discussion that enables me to set ground rules for classroom discourse: everyone should be heard, but no one should insult or otherwise hurt anyone else. Rather than laying down the law, I acknowledge that we all have different ideas and backgrounds and introduce the idea that the classroom is a place to explore difference. Then I talk about how much every student's safety matters to me. At that point, I ask what kind of rules we might set that would ensure everyone's safety. If the students generate the rules, they will be more invested in keeping to them. You may need to help students to use only statements about themselves and the texts and to never judge or insult their peers.

Once I am sure that my students are comfortable and safe, I can turn to looking closely at the texts with them. For the purpose of this essay, I will be using *Richard II* as an example of a text to teach through the lenses of queerness and LGBT identities.

Like the other history plays, *Richard II* was, of course, written in conversation with other texts, including Holinshed's *Chronicles*, and also with Shakespeare's (and his audience's) knowledge of the past and beliefs about their own rulers and nobles. Since Richard died in 1400 and Shakespeare was born in 1554, Richard's life and death was old history to Shakespeare. Where I teach, I can assume that my students do not know much about this history, so I fill them in, especially about the social roles and relations of the play's characters. If students are to understand what they are reading in *Richard II*, they need to know that the dukes in the play are far more powerful than the knights. How much land these men own and how they raise and control armies is also crucial information for students.[1] In this play as in the other history plays, power relations are intimately involved with sexual, love, and gender relations. I want students to understand that Shakespeare is depicting relations among elite, powerful men and women from England's past, people not like those among whom he grew up, and that he is getting his information from chronicle history and other texts and then doing what he wants with those texts, in the same way TV and film writers today use history to tell the stories they want to tell. Teaching queer and LGBT issues in the history plays is, for me, enhanced by historical understanding.[2] A discussion of today's rapidly changing cultural context in relation to sexuality and gender in the United States is a good introduction to the notion that four hundred years ago in England people might have seen such things differently and that we cannot assume otherwise. Although I would caution students that each particular play cannot be evidence for large claims about such issues as sexuality and gender, I also want them to notice what is remarkable and unremarkable in each play's world; this is another way of noticing what might seem normative for Shakespeare, what his audiences would take for granted.

I run a student-centered classroom, asking students to collect evidence while they read, asking open-ended discussion questions, and only inserting brief lectures when students need factual information. Thus, when I teach queer and LGBT issues in Shakespeare's plays, I will usually ask students to collect references to subjects and words such as *love, sex, boys, women, men*, and *marriage*. These are, for me, transhistorical categories, but I encourage students not to assume that they know what characters mean when these subjects and words appear. I remind them that although these categories may be transhistorical, they are also loaded with meanings and mean different things to different people. When students look for those references, they find great material for discussion. In the rest of this essay, I will discuss what students may uncover when looking for such references in *Richard II* and how to frame discussions based on their discoveries. I introduce historical information as subjects come up. If you are teaching mainly through lecture, you might introduce the historical material on sexuality and gender in an opening lecture and then talk about the examples I discuss with that knowledge in mind.[3]

I ask students to collect love language and behavior regardless of speaker or context. What they find can surprise them. The vocabulary and gestures of love permeate political relations in *Richard II*, as they do in all the history plays. For example, Bolingbroke initially greets Richard as his "most loving liege" and then says to Richard that he brings his suit against Mowbray "[i]n the devotion of a subject's love" (21, 31). In turn, Mowbray calls the King his "dear, dear Lord" (1.1.176). At the lists, Bolingbroke asks to kiss Richard's hand (1.3.46), and Richard descends from his throne to "fold him in [his] arms" (54). Subsequently, when Richard cancels the combat and banishes both men, he cautions them not to "[e]mbrace each other's love in banishment" (178). Later in the play, when he believes his former favorite advisers have deserted him, Richard responds with vituperative aggression. Sir Stephen Scrope says, "Sweet love, I see, changing his property, / Turns to the sourest and most deadly hate" (3.2.132–33). This language is not limited to the king and his courtiers. When Bolingbroke returns to England, traveling with the Earl of Northumberland, the Earl says, "your fair discourse hath been as sugar, / Making the hard way sweet and delectable" (2.3.6–7). Later in their conversation, Northumberland's son, Harry Percy, offers his service to Bolingbroke, who accepts it and promises, in the language of love, to return the favor when he rises in fortune: "And as my fortune ripens with thy love, / It shall be still thy true love's recompense. / My heart this covenant makes; my hand thus seals it" (2.3.48–50).

I open the class by asking what students have found when they looked for love language and behavior. By the time they have finished telling the class, the board is covered with their collective evidence. Looking at the range of evidence helps us to talk about it. Some questions to ask include: Is this love language meaningless or meaningful? Is it a disguise for political intentions? Does it reflect true feelings? Is the love language political instrumentalism reflected as emotional truth? Is the love language and behavior different in kind from or just as superficial as the way politicians talk and act today? We see politicians hugging one another on occasions such as debates, but could we imagine one publically saying, "We will descend and fold him in our arms"? Richard's royal "we" is a good occasion to ask what his identity looks like throughout the play and how that identity might be conditioned on love between and among men. I also ask what it might mean for social and sexual relations between men that men lived in a world in which politics and business were distinctly and manifestly personal and affective realms.

When the discussion seems to warrant more background, I introduce some social facts of medieval and Renaissance daily life. Students don't generally know that when traveling together, men like Northumberland and Bolingbroke often slept in the same rooms and even in the same beds. When students notice that Richard and his queen do not occupy the same household through much of the play, I let them know as well that this accurately reflects the arrangements in many elite Renaissance households, which were often divided so that men were sleeping with men and women with women. I think it is a good idea both not to imply that these sleeping arrangements indicated erotic affection or intentions and also not to rule that out. I ask students to think about what proof the text offers that people are having sex and what such proof or lack of proof might mean.

The proof of sexual relations actually mentioned in the play is another thing that might look queer to us and our students. I ask students to look for evidence of sex inside and outside marriage in the play. Students often provide the Duchess of York's contention that her husband's willingness to denounce their son, Aumerle, for treason must be because he thinks Aumerle is someone else's child: "thou dost suspect / That I have been disloyal to thy bed, /And that he is a bastard, not thy son" (5.2.104–06). Using York's "bed" as a metonym for their sexual relationship, the Duchess easily asserts the possibility and also the untruth of her infidelity and pregnancy by another man. Earlier in the play, the Duchess of Gloucester also uses "bed" as a metonym for sexual intercourse, saying to John of Gaunt, "That bed, that womb, / That mettle, that self mould that fashioned thee, / Made him a man" (1.2.22–24). Her dead husband, she claims, came from the same "bed," a sexual act between the same people, that formed his brother, Gaunt, and therefore Gaunt should revenge his brother's (her husband's) death. In these speeches, a child indicates sexual intercourse, but marriage clearly does not guarantee parentage. I ask students why it is the women who talk of beds, and I tell them about the fear of cuckoldry and illegitimacy that haunts marriage and family in a patriarchal system where inheritance is governed by primogeniture.[4]

Another good thing to have students look for is how characters talk about their parents. This usually uncovers Bolingbroke's more obfuscated reference to his origins in a parental sex act. He calls his father, Gaunt, "the earthly author of my blood" (1.3.69). I ask students to discuss the differences between Bolingbroke's name for his father and the Duchesses' two speeches. Unlike the women, Bolingbroke avoids even a metonymic reference to sexual intercourse. The Duchess of Gloucester invokes her mother-in-law's "womb," but Bolingbroke does not mention his mother's body or his parents' bed, and he only invokes his father by calling him an "earthly author," removing bodies from his origin as if Gaunt spoke or wrote him into existence. Calling Gaunt an "earthly author" also implies that he has another, nonearthly author, God in heaven. These creators together, he says, have given him his "blood." "Blood," like "bed," is a keyword in this text. The audience has just heard Bolingbroke's aunt, the Duchess of Gloucester, twice call that same blood, the blood of his grandfather, Edward III, "sacred" in the speech in which she refers to Edward's "bed" (1.2.12, 17). She, however, like the other duchess, does not shy away from bodies. This evidence shows students how Shakespeare's texts associate sex and desire with women much more than with elite men, an association that might look queer to us since men are still often seen as more desirous than women.

Recently, some students have brought in evidence about sexual desire from songs and television and the news, and we have wonderful classroom discussions about that evidence in relation to what we are seeing in the plays.

Discussion of marital sex usually includes Bolingbroke's public denunciation of Richard's favorites, Bushy and Green:

> You have in manner, with your sinful hours
> Made a divorce betwixt his queen and him,
> Broke the possession of a royal bed,
> And stained the beauty of a fair queen's cheeks
> With tears drawn from her eyes by your foul wrongs.   (3.1.11–15)

The *Norton Shakespeare* explains these lines with a footnote: "Bolingbroke implies that Bushy and Green had homosexual relations with Richard; Holinshed claims that they procured female paramours for him" (1011n2). I ask students how else they could interpret Bolingbroke's words. Exploring all the interpretive options here is a great way to show students how different ideas about sex were in the past. As Andrew Gurr points out, "Commentators have variously taken this allegation, not detailed in Holinshed, to mean adultery [or] homosexuality" (*Norton Shakespeare* 1013n13). Can we use this accusation to identify Richard (and Bushy and Green) as homosexual? It is hard to see this accusation as giving Richard a sexual identity, although it is certainly possible that Bolingbroke is talking about acts of sex between men. If you are looking for an assignment around issues of queer and LGBT identities, you can ask students to look at different editions of the play to see the history of commentary, or lack of commentary, around this accusation. Some prominent editions, including the Longman and Riverside, do not comment on these lines, which seems quite odd given that, as the Arden edition points out, Bolingbroke's accusation is "inconsistent with the portrayal of Isabel's relations with Richard in the rest of the play" (91n.).

Asking students to look for comments about gender is equally productive for discussion. In *Richard II*'s third act, Scrope informs Richard that the commons have taken Bolingbroke's side and risen against him; Scrope says that "Boys with women's voices / Strive to speak big, and clap their female joints / In stiff unwieldy arms against thy crown" (3.2.109–11). This image of boys as female reappears later when Bolingbroke, now King Henry, asks Harry Percy to tell him about his son, Prince Hal. Henry calls Hal a "young, wanton and effeminate boy" (5.3.10). In this conversation, gender and sexuality are both in play. Harry Percy says that when he told the prince of the triumphs at Oxford, Hal said he would participate by going to whorehouses, taking "a glove" from the most common whore and wearing it when competing (5.3.14–19). What are we, four hundred or so years away from Shakespeare's play and six hundred or so away from Richard II, to make of this picture of a feminine boy who frequents whorehouses? This and other useful questions, such as why the play is so interested in male-male love and so much less interested in female-female love, are great ways to help students explore the history plays and history as spaces of difference, spaces that can challenge them to see their own worlds and norms differently as well.

NOTES

[1] In the introduction to the *Norton Shakespeare*, Katharine Eisaman Maus has two paragraphs that directly address property and noble status; a look in class at those paragraphs can be a good way to introduce those topics (976).

[2] See Madhavi Menon's introduction for a position on queering Shakespeare that rejects historicizing. Valerie Traub has a wonderful commentary on the conversation about queerness and history ("New Unhistoricism").

[3] See Mario DiGangi, "Sex," for a great bibliography of materials that one could use to craft such a lecture. Some more recent important books include Bromley and Stockton; DiGangi, *Sexual Types*; Fisher; and Traub, *Renaissance*.

[4] Another interesting bit of evidence in relation to marriage and women's power is Richard's list of causes of the "death of kings," which includes "some poisoned by their wives" (3.2.155).

Dangerous Men in Drama:
Teaching the Cade Rebellion in 2 *Henry VI*

Ronda Arab

I teach 2 *Henry VI* as part of a course on masculinity in early modern drama; while we do study the brutal squabbles among the nobility, for this essay I will focus primarily on the artisan rebellion led by Jack Cade. My objectives in examining the Cade rebellion are, first, for students to understand the complex responses good drama can elicit, through understanding how much of the play's pleasure is created by the brave, manly, witty, but horrific and frightening artisan rebels. This is something our students, astute and sophisticated watchers of TV dramas such as *Breaking Bad, Dexter*, and *The Sopranos*, will get. Second, I aim for students to learn about early modern discourses of work and working men, discourses that reflect both appreciation and fear of the working man's perceived powerful physicality.[1]

I start with a close reading of York's description of Cade in battle against the Irish, the reader's introduction to Cade:

> In Ireland have I seen this stubborn Cade
> Oppose himself against a troop of kerns,
> And fought so long, till that his thighs with darts
> Were almost like a sharp-quilled porcupine:
> And, in the end being rescued, I have seen
> Him caper upright like a wild Morisco,
> Shaking the bloody darts as he his bells.
> Full often, like the shag haired crafty kern
> Hath he conversèd with the enemy,
> And undiscovered, come to me again,
> And given me notice of their villanies.   (3.1.360–70)

After one student reads the passage out loud, students do a close reading exercise with colored pencils, looking for patterns and repetitions. Students note a word, structure, or image (visual, aural, tactile, etc.), circle it in one of four different colors, and proceed through the passage circling similar examples of the detail in the same color. After doing this they create a legend that names, explains, and categorizes the mark-ups according to color, and then use their markings to consider what effects the writer intends and how those effects are achieved. This rich passage will easily yield the most important aspects of Cade: he's a stubborn warrior singlehandedly capable of taking on an entire troop of Irish foot soldiers, so fierce he shakes off the arrows piercing his thighs with the physical force of a morris-dancing caper. Cade exudes strength, power, manliness, and suitability for war. Astute students will notice the repetition of "kern" and the paradox of its double usage: Cade fights the kerns, but he also can pass as a "shag haired crafty kern" in order to infiltrate their camps and provide intelligence to the Duke of York. Given that the Irish were an enemy associated with savagery, craftiness, vagrancy, and rebellion, Cade's double agency suggests danger. Questioning York's attitude toward Cade will lead students to note that his admiration is begrudging: Cade is described as "stubborn" but not brave or valiant; he is "crafty," not intelligent or full of wit; the animal he most resembles is a "porcupine," not a lion or a hawk.

Students will note the central metaphor of Cade as a morris dancer, and it will be necessary to explain the morris dance as a physically demanding, highly skilled, festive spectacle often linked with war. Early-sixteenth-century urban watch processions advertising martial readiness included morris dancers; morris dances became part of May game and other festive celebrations in the mid-sixteenth century and continued to be performed on the stage throughout the 1590s.[2] Students should understand that cultural controversy surrounded popular festivities such as May games because of their inversions of order and parodies of authority; I suggest having students read Phillip Stubbes's "Lordes of Misrule in Ailgna" from his *Anatomie of Abuses*, in which he demonizes these dancers as outlaws who pose a threat to social order by dancing on the Sabbath, disrupting church services, and "fight[ing] under the banner and standard of the devil against Christ Jesus, and all his lawes" (171). He also describes the dancers in wonderful detail. York's description of Cade as a morris dancer shows part of York's disdain, as morris dancing and popular festivities were commonly considered by the higher estates to be rustic, uncouth, and unsophisticated. In questioning the potential staging of the scene, students might speculate that Cade dances on one part of the stage, a visual spectacle with audience appeal, as York describes him from another. The mixed responses Cade generates here—York's paradoxically contemptuous esteem versus audience pleasure—can lead to a discussion of the complexities of theatrical messages and audience responses to characters, a useful preparative for further analysis of the rebel laborers.

Instructors might follow York's introduction of Cade with short excerpts from early modern military manuals. I bring these short documents into class, rather than assign them in advance, and have students read them alone or in small groups after an initial close reading of the passage. Their analysis of York's description will allow them to see relevant details in the archival excerpts, whereas reading the excerpts cold might produce only bored incomprehension. In *Of the Knowledge and Conducte of Warre* (1578), Thomas Proctor designates ploughmen and craftsmen as ideal soldiers, their muscles having been strengthened by hard work and their bodies accustomed to rough conditions:

> [F]or their exercyse or trade of lyfe, first it is cleare, that the stronger, better breathed, and harder man of bodie by nature or custome, is the more avaylable for warres: and therefore it is to conclude, that men of

such occupations, as are accustomed most to labour with the strength of their armes, are to bee preferred for this purpose, as smythes, butchers, masons, dyggers in mynes, Carpenters, & most principallye the husband-man, both for his wonted enduringe of hardnes in fare, and of all weathers and toyle in the fielde.   (F1v–F2r)

Matthew Sutcliffe similarly writes that when choosing soldiers, one must consider the "trade of their living":

For many to win themselves a living, are oftentimes driven to follow base occupations, that otherwise are couragious, & of liberall disposition, & have bodies fit for labour. So that although the *Spartans* and the *Romans* refused such for souldiers, as exercised manual occupations, and kept shops, yet do I not thinke they deserve generally to be refused, but onely such of them that are weake, tender, and effeminate. All those that are hardened with labour; as husbandmen for the most part, and those that can suffer raine, heate, and cold, and use to fare hard, and lie hard, and sleepe little proove brave men.   (M2r)

Sutcliffe's anxiety about the apparent contradiction between the low birth of laboring men and their suitability for honorable service in a militia is a useful discussion point given that the artisan Cade is both a rebel and a powerful soldier. It also can work well with the discussion of York's mercurial attitude toward Cade.

After introducing this ambivalent attitude toward artisans as soldiers, instructors might find contemporary context for Shakespeare's depiction of the Cade rebellion useful, including the historical reality of late-sixteenth-century fears of artisan-led uprisings. A few facts: historians cite thirty-five general outbreaks of disorder in London between 1581 and 1602, forty food-related riots in England between 1586 and 1631, and hundreds of riots between 1530 and 1640 over changes in land usage in the country (Manning 3, 187; Sharp 10). Artisans, laborers, and rural cottagers were the most active participants in these riots, as they were the most affected by bad harvests, food prices, and, in the country, landlords' contentious enclosures of land for raising sheep, which denied the poor right of access to formerly common lands in which they could gather fuel and foodstuffs, graze animals, or even fish and hunt fowl (Everitt 169–70). The clothmaking regions were especially volatile, and Shakespeare, notably, makes Cade a clothier, although he is not named as such in the historical sources. Shakespeare also references the practice of enclosures by having humble petitioners complain about the Duke of Suffolk's unfair land enclosures in act 1, scene 3, a detail also not found in the play's sources.

I move next to the rebels' first congregation scene, where the play imagines the rebels gruesomely putting their artisanal skills to work in battle; here the class continues discussing the artisans' dual representation as frightening but admirably bellicose:

> HOLLAND. There's Best's son, the tanner of Wingham—
> BEVIS. He shall have the skins of our enemies to make dog's leather of.
> HOLLAND. And Dick the butcher—
> BEVIS. Then is sin struck down like an ox, and iniquity's throat cut like a calf.
> HOLLAND. And Smith the weaver—
> BEVIS. Argo, their thread of life is spun.   (4.2.19–27)

Having seen that low-born working men had potentially dangerous physical strength and endurance, here students will note that their specific artisanal skills offer the techniques and tools for carnage: the butcher will slaughter the enemy by slashing their throats like the beasts in his abattoir and the tanner will make gloves from their skins. The images are horrific; however, the verbal play is clever, moving as it does from ghoulish association (human skin to leather) to rhetorically lofty declaration to pun: horror and amusement are simultaneously evoked. From here I jump immediately to a short passage in the next scene, wherein Cade congratulates Dick the butcher after the battle in Blackheath:[3] "They fell before thee like sheep and oxen, and thou behaved'st thyself as if thou hadst been in thine own slaughter-house"(4.3.3–4). While establishing an alarming connection between artisanal work and violent power, both passages contribute to the play's aesthetic of conjuring thrills through the imagination of gruesome and wicked acts.

Audience pleasure is aroused by the artisan rebels' clever wordplay and control of rhetoric and humor in other scenes as well, further affectively bonding the audience to the artisans despite their dubious morality. The next passage we focus on is 4.2.29–58, wherein Cade makes self-elevating claims that the butcher deflates with punning jokes about Cade's common status. These jokes need not be seen as asides, as neither Cade nor the rebels actually believe his claim to be Mortimer (52);[4] Cade admits the lie at line 145. The openness of the mockery casts it as a triumphant, carnivalesque reclaiming of what dominant discourses considered low and shameful, demonstrating how little respect the rebels have for established hierarchies. Cade is associated with vagabondage and the life of the so-called sturdy beggar multiple times: he is born in a field to homeless vagrants; his father's best shelter was the "cage," or prison; his father-in-law was a pedlar, an occupation considered fraudulent and outlawed by the Vagrancy Acts of 1572 and 1597 (Beier 86, 89); and Cade himself has been whipped in the marketplace for beggary and branded for stealing sheep. Students should see that Cade's criminal history is that of a poor man seeking food. They should also understand that not all members of Elizabethan society believed the Poor Laws that would criminalize him were just; that Cade is branded for stealing sheep is especially significant, as it was for grazing sheep that landlords were enclosing common lands. The rebels use witty self-mockery to own their poverty and low social status; simultaneously, these well-known grievances are articulated to a public that might well see legitimacy in them.

One might also look at moments the rebels' spirited responses call attention to charged contemporary debates over the honor or dishonor of manual work; I suggest Christopher Hill's "The Industrious Sort of People" for straightforward lecture guidance on early modern valuations of labor; I also write on the board Parson John Ball's famous words from the 1381 Peasants' Rebellion—"When Adam delved, and Eve span, / Who was then a Gentleman?" (Holinshed, *Chronicles*, 1807–08, 2: 749)—and explain their historical place and meaning. With these introductions I move back to Bevis and Holland, 4.2.1–18, where they interpret the Elizabethan "Homily against Idleness" as authorizing manually laboring men for positions as magistrates and expose the hypocrisy of official discourses claiming to value work. I then move further into the scene wherein Cade's claiming of the throne has Stafford respond, "Villain! thy father was a plasterer; / And thyself a shearman, art thou not?" Cade retorts, "And Adam was a gardener" to which Stafford's brother asks, "What of that?" (4.2.119–23). Cade's defiant audacity and shrewd manipulation of an old and well-known political refrain honoring laborers likely appealed to the many working people of the audience, while the contempt for manual labor of the proud nobles and their oblivious response to a conventional reminder of all of humankind's humility reveals their arrogance.

Further attention to political and economic issues of land use and food distribution offers more opportunity for discussion of the audience's potential sympathies with the rebels. I have students take five to ten minutes to write about the objectives of the artisans' rebellion. From the multiple possible responses, the discussion will eventually get around to food and drink, at which point we read the following passages:

> CADE. There shall be in England seven halfpenny loaves for a penny. The three-hooped pot shall have ten hoops, and I will make it felony to drink small beer. All the realm shall be in common, and in Cheapside shall my paltrey go to grass. And when I am king, as king I will be—
> ALL CADE'S FOLLOWERS. God save your majesty!
> CADE. I thank you good people!—there shall be no money, all shall eat and drink on my score, and I will apparel them all in one livery that they may agree like brothers, and worship me their lord.   (4.2.60–69)
> CADE. I charge and command that, of the city's cost, the Pissing Conduit run nothing but claret wine this first year of our reign. And now henceforth it shall be treason for any that calls me otherwise than Lord Mortimer.
>   (4.6.2–5)

The paradoxes here encapsulate the play's representation of the rebels and make for good debate between students who admire Cade and those who do not: he offers a festive, utopian vision of abundant food and drink and common land usage, but it is embedded in his authoritarian, brutal desire to wield absolute power.

We end our study by considering theatricality directly, along with the aesthetics of manliness and the power of spectator identification with human forms on display. I have students read a short excerpt from Jean Howard and Phyllis Rackin's *Engendering a Nation*, which cites Thomas Heywood and Thomas Nashe on how heroic men on stage inspire audience members to emulate their bravery and manly English patriotism, as well as an additional short passage from Heywood's *An Apology for Actors* on how audiences are warned into moral behavior by the "untimely ends" of rebels and evildoers presented in stage plays.[5] I ask students how accurate they find these theories based on their own theater, film, and TV viewing experience and have them consider the early modern antitheatricalist position that believed illicit behavior enacted on stage encouraged wickedness in viewers. I then move on to possible responses to the characters in *2 Henry VI*, asking students to consider the implications of Heywood's and Nashe's models for a play with a weak king, corrupt noblemen, and vicious rebels. My questions include the following: Does the play present admirable characters and if so, who? How might a largely commoner audience respond to these characters? Why might audiences enjoy watching Cade and his fellow rebels—what satisfactions or pleasures lie therein? Why are strong, charismatic, but bad characters enjoyable to watch? What processes of identification or disidentification take place? To facilitate thoughtful responses, I divide the class into small groups and assign each a question or two before reconvening for a full class discussion.

Students will, of course, have a range of responses. My general aim is to discuss how Heywood's easy moralizing, about how punishing evildoers acts as a deterrent, ignores more complex ways audiences respond to characters. Cade is punished in the end, as are Dexter and Walter White in recent TV dramas (*Dexter* and *Breaking Bad*), but he is probably the most exciting character on the stage to many audience members, especially given the lack of admirable models among the upper class characters, except for Gloucester, who is stripped of power and murdered early on. Are punishments anything more than a conventional bow to hegemonic morality when the dangerous body has elicited aesthetic admiration for his powerful masculinity throughout the performance? We end the class with discussion of the fantasies and desires that theater and other performance media allow audiences to vicariously enjoy, which are not necessarily acceptable or even personally desirable in one's social world outside the theater context. Cade and the rebels, like Dexter and Walter White, defy the conventional morality and restrictive hierarchies and social institutions that can be painfully constricting to their audiences. But are these vicarious fantasies socially beneficial escape valves or dangerous incitements to violence?

NOTES

[1] Some of the pedagogical approaches described in this essay are based on analyses of *2 Henry VI* in my *Manly Mechanicals on the Early Modern English Stage*.

[2] See John Forrest's *The History of Morris Dancing, 1458–1750*.

[3] The butcher's prowess harkens back to the play's first uses of butchery as a signifier for brutal execution, in the politically motivated assassination of the Duke of Gloucester. I have the class look at act 3, where King Henry laments that Gloucester is imprisoned like a calf taken to a butcher's slaughterhouse (3.1.210–12), where Warwick names the dead Duke as a "heifer dead and bleeding fresh" (3.2.188), and where Margaret denies the role of her faction in his death, asking Suffolk (sardonically, I imagine), "Are you the butcher, Suffolk? Where's your knife?" (195). Violent butchery functions as an image that creates a significant correspondence between the lower orders and the nobility. King Henry's lamentation is meaningful as well, as his feminized self-representation as a weeping "dam" who "can do naught but wail her darling's loss" indicates his weakness as a king (3.1.214–18), a significant point for discussions of manliness.

[4] The Folio does not indicate asides after these speeches, although usual practice is to write them in.

[5] The Howard and Rackin excerpt starts on the top of page 18 with "The number of dramatic histories which Shakespeare wrote" and ends on page 19. The Heywood passage is on F3v of the 1612 edition; it begins with "Playes are writ with this ayme"; one can decide how much of the two paragraphs to include.

Ghost Stories: Lost Fathers and Abandoned Sons in the History Plays

Joyce Green MacDonald

Putting down Jack Cade's rebellion in *2 Henry VI*, Lord Clifford tries to make Cade's followers remember their duty to their king by reminding them of Henry's noble origins:

> Who loves the king, and will embrace his pardon,
> Fling up his cap and say, "God save his majesty!"
> Who hateth him and honors not his father,
> Henry the Fifth, that made all France to quake,
> Shake he his weapon at us and pass by. (4.7.167–71)

The memory of dead fathers who performed great deeds on behalf of the nation is summoned again by Young Clifford, vowing revenge after his own father's death at the hands of the Duke of York at the Battle of Saint Albans. "In cruelty will I seek out my fame," he tells us, lifting his father's body in his arms:

> Come, thou new ruin of old Clifford's house:
> As did Aeneas old Anchises bear,
> So bear I thee upon my manly shoulders:
> But then Aeneas bare a living load,
> Nothing so heavy as these woes of mine. (5.3.60, 61–65)

These two invocations of dead fathers—one the English king, the memory of whose greatness stands to be swallowed up in current civil rebellion, the other the mythological ancestor of all Britons—offer powerful illustrations of the role of fatherhood in shaping Shakespeare's history plays. The notion that present-day Britons were descended from Brutus, the great-grandson of Aeneas, imaginatively inscribed the significance of patrilineal inheritance into British identity. Lord Clifford's invocation of Henry V emphasized the blood tie of resemblance between fathers and sons, but the play subsumes Young Clifford's personal grief into a larger existential crisis. Losing his father, he has also lost his place in a line of heroes and founders. The Cliffords speak during a national emergency that will force fatherless young men to figure out how to revive the example of paternal glory through their own deeds, forging their own manhoods out of absence, grief, and loss.

Missing fathers can serve as a useful classroom tool for teaching Shakespeare's history plays. In my fall 2012 section of our university's large-lecture Shakespeare course, I was repeatedly struck by the significance of characters' relations to the memories of their fathers (and father figures) as they struggled to make themselves whole in the present. Especially as we moved through a group of plays printed or first performed between 1598 and 1600—*1 Henry IV*, *Julius Caesar*, and *Hamlet*—dead fathers and ghosts of the past repeatedly emerged as principles that shaped both characterization and structure. But the significance of paternal inheritance first made an appearance in our discussion of *Richard II*.

Richard's character is unfamiliar to many students, and he is not necessarily the kind of Shakespearean king to which they're drawn. I used the BBC/Time-Life production of the play starring Derek Jacobi as Richard, and the power of his performance helped a great deal in selling the play and the role to them. The video also helpfully visualized the generational divide between the elderly York and Gaunt and the younger cousins Richard and Henry Bolingbroke. The production's emphasis on generational difference succeeded in part because of the luxury of having John Gielgud play Gaunt. Gielgud's memorable performance helped me return to one of the course's running threads—the Shakespearean careers of the actors in the video clips I used to illustrate scenes from our plays—and I remarked that Gielgud had been an acclaimed Richard in his own youth. More than forty years later, here he was still engaged with the play. Derek Jacobi took part in the 2013 PBS series *Shakespeare Uncovered*, where he talked about playing Richard for the BBC series and discussed the role with actors then preparing for a Globe Theatre production of the play. Jacobi played Hamlet in the BBC series, and would play Hamlet's uncle Claudius in Kenneth Branagh's 1996 film. Generational transmission and connection manifested itself in many such moments from Shakespearean productions I chose for the class, providing a metatheatrical framing for our emerging interest in fathers and sons in the plays.

Although I doubt that the actors connected along the daisy chain of *Richard II* would talk of their work in terms of paternal legacy, I noted the value of the idea of passing something down—already implicit in the text with the comparisons between Richard and his father, the Black Prince, whom he lost when he was nine years old. Our next history play that semester was *1 Henry IV*, where students were pleased to see Shakespeare continue the story of Bolingbroke, about whom they had decidedly mixed feelings. They were quick to note that the play repeated the generational conflict we had observed in *Richard II*, except this time with greater complexity: the king deserved his son's support even if he stood on shaky ethical ground. Falstaff would have been an engaging father figure in an alternative history of political obligation, and Hotspur—who perhaps needed a father's guidance most of all—could not trust the men whose moral obligation it should have been to raise him to proper manhood. In this play, sons have living fathers, but those fathers can't be trusted to lead them safely into the worlds of war and politics. The sons build themselves from scratch in a system whose notional reliance on relationship and orderly descent had already been proved a violent fraud with the deposition of Richard II.

The classic progression at this point of a Shakespeare survey syllabus would be something like *Richard II*, *1 Henry IV*, and then either *2 Henry IV* or *Henry V*. Instead, I chose to follow *1 Henry IV* with *Julius Caesar*. It was a presidential election year, and I wanted students to engage with questions about civic life and the role and obligations of leadership. Yet, when we started *Julius Caesar*, fathers and father figures brought themselves to the forefront of discussion again. The historical Mark Antony was distantly related to Julius Caesar on his mother's side, but in Shakespeare's play he assumes an almost filial loyalty to him as he seeks justice, by "indirect crook'd paths" (*2H4* 4.3.313), for his murder. Antony's private watchfulness in the face of public chaos, his mastery at manipulating public opinion, the intensity of his personal loyalties were all familiar from our earlier observations of Bolingbroke and his son. Although he was not Caesar's son—that distinction belongs to Octavius, a very different kind of Shakespearean hero—Antony identifies so powerfully with Caesar's cause and Caesar's memory that he resembled the other questing sons of absent or culpable fathers that we had studied. In class, I pursued the contrast between his unwavering commitment to Caesar and Prince Harry's delay in rallying to the side of his own father, although ultimately the latter does rise up and help defeat his father's enemies.

The competing funeral orations spoken over Caesar's body in act 3, scene 2, turn on how to place great men in history and what their survivors should take away from their example. Brutus in effect places Rome's value over Caesar's, divorcing the progress of the nation from the man to whom it was entrusted. He conspired against him, "not that I loved Caesar less, but that I loved / Rome more" (21–22). Antony, in contrast, cannot sever Rome from Caesar, insisting that all his actions, whether ambitious or not, were aimed at securing Rome's greater glory. His identification with Caesar's cause and Caesar's devotion to Rome is complete, or so he tells the crowd: "My heart is in the coffin there with Caesar, / And I must pause till it come back to me" (107–08). The image is striking. Antony is simultaneously living and dead, speaking to the crowd in this moment yet emotionally bound to the corpse on display in front of them. As it is impossible for him to separate Caesar's cause from Rome's, it is also impossible for him to separate himself from his loyalty to Caesar's cause; his heart belongs with the dead, so that political loyalties and personal loyalties merge into one.

Although he protests Caesar's commitment to Rome, what matters here at least as much—if not actually more—is Antony's commitment to Caesar. He insistently embodies and physicalizes that commitment, swearing that knowledge of its depth would compel the plebeians to "kiss dead Caesar's wounds, / And dip their napkins in his blood," inviting them to "make a ring about the corpse of Caesar" and prepare to discover how deeply he regarded them all as "his heirs" (133–34, 159, 146). Through the medium of Caesar's dead body, Antony conjures a bloodstained vision of membership in an imperial family that transcends politics or status. In Caesar's blood, through the provisions of his will wherein he remembered them, and in their acts of vengeance on his behalf, the plebeians will become Caesar's children. For Prince Harry, however, the battle to vindicate a father's honor is even more personal than it is for Antony; he fights not only for his father's right to rule but also to make Hotspur pay for usurping Harry's rightful place in his father's esteem. He swears to his father that he "will wear a garment all of blood" (*2H4* 3.3.135), blood powerful enough to wash away his own "shame" (137) as he is newly baptized into filial duty. The English history play invokes an image of family that, even if founded in blood, is much more literally organized around paternal inheritance.

I used the classical studies section of *Oxford Reference Online* for a quick class presentation on the Lupercalia, the festival where *Julius Caesar* intro-duces Antony. Held in memory of the she-wolf who suckled Romulus and Re-mus, it celebrated nurture, fraternity, and dynasty, since the twin infants would grow up to be the historical founders of Rome. (Indeed, the role of masculin-ity in Rome's origins anticipates the place of the father-son bond in the En-glish history plays, although I was working on the fly with the classical materials and didn't think to make the connection in class.) Women seeking to become pregnant, like the barren Calpurnia, would offer themselves to be ceremonially struck with goatskin thongs by naked runners racing around the ancient walls of the city. Thus associated with fertility and with biological, familial acts of civic foundation, Antony's first appearance in *Julius Caesar* shadows the family connection he conjures at the funeral. Indeed, Caesar invites him into a proxy relationship with his wife and thus his own bloodline when he tells Calpurnia to "[s]tand . . . directly in Antonio's way" as he runs the course (1.2.5). As both a son and a kind of husband, Antony's rhetorical animation of a new Roman family at the funeral is all the more powerful because it takes place in the face of death and sterility. He makes something new out of blood and violence and loss.

Although I did not follow *Julius Caesar* with *Antony and Cleopatra* that se-mester, the later Roman history clearly shows him acting out these intimations of new imperial family structures as he and Cleopatra rebel against Octavius— Caesar's adopted son—with plans to place their own children on Egypt's throne. But the rhetorical and political labor Antony performs in the earlier play, with its bodily props, also usefully points us back to the *Henry VI* plays. After the battle of Saint Albans, the Duke of York and his sons and supporters gather to count their spoils. Edward shows his sword stained with the Duke of Buckingham's blood, and Warwick's son Montague proudly displays the Earl of Wiltshire's. But Richard of Gloucester outdoes them both when he shows off a severed head: "Speak thou for me," he says memorably and chillingly, "and tell them what I did" (1.1.16). Here, as in *Julius Caesar*, bodies—or at least body parts—achieve the power of speech as they announce a newly literal commit-ment to familial unity and paternal likeness. "Richard hath best deserved of all my sons" (12.1.17), York proudly observes in response, like a cruel god ap-peased by human sacrifice. As we saw in the aftermath of Antony's funeral ora-tion and in Young Clifford's consecration of himself to "cruelty," the assertion of paternal descent can just as easily devolve into violence as it can soar into the will to reenact the fathers' greatness.

Caesar's wounded body and Somerset's severed head are physical reminders of the mixed currents of paternal homage, blood and violence swirling through Shakespeare's English and Roman histories. Beyond the physical bodies they represent, ghosts in these plays most powerfully summon their notions of fatherhood and of filial duty. As capable of rousing "fear and wonder" (*Ham.* 1.1.42) as of rousing admiration and certainty, fathers' ghostly appearances to their haunted and uncertain sons are pedagogically useful in leading discussion toward the emotional weight attached to intergenerational bonds in a political context.

Absent fathers and disappearing images of paternal guidance made a powerful first appearance on our syllabus with *Richard II*, in which Richard flippantly disrespects the dying Gaunt and the elderly York ineffectually attempts to intervene in his son's and nephew's courses of action. I brought in material on the historical Richard's father, the Black Prince, whose warrior status and annexation of large swaths of French territory during the Hundred Years' War made him the kind of absent father who commands unquestioning respect in the history plays: strong, successful, committed to the welfare of the nation. My students saw that Richard's own lack of a male heir, whatever legitimacy he gained from being a crowned king, made him politically vulnerable and somehow socially suspect. The effects of his sonlessness were aggravated—or even perhaps made manifest—by an equally serious lack of filial gratitude and respect for the accomplishments of his father's generation.

When the ghost of Julius Caesar appears to Brutus the night before the battle of Philippi, it has relatively little to say. He is Brutus's "evil spirit" (*JC* 4.2.333), who will see him again at the battlefield. Coming after the disheartening dispute with Cassius and the news of Portia's suicide, however, the ghost makes himself literally known only to Brutus; the sleep of others in his tent is disturbed, but only Brutus actually sees and remembers it. He carries this unsettling memory with him onto the battlefield and knows, when he sees Cassius's body, that the ghost only he saw is responsible for the current disaster: "O Julius Caesar, thou art mighty yet! / Thy spirit walks abroad and turns our swords / In our own proper entrails" (5.3.93–95). Interestingly, only the First Folio's stage directions identify the apparition as the ghost of Caesar; the ghost never so identifies itself, yet Brutus knows what it is and the power it holds over his fate. The ghost's import is impressed most powerfully on the character who needs most urgently to recognize it. Caesar's "sons" Octavius and Antony know what is at stake and so the ghost does not appear to them. Brutus, so deeply aware of the future impact of the assassination, so confident that he can communicate its meaning to the horrified citizens through his logical rhetorical framing, is at the moment of crisis forcibly reminded that he utterly failed to grasp Caesar's true "spirit."

In contrast to Brutus's private confrontation with the ghost, the spirit of Hamlet's father appears to all the young men of the watch, although he will only communicate with his son. His son is the one most intimately obligated to listen, to hear, to understand and remember his father's living presence. Coming after *Julius Caesar* on our syllabus, *Hamlet* offered us the opportunity to compare the prince of Denmark with Bolingbroke, Richard II, and Mark Antony in terms of their commitment to past paternal ideals. We had the opportunity to see how the father-son bond worked in two English histories and a Roman history, but removing a political framework—or at least being somewhat distanced from it—gave us a theoretically less obstructed view of the familial dynamic.

Looking at different video versions of Hamlet's first ghost scene helped us to talk about the emotional places occupied by fathers and by fatherhood itself in the play. Students were taken by the creepy visuals, black and white photography, and striking camera work of the 1948 Laurence Olivier version. The scene vibrates with anxiety, replicating Hamlet's own emotional state as the camera slides in and out of focus. His fear marks the magnitude of the task facing him, and the scene ends with him fainting. In contrast, Franco Zeffirelli's 1990 film puts the focus of the scene on Paul Scofield's reserved, sorrowful ghost instead of on Mel Gibson's Hamlet; the ghost weeps and stretches his arms out toward his son as he softly tells him to "[r]emember me" and then disappears (1.5.91). In Gregory Doran's 2009 BBC *Hamlet* with David Tennant, the prince falls to his knees in shock as he finds out the horrifying truth about his father's murder, but Patrick Stewart's ghost is more demonstrative than the character in either of the other two versions. At "[i]f thou hast nature in thee" (1.5.81), he seizes the kneeling Tennant by the shoulders as if to harangue him on the necessity of seeking revenge, then enfolds him in an embrace as he tells him not to persecute Gertrude. As he disappears, he shouts, "Remember me!," charging his son with an unavoidable duty. The intensity and physicality of this ghostly father makes Hamlet's connection to him and his current sense of loss more urgently real in the midst of his own confusion. That Stewart plays both Hamlet's dead father and his murderous uncle keeps the prince's emotional confusion always visible to the audience. His father is gone but still present, and the son can never escape reminders of his duty to vindicate his blood.

Hamlet, of course, is not a history play. But coming chronologically after *Henry V* and *Julius Caesar*—plays that turn on the bonds between fathers and sons and on the pressures sons face to justify themselves as worthy inheritors of their fathers' greatness—it can make powerful contributions to a semester organized around the topic of paternity and male gender identity in Shakespeare. These themes cross Roman and English history plays, as we have seen, and are present in Shakespeare from the beginning of his career. Putting examples of filial connection in the plays in touch with what we know about principles of patrilineage in Renaissance society—beginning, perhaps, with the haunting image of Young Clifford carrying away the wreckage of empire in the shape of his dead father—can be a powerful way of showing students what is at stake when Shakespeare's historical actors attempt to speak with, and of, the past.

Historiography and Hives:
"Research Notebooks" as Prewriting Exercises

Joshua Calhoun

In one of my last graduate classes, I was asked to complete a series of seemingly pointless exercises. They were not part of a longer, potentially publishable essay. They were not paper-length explorations delivered at a conference. They were focused drills. The word "EXERCISES" in all caps appeared on the first page of the syllabus along with an explanation that began, "Short exercises are central to the course." For each weekly meeting, in addition to reading primary and secondary texts, we were expected to complete two to three exercises directing us to do such things as "[t]ake any one of the 'Commodities' that Hariot describes and find out as much about it as you can in half an hour, using the *OED*, EEBO, British History Online, and the Proceedings of the Old Bailey. . . . Write two pages of notes" (Stallybrass, Syllabus 1, 5).

The experience of completing focused fact-finding missions changed not only my research habits but also the way I read student essays. I grew impatient with rhetoric-heavy, research-lite papers. Why were most of their secondary sources decades-old articles from *JSTOR*? With a World Wide Web of information at their digit-tips, why weren't the digital natives in my undergraduate classes digging deeper than *Google* searches? Talking to students, I learned that many felt overwhelmed. Inundated with information, most undergraduate junior and senior English majors I was teaching had settled into a research rut. They used two or maybe three research resources beyond *Google*. And one was *Wikipedia*.

Drawing on the focused exercises I was asked to complete in graduate school, I created a semester-long assignment to teach undergraduate students to perform careful, extended, nuanced research and to show them that such research does not need to be significantly more time-consuming than rewording the sort of shallow results that appear on the first page of a *Google* search. The research notebook assignment (hereafter RNBs) is still under construction, but it is one that, even in its early versions, has helped me help students feel less overwhelmed as researchers and more capable as writers. Having honed their research skills while completing RNBs, students routinely turn in essays that are more persuasive, precise, and interesting. As one student commented on an anonymous course evaluation:

> Normally when you are writing a paper you begin thinking, ok what can I make an argument out of? This assignment turned it around and had us just look for stuff that is interesting . . . and compile the research just for the sake of research, only looking for arguments later. This really changed the process of writing for me.

A bonus outcome, one I had not calculated, was that the assignment upended class discussion in the best of ways, helping address a problem with class dynamics that has frustrated me (and many of my colleagues): the most talkative students talk even when they have nothing particularly insightful to say. RNBs shifted our conversation from rhetoric to research, inviting hard-earned research insights to drive class conversations. As a result, those whose ideas most shaped individual discussions—and, ultimately, the trajectory of the course—tended to be the brightest students, not the most uninhibited.

The RNBs have worked particularly well in a class I teach on Shakespeare's second tetralogy titled How to Kill a King: Reading, Writing, and History Making in Shakespeare. The class examines what Shakespeare read and how he blended varied sources to make (and kill) his character-kings, and the RNB assignment asks students to do a similar kind of analogic reading, research, and narrative weaving.[1] In this essay, I outline the project as it now exists after four semesters of testing and tweaking. Two former students, Sophie Heywood and Ethan Kay, volunteered their time as part of a collaborative project to improve the assignment and to create *The RNB Hive*, a Web site that will serve as a tutorial and resource center for future classes; it is my hope that the site will also be useful to colleagues interested in adopting or adapting this assignment.[2]

Overview

The RNB assignment asks students to spend approximately four to five hours completing independent research for each of the plays we read in class.

Ultimately, the RNBs are linked to essay writing, but at the outset RNBs offer students the chance to gather data, ask questions, explore interests, and chase down leads without worrying about making a rhetorical point. We spend two weeks reading each play, and RNBs are due on the last class day for each play. As the assignment is currently conceived, students have a menu of exercises to choose from (see table 1). For each RNB, students complete four exercises of their choosing, generating the equivalent of one page of typed notes per exercise. I suggest that each exercise take about an hour of focused research. Students may type or handwrite their notes. The last part of each RNB is a short summary paragraph (approximately two hundred words) in which students highlight their best discovery. I urge students to make sense of the assignment by doing: get to work on an exercise and see where it goes. The RNB project is designed to be more doable than thinkable at the outset.

Exercises

While students choose just four exercises each week from the menu of ten below, ultimately they must complete each exercise twice, which means they work their way through the entire list over the course of the semester, trying out different kinds of research. The exercise options are tailored to the course. In a different course one might include more options related to stage history, gender politics, religious conflict, and so on. Detailed descriptions of each exercise are available at *The RNB Hive*; here, I offer a brief walkthrough.

Reading *Richard II*, a student might feel especially drawn to act 3, scene 2, in which a resigned King Richard says, "Let's talk of graves, of worms, and epitaphs, / Make dust our paper, and with rainy eyes / Write sorrow on the bosom of the earth" (141–43). Deciding to complete a bibliographic comparison (see table 1), this student might go to special collections, call up the 1632 Second Folio, and begin comparing it with the course text. She may notice, among other things, that the stage directions in her copy, "*Enter the King*" (Barnet 54), differ from the Second Folio's "Enter Richard." Curious about this uncrowning, she may turn back and find that the last time Richard was introduced by a stage direction in the Second Folio, he was called "King." Here, at the beginning of the scene in which he realizes all hope is lost, he is stripped of his title. Catching the research bug, she might settle in, search carefully, and find that all Second Folio stage directions call Richard "King" before 3.2 and "Richard" from 3.2 on—with one exception in 5.6: "*Enter Exton . . . with the coffin*" (Barnet 109). This striking insight is not, however, a hypothetical discovery. It is an example from a former student's RNB.

A page of notes or an hour later, the student has learned how to begin archival research. She might stay in the archives to complete a reappropriations exercise by delving into the collection's intriguing Shakespeareana. Later in the week,

Table 1: RNB Exercise Menu

Exercise	Focus	Outcomes
Word study	*One or two words from the play*	Information about etymology, development, usage in Shakespeare and/or other Renaissance texts
Scene study (film)	*Two film versions of one scene*	Observations about setting, line editing, casting, costuming, camera angles, etc.
Stage adaptations	*Two or three stage adaptations of the play*	Observations about staging, casting, costuming, public response, etc.
Character investigation	*One character*	Information about historical person, history of representation on stage and film, character afterlife, etc.
Annotated bibliography	*Two academic essays, one electronic and one print*	Four or five sentence annotations that put the two essays in conversation
Publication history	*Sixteenth- and seventeenth-century print sources*	Annotated catalog of early printing of the play and of secondary resources related to the play
Bibliographic comparison	*Two print versions of One scene*	Observations on similarities and differences between a scene in the course text and in a pre-1900 printed version of the play; must be completed in special collections
Environmental interpretation	*Social ecology and representations of the natural world*	Investigation of the history and usage of one plant, animal, or mineral mentioned in the play
Reappropria-tion	*A cultural object that reenvisions the play and converts it into a surprising format*	Description of object, information about its creation, observations about its relation to the play
Prosody	*Analysis of sounds and rhetorical patterns in a selection of lines*	Insights about patterns, sound, rhythm, and rhyme; information about the vocabulary used to describe poetry

she might watch the BBC's 2012 version of *Richard II* (*The Hollow Crown* series) and complete a scene study on 3.2 noting, among other things, that nearly forty lines, or more than fifteen percent of the scene, are cut and that cutting of plays often happens in small sections—a line or two here and there. At this point, the student has just one more exercise left, lots of paper options, and plenty of momentum.

Evaluation

Honed research skills, improved class discussion, and sharper student writing are the outcomes that matter most to me, but a grading scheme is crucial, too, for a project worth thirty-five percent of the course grade. For each RNB, each of the five sections (four exercises plus the summary) are worth three points. Completing all the basic requirements for all RNBs (five total) earns seventy-five points.

Most students compile RNBs electronically, but at periodic checkpoints and at the end of the semester, hard copies are required. While I am hesitant to standardize the physical format of RNBs—I want students to take ownership and explore ways of compiling research—I do have a few basic formatting rules. Students appreciate the guidelines, and I appreciate a degree of uniformity when grading. Formatting is worth another five points, bringing the total to eighty points overall.

For each RNB, students are encouraged to get carried away with the research by completing a nonrequired "wildcard" section. This section might extend a student's favorite exercise (if a particular exercise inspires research over and above the requirement) or it might take research in a completely different direction. One student who was simultaneously completing her resident teaching at a local grade school created lesson plans for teaching Shakespeare to third graders, while a premed student spent extra time in special collections learning about Galenic medicine and early modern herbals. Wildcards are worth up to four points each, so completing three wildcards during the semester can bump a student's final RNB grade from the B range up into the A range. I frame the wildcard as a nonrequired, curious adventure of the student's choosing. I have considered dropping wildcards—I do get occasional complaints about the fairness of giving a B for completing the basic requirements—but I find they effectively reinforce the value that RNBs place on intellectual curiosity, diligence, and initiative.

Outcomes

Writing: Final Essay

At the end of the semester, students use their RNBs to write a final essay—but they can use only sources cited in their RNBs. When citing research in final essays, students are required to cite both the original source and an RNB page number. So, for example, an in-text citation would appear as (Smith 38; RNB 15). Final essays and final RNBs are turned in and graded together.

The writing prompt for the final essay draws on Gerald Graff and Cathy Birkenstein's claim that "[e]ffective persuasive writers do more than make well-supported claims ("I say")"; they also map those claims relative to the claims of others ("they say") (xii). The final essay is an exercise in mapping the research evidence produced in the RNB relative to the scholarly conversations students have been engaging in all semester. Graff and Birkenstein advocate the use of writing templates that "have a generative quality, prompting students to make moves in their writing that they might not otherwise make or even know how to make" (xiii). Adapting one of their templates they call "Establishing Why Your Claims Matter," I ask students to craft a final essay around this sentence (or some slightly revised version of it): "Although [insert something your research turned up] may seem trivial, it turns out to be significant in Shakespeare's [insert play or plays] because [reason]." I call this the "seems/is" template, and we spend time in class discussing how concrete research allows us to move from "It just really seems to me" and "I just think/feel/believe" to a more precise set of observations. Often, the "seems" side of the equation is the thing a student assumed or wanted to argue before careful research—the very kind of claim students were struggling to buttress with rhetorical questions and thesaurus bombs in the classes that inspired the assignment.

In their review of the data, student collaborators Heywood and Kay counted the number of sources cited in each RNB and the number of sources cited in each final essay. They found that

1. Students with 30+ sources in their RNB consistently earned final essay and RNB grades that were ≥ 90%
2. Students who cited their RNB 10+ times on the final essays always earned a final essay grade ≥ 90%

The data indicate that students who took the research seriously and who actively integrated that research into their final essays excelled. In another analysis, Heywood and Kay found a direct correlation between the number of sources students included in their RNBs and the level of detail and specificity present in introductions and conclusions to final papers. Student feedback on anonymous end-of-semester evaluations reinforced the value of using RNBs as a precursor to final essays. One student claimed:

> I was hesitant about the RNBs, but I think they are probably one of the most useful assignments I've had in my college career so far. It was so rewarding to be researching something just for the sake of researching and not with the goal of a specific essay in mind; I felt really satisfied when I could tie it all together at the end.

Discussion: RNB Days

Something I failed to understand when designing the assignment was how enthusiastically students would discuss their research if given time to do so in class. I stumbled upon this accidentally on the day the *Richard II* RNB was due. I started class by asking students to gather in groups of three and talk about the best discovery each had made. The question was designed as a ten-minute opening icebreaker. The class erupted into conversation that went on for twenty minutes without a lull. When we reconvened as a class, I asked the students "What's the best thing someone in your group, besides you, discovered this time around?" As soon as one student would offer up an insight, students in another group would eagerly jump in to add what someone in their group had discovered. One student's word study had tracked the use of *base* across the Shakespearean canon, noting not only that the word appears more often in *Richard II* than any other plays but also that it appears more often in histories (7.7 times per play) than in tragedies or comedies (6.1 and 4.1 times per play, respectively). Another had tracked down theater reviews of Edwin Booth's (brother to John Wilkes Booth) 1875 staging of the play as part of an adaptation study. In class discussion, students nearly lost track of time and easily filled an hour and fifteen minutes with engaged speaking and listening that centered not on off-the-cuff remarks but on hard-earned facts and impressive insights.

Over the course of the semester, RNB days were days when we could take the conversation in new directions based on students' interests. Student evaluations identified RNB days as some of their favorite class days. In at least one student's experience, "The opportunity to discuss our findings with other students was even more interesting and educational than the assignment itself." This remark, suggesting that an outcome of the assignment can be more productive than the assignment itself, emphasizes a final point worth making: as offbeat as the assignment may seem at first, it quickly becomes part of the class rhythm and routine. What seems complex and unfeasible in week one becomes part of a collaborative research flow that involves active feedback from peers and the professor. One student shares a notable insight about stage directions for *Richard II*; two weeks later, five students are making intriguing discoveries about stage directions and speech prefixes in *1 Henry IV*. I am still perfecting the beginning-of-the-semester pitch—creating *The RNB Hive* is part of that effort—but it is worth the work. Asking students to do research for the sake of research in the form of focused exercises generates more vibrant, diverse, intelligent class discussion and student writing.

NOTES

Student collaborators Sophie Heywood and Ethan Kay made this essay possible. I am grateful to Peter Stallybrass, who continues to inspire my research and teaching.
    [1]Before students begin RNBs, we read and discuss "Elizabethan Reading" (Miola 1–17), in which Robert Miola demonstrates that "Elizabethans moved rapidly, eclectically, and associatively from text to text looking for connections, following impulses, working and playing. . . . They read analogically" (4). Peter Stallybrass's short essay

"Against Thinking" is also required pre-RNB reading, and it provides a useful framework to help students move from passive thinking to productive working.

[2]See Calhoun and Kay. A Hilldale Fellowship from the University of Wisconsin-Madison funded the collaborative research that allowed Ethan Kay and me to create the site.

Teaching the Henriad:
Reading, Dramaturgy, Performance

Paula Marantz Cohen

For many years, I taught an introductory Shakespeare course, following a basic approach that fit well with my university's ten-week terms. I devoted two weeks to each of the four plays, selected from each of the four principal genres (history, comedy, tragedy, and romance), and spent the two weeks at the end on a selection from the sonnets. As the years passed, I began to closely gauge which plays my students liked more and which less. In general, the more I liked a play, the more they liked it. But there were two notable exceptions. Students always loved *1 Henry IV* and they always loathed *Richard II*, however much I came to know and like it. If only students could see how *Richard II* fit within the second tetralogy, I often thought, they would like it more. At the same time that I pondered this, I was also wrestling with other concerns about my teaching of Shakespeare. Although I loved dealing closely with the text, I knew that I was giving students a narrow sort of appreciation; I was ignoring the production aspect of the plays.

One day, I had lunch with Adelle Rubin, then theater director at Drexel (since retired), who had staged a number of Shakespeare plays in the course of her career. Over the years, she had sent some of her best performing arts students into my class to act out scenes from plays we were reading. Adelle and I hit on an ambitious idea: courses that would span three ten-week terms and would include not just reading but also dramaturgy and performance. Students would read all four plays in the second tetralogy in the first term and sketch out a script that would include excerpts and narration in the second term. In the third term, they would audition for parts and rehearse under the direction of Adelle, with a performance as the culminating event.

The three courses we eventually offered fell under the titles Introduction to Reading Shakespeare: The Henriad; Introduction to Shakespearean Dramaturgy: The Henriad; and Introduction to Shakespearean Performance: The Henriad. We juggled the terminology to fit categories in the curriculum. (Reading would be under the English rubric; dramaturgy under the writing rubric; and performance under the theater rubric.) We also stipulated that while students could drop out at any point, new students could not enroll after the first term. We enrolled more students in the first course than we would need for the final performance in the third with this idea in mind. Beginning the first class with twenty-five, we ended in the third with twelve.

The first course, Introduction to Reading Shakespeare: The Henriad, might seem like a misnomer, raising the question of whether a single genre, in this case history plays—and a narrowly contiguous group of history plays at that— is appropriate for an introductory course. I had thus far operated under the assumption that an introduction to Shakespeare should span at least three of the major genres. (I had already deviated from my initial need to cover four genres and, instead, to include problem plays and lesser-known plays in place of the "big names" in each genre.) But having taught Shakespeare at this point for over a decade, I saw things differently. It was nice to introduce students to the range of Shakespeare's genre choices, but it wasn't wrong to focus more narrowly, even in an introductory course, in order to give a sense of the continuity of Shakespeare's vision. If my standard introductory course provided a sense of breadth, this version gave depth. It also provided material that could be especially useful to students coming from a range of disciplines—not only history but political science, psychology, sociology, even business and education. The predictable excerpts from Holinshed's *Chronicles* and standard critical commentary on the plays, which I used in my conventional introductory course, were supplemented by readings in family dynamics, the genealogy of family and society, and in political theory and strategy. Some of the most successful readings in this context included excerpts from Machiavelli's *The Prince* (itself a possible source for the Henriad), Freud's *Civilization and Its Discontents*, Gregory Bateson's *Towards a Theory of Schizophrenia*, R. D. Laing's *The Politics of the Family*, and Erik Erikson's *Childhood and Society*. I also included readings on family history, like Edward Shorter's *The Making of the Modern Family*.

As for the dramaturgical element of the second term, here the focus was initially on highlighting favorite scenes from the four plays, coming to a consensus about which should be included in the final term's performance, and then writing connective commentary. But this process was also highly deliberative and not without a theoretical component. We spent time discussing how dramaturgy is critical commentary transferred to a performance text and that the act of choosing scenes and then deciding how to connect them invariably means imposing an interpretive gloss on the play. Some of the most interesting moments in the course involved quarreling over what was important and why and how certain scenes could be best set up for an audience unfamiliar with the plays.

In preparing to write the script, we watched various versions of the plays, including Orson Welles's composite *Chimes at Midnight* and Kenneth Branagh's *Henry V*, which contains flashbacks from *1* and *2 Henry IV*. I was personally helped by reading Ace G. Pilkington's analysis of the various BBC productions of the Henriad, which includes statements by the various directors about how they interpreted and cast the plays.

The script for the final course began with John of Gaunt's speech in act 2, scene 1 of *Richard II* and was prefaced by the following overview that the students, after much wrangling, felt gave adequate background in a simple but engaging style:

> The time is the late fourteenth century. The place—England, where the young Richard II reigns as the divinely anointed king. As a ruler, Richard is a disaster. He has leased out English land and confiscated the wealth

of his nobles in order to finance his own extravagant lifestyle. Both the nobility and the people have grown increasingly dissatisfied with his rule. Among his most vocal critics is his uncle, John of Gaunt, whose eldest son, Henry Bolingbroke, has been capriciously exiled by Richard. As our first scene begins, we see Gaunt on his deathbed, prepared to tell his king the truth about his actions. Gaunt's last words are a prophetic speech on the fate of England under its present ruler.

This preface, a collaborative effort, was not easy to write. Though it seems balanced, there were some in the class who took issue with the words "divinely anointed king." They felt that more explanation about divine right was needed here, though others believed this was clear enough, especially if the narrator gave it proper emphasis in performance (whether that meant ironizing it or simply underlining it remained a matter of controversy). We were helped in achieving a balanced view on this subject by reading Virginia M. Carr's discussion of a "two-eyed" view of *Richard II*. This perspective understands both the usefulness of the divine-right idea of kingship and the allure of the Machiavellian one (which might also be termed the idea of meritocracy). Another site of dispute was the phrase "capriciously exiled." Some felt that Bolingbroke's banishment was not capricious, even if it was impolitic or at best problematic. In the end, we had to compromise for the sake of succinctness and coherence. Sometimes that meant simply taking a vote on a choice of word or phrase.

Some predictable scenes were included in the script because they moved the plot forward and were notably dramatic or amusing: Richard uncrowning himself ("mark me how I will undo myself") in *Richard II* (4.1.203); the encounter on the battlefield of Hotspur and Hal in *1 Henry IV*; the repudiation of Falstaff by Hal, now Henry V, in *2 Henry IV*; and the Saint Crispin's Day Speech in *Henry V*. But the script also included Hotspur's wrangling with his wife and the scene between Hal and Falstaff, in which they play at being Hal and his father in *1 Henry IV*; the confrontation between Hal and his father in *2 Henry IV*; and the courtship scene between Henry and Catherine in *Henry V*. These scenes were important in establishing aspects of these characters that couldn't be grasped through other means.

The third term was taught by Adelle, who held the auditions and directed the performance. Although I did not teach, I was involved in a way that was enormously significant for me. I allowed myself to be cast as Alice, maid to Catherine, in the scene of courtship in *Henry V*. I was the only member of the class who knew French, which made for an interesting overlay. In the scene, the maid appears to know some English and is helping the princess communicate with her royal suitor. In playing this role, I was struck most by how hierarchy was both retained and subverted, both by Shakespeare inside the play (the maid teaching her mistress so that Catherine can achieve a more powerful role) and in the enactment of the scene (the professor acting a bit part that drew on a certain knowledge her students lacked).

Performing with my students was an exhilarating and humbling experience. I am no actress. Learning those few lines by heart was hard, and standing on the stage and mouthing them with any degree of poise, even harder. I felt the strain on my authority—of being mediocre in the role and of placing myself in a vulnerable position with respect to the director as well as my students.

Yet this addition was also exciting and, I think, pedagogically valuable. The class bonded in a strange and uneven way in the course of rehearsals, and I became, briefly, part of a performance ensemble. It made me think about how Shakespeare might have felt writing the plays but also performing in them. I had never thought about the strains and the satisfactions that this double role might have engendered, but the course made me do so in concrete as well as theoretical terms. I was able to see the idea enacted, literally, in my own person.

An additional boon that resulted from this approach was that students' dislike of *Richard II* decreased. Even though they hadn't liked Richard when they read the play in the first of the three terms, in the second and third terms their sympathy for him was much greater. By having to piece together the four plays and then perform them, they could see issues in starker relief than in the first term when reading the plays in succession. They were better able to understand the dire consequences of Richard's usurpation and could compare elements of his weakness with Henry's and Hal's cold-bloodedness and calculation. They could now perform his prophetic speech knowing that what he prophesied would come to pass—that betrayal would carry through into future generations and would be reenacted on a microcosmic level in the repudiation of Falstaff by Hal, which many students found repugnant while others found necessary. Students obtained, in other words, Carr's "two-eyed" view. The discussion after the performance, where we argued for or against the usurpation of Richard, seemed exceptionally nuanced. Students who had favored Bolingbroke and loved Hal were able to see more clearly the price paid for this predilection than they would otherwise have done.

Our final performance drew a smattering of attendees—mostly friends and family of our performers and some stray faculty. But the result was satisfying beyond the number of people present. The course represented a triumph of continuity and a multileveled and multifaceted engagement with Shakespeare. It made me a better teacher of the plays and my students more appreciative of Shakespeare's genius.

The Character of Richard III

Yu Jin Ko

Because I have taught *Richard III* only in courses that focus on Shakespeare in performance, my discussion of Richard's character will remain stage-centered. I thus begin with a challenge that is familiar to actors who have performed in the play: how to handle the highly patterned, rhetorical formality of the language. One need look no further than Richard's famous opening soliloquy to encounter the characteristic profusion of rhetorical devices that manuals of rhetoric would have made familiar to early moderns:[1] the repetitions (e.g., anaphora, ploce), the finely calibrated antitheses and parallel structures (e.g., isocolon), the alliterations, and tropes such as personification. One of the first challenges for the modern actor is to make the highly wrought language organic; while respecting the formal properties to lend precision, structure, rhythm, and poetic power to the thought, an actor must treat the words as living speech that an individual utters because of particular motives, needs, and intentions. Similarly for the student, for the play to become more than a bewildering medley of remote historical figures and stylized figures of speech in which the element of artifice stands in for "Shakespeare," or merely betokens "the way they talked back then," it is crucial to discover the contours of a living character in Richard.

Hence, after a short historical introduction that highlights some of the salient details of the Wars of the Roses (and expands on an assigned historical reading[2]), I often move straight into an in-class rehearsal exercise on the first speech. In preparation, however, I usually assign for the first class a preliminary exercise in which students create a line-by-line paraphrase of the first thirty-two lines of the soliloquy. Further, as we switch to the in-class exercise, I remind the students of the play's original stage conditions and point to one in particular that is generally retained for this play even today. Richard delivers his first speech directly to the audience, which gives him his first opportunity to develop a rapport with it. Whether the actor uses the speech to charm and disarm, to terrify, to promise a great ride together, or to offer another intention, the actor establishes an open, interactive dynamic with the audience and therefore places the play in the volatile, shared space of early modern drama in which stage illusion and participatory, metatheatrical awareness exist together. The exercise draws on widespread practices (following those of Constantin Stanislavsky and Uta Hagen) and asks the students to consider several overlapping components in any order:

1. Explore the five W's and H: who, what, where, when, why, and how?
2. Associate an active verb with each phrase or rhetorical unit.
3. Imagine the physical actions that might accompany the words.
4. Reexamine the prepared paraphrases in the light of the above considerations.

To indicate the potential for this exercise to open up the play in exciting ways for the students (and the teacher), I will give a composite account of discussions that began with the question of who, or more specifically, who is Richard? In addition to pointing out that he is a Yorkist duke and brother to the king, the students immediately and predictably point out that Richard is deformed. As they examine the lines that speak of his deformity more closely, however, new insights may arise: the physical characterizations are often expressed in the passive voice, suggesting victimization ("I that am rudely stamped . . . curtailed of this fair proportion, / Cheated of feature by dissembling Nature" [1.1.16–19]); they come tumbling together, punctuated by repetitions of "I," as though he is repeating things that others said about him over and over (and indeed, actors often look for what others say about a character as a clue to characterization); his physical deformities are continually placed in opposition to amorous pleasures, the latter of which are frequently belittled in a language of trivialized sensuality (even "love's majesty" would enable him only to "strut before a wanton ambling nymph" [16–17]). In using close reading to answer the question of who Richard is, and thinking about what their paraphrases might not have fully translated, the students can develop a sense of why Richard uses the words he does. Is he speaking from a place of emotional injury, returning the cruelty he has himself suffered? Does he simply rationalize his "treacherous" (37) ambitions? Are his characterizations of lovers' "sportive tricks" (14) a sign of thwarted longing? sardonic contempt? simple resignation?

And what action might the actor give each line or unit? I am not talking principally of the gestures that might accompany a line but the action (embodied in a concrete, active verb) that the line itself performs. "But I, that am not shaped for sportive tricks," Richard says (1.1.14)—does he simply catalog those tricks? explain and share? lament? protest? accuse? curse? If the last, whom does he curse? Does he relive his misery as he recounts? Or does he send himself up (i.e., delight in mocking himself, especially as the litany reaches a kind of self-pitying peak at "dogs bark at me" [23])? For each line or unit, the particular verb could very well differ, which adds not only different shades to the speech itself but to Richard the character, even as a relationship with the audience gets shaped. Further, other questions—What does he want? How will he get it? When does he want it? Where is he?—naturally arise and reference other parts of the opening scene or even other scenes. Often the most fully debated question is why? The consideration of that question can complicate the question and bring in more historical material and reception history. Because the class will often focus on psychological explanations, I introduce alternative models and ideas that are familiar to scholars: first, the thought as expressed by so many characters that physical deformity is the outward manifestation of inner depravity; related to this, the stage tradition of the Vice figure and the attendant theatricality; and finally, the historico-providential model (Tudor myth) that sees Richard as the evil embodiment of England's punishment during the Wars of the Roses for the sin of regicide (Richard II), which the Tudor Richmond's victory over Richard purges. As these ideas get introduced and debated, the discussion starts to broaden in scope and anticipate further discussions that will occur more fully in later classes, including the important one of how we are to understand the mechanism of history in this play.

I should add that, while we're still on the opening soliloquy and the first scene, even the question of when—When does Richard want to achieve his ends?—can open up the play in multiple ways. We know that Richard explicitly plans for Clarence to be confined "this day" (1.1.38) and further uses metaphors that signal haste, as when he announces his plan to send Clarence "with post-horse up to Heaven" (1.1.146).[3] The last phrase looks forward, of course, with delicious dramatic irony to the most famous line in the play as Richard seeks another horse with reckless urgency: "A horse! A horse! My kingdom for a horse!" (5.7.7). We can recognize from very early on not only the play's intricately patterned language but also the dramatic structure, with its set-piece like moments when prophecies, curses, and unwitting self-curses are fulfilled and reflected on. The emphasis on character and psychology can thus lead to broader thematic questions like which forces, individual or impersonal and metaphysical, might be responsible for the emblematic pattern—or is it the bloody march?—of history.

To close the teaching sequence initiated by the exercise, I often show (time permitting) two versions of the opening soliloquy: the English Shakespeare Company's recorded stage version with Derek Jarvis (1990) and Richard Loncraine's film version with Ian McKellen (1995). With each I include a shortened clip of the rather lengthy preludes to the soliloquies themselves, because they contextualize Richard's position quite differently from one another and resonate with some of the questions and issues raised in the exercise. Whether on film or on stage, the opening establishes a relationship between Richard and the audience (in McKellen's case with a direct address to the camera) and sets in motion the forces that operate in the play world. This teaching sequence does take up quite a bit of time (usually an entire class), but as an introduction to the play, it has been fruitful.

The second large teaching sequence follows from the first and similarly takes up a lot of classroom time, but it too helps to establish a vocabulary that allows the students to range more broadly in later classes. In this instance, we treat Richard's notorious wooing of Anne by getting on our feet and performing the scene. While some students come into the class relishing the chutzpah and theatrical bravura Richard displays in wooing her under the most preposterous of circumstances, many more start off troubled and question everything from the plausibility of Anne's capitulation (or seduction) to assumptions about what Anne later calls a "woman's heart" in her representation (4.1.78). While I address these concerns and try to engage the students in discussing them, I try to use the discussion as a springboard to the dynamics of the wooing and the brazen artistry Richard deploys. I have found it useful to frame the scene as a sale, in part because it allows me to draw on my experience doing cold sales in

New York during my graduate school days (one year vacuum cleaners and the next dictionaries). Though one surely does not want to impose the template of a sale too closely onto the scene, some striking similarities do arise. The rapid-fire exchange of the stichomythia recalls the rhythm and practice of quickly countering objections in which salesmen are trained. (The first objection was often, "There's no soliciting here," which we were trained to counter with the glaringly self-evident untruth, "Oh, it's not like that." More often than not this had the effect of throwing the potential buyer off balance enough to start the pitch.) Other lessons and strategies also resonate. Take control and avoid using the phrase "let me," because it shifts the initiative to the buyer. (Earlier in the wooing, Richard uses variants of the phrase, as in "give me leave" [1.2.76].) However, persuading and winning points mean nothing without closing the sale ("He that bereft thee, lady, of thy husband, / Did it to help thee to a better hus-band" [138–39]). As popularized in the film *Wolf of Wall Street*, when a silent pause follows the decisive offer, the one who speaks first loses ("Take up the sword again, or take up me" [171]). Start writing out the sale to force the close ("Look how my ring encompasseth thy finger" [191]). I point these things out to reinforce the sense that, as in a sale, there is a clear objective (marriage) and every little moment either leads to or is an obstacle to be overcome on the way to the objective (and the larger objective, or super-objective, of acquiring the crown). The fun is in enacting the battle with a vested interest.

With all this in mind, I give each student a handout with text (from 1.2.49–212, though shorter also works) and divide the class into two lines (one for Anne and one for Richard) that face each other. For each character, one student in turn (down the line) speaks one line, trying to follow seamlessly from the previ-ous line when the character speaks multiple lines. Here again, we emphasize associating an active verb with the line while always keeping the ultimate ob-jective of marriage in view. Does Richard plead? instruct? taunt? command? charm? flatter? warn? cajole? confess? retaliate? concede to cut off and move on? Playing an active verb also helps the students understand that third-person descriptions—that Richard is perversely funny or charismatic or seductive—are consequences of specific line readings and choices. (Indeed, laughter sometimes erupts at highly unexpected moments.) The same applies for Anne, though in reverse. To physicalize the exchange, and reinforce the sense that a battle of wills is taking place, I ask the students, as a line, to take a step forward or backward when they feel that a character has said something especially ef-fective or weak. Though at first this can be rather chaotic, it's remarkable how the actions can become quite synchronized by the end as the students develop a collective sense of the power dynamics and shifts in momentum. When the exercise goes off well (and it doesn't always), the students experience firsthand how artifice—the chiming and aggressively ricocheting stichomythia—can be used to advantage in achieving a very specific, psychologically real objective. The insights gathered will also resonate in other scenes, especially the cognate scene of Richard's (failed) wooing of Elizabeth.

To counterpoint the above exercise, I introduce a different exercise that can be repeated with variations in later classes. As a reminder that naturalism or psychological realism alone is often inadequate for the play's heterogeneous dramaturgy, I look at a scene like the group exchange in 2.2 when Queen Elizabeth, the Duchess of York and Clarence's children compete in a collective lament for what Margaret later calls "seniory" in woe (4.4.36):

CHILDREN. Ah, for our father, for our dear lord Clarence!
DUCHESS. Alas, for both, both mine, Edward and Clarence!
ELIZABETH. What stay had I but Edward, and he's gone?
CHILDREN. What stay had we but Clarence, and he's gone.   (2.2.72–75)

The students generally note the stylization and even mannered artifice in the exchange, and I reinforce their discomfort by showing a short clip from the 1983 BBC production, in which the actors, especially the children, awkwardly try to play the scene naturalistically but render it unnaturally flat. Thus, as an antidote, I ask the students to spread themselves around the room, randomly facing different directions (even the wall) and at different heights (on chairs, or even tables!), and then take turns delivering the lines as forcefully as possible, with a specific verb again (e.g., accuse the gods) but as though a part of a ritual chant rather than an interpersonal exchange. The sound of voices bouncing and echoing around the room has a strong effect, particularly in providing a sense of the impersonal, epic element of history. In this exercise what matters is not keeping the characters and their relationships straight but conveying the sense, with choric anonymity, that death is pervasive as the violent machinery of history litters the land with dead fathers, sons, and husbands. While reading act 4, scene 4 when Margaret, Elizabeth, and the Duchess again engage in a chorus of competing laments ("I had an Edward, till a Richard killed him" [40]), a similar exercise can be performed; because names echo each other in the laments ("Thou hadst an Edward, till a Richard killed him" [42]), the precise identities of the victims blur, even as paradoxically specific individuals have fallen in the general carnage.

As should be clear, I have not attempted to provide a comprehensive teaching plan or approach. However, taken together, the exercises I have outlined can offer insights and methods that can be applied to other scenes and characters while also allowing the students to reflect more broadly on the play. Whether the character in question is Clarence, Murderer 1, or Margaret, taking an actorly, insider approach can help the students develop a more intimate and emotionally vested connection to the character. The students can also engage more concretely with the characters' trajectories, asking, for instance, what drives Richard's determination to kill off the princes or how he struggles with his "dream" on the eve of the Battle of Bosworth Field. At the same time, enlarging the boundaries of character by considering nonnaturalistic performative possibilities (from shared addresses to the audience to ritualistic deliveries) can help the students understand more fully the nature of the world that the characters, as Richard says, bustle in.

NOTES

¹Two obvious texts are George Puttenham, *The Arte of English Poesie* (1569), now available online, and Henry Peacham, *The Garden of Eloquence* (1593), also online.

²I often assign the chapter titled "History and History Plays" in Saccio, 3–12.

³The Norton editors replace "horse" with "haste," even though both the quarto and the folio use "horse."

Close Reading, Politics, and Shakespeare's *1 Henry IV*

Patricia Marchesi

With the notable exception of students who love to read historical fiction, the world of Plantagenets, Yorks, and Lancasters can strike modern-day students as obscure, confusing, and irrelevant. Put that unfamiliar world together with Shakespeare's four-hundred-year-old language, and you get a play that can be a challenge to teach. Yet in spite of unfamiliarity with the intricacies of royalty and the often complex historic panorama of the British monarchy, students can come to enjoy *1 Henry IV*, engage closely with Shakespeare's language, and produce complex and original interpretations. Since Hal and Hotspur are rivals for the same position, I often encourage students—through a series of close reading exercises—to think about them the way they might think about presidential candidates. Students usually have little practice noticing word choice and its connection to character, and yet they understand the power of language when it comes to political campaigning. Framing the play as a political clash between two different parties and their representatives provides students with a contemporary situation they can relate to and makes close reading exercises more meaningful and relevant. Once students understand the link between language and worldview, they have the tools to evaluate characters' personalities and political strategies. My goal is for students to engage closely with Shakespeare's language, so that by the end of act 1 they can answer the following question: if Hal and Hotspur were both running for president, for whom would you vote?

In order to impress on students the notion that Shakespeare presents us with two opposing forces—political parties—we create a list of characters based on their allegiance:

For the King	*Against the King*
King Henry IV	Northumberland (Henry Percy)
Prince Henry / "Hal" (his son)	Henry "Hotspur" Percy (his son)
John of Lancaster (Hal's brother)	Lady Percy (Hotspur's wife)
Westmoreland	Worcester (Hotspur's uncle)
Sir Walter Blunt	Mortimer
	Lady Mortimer
	Glyndŵr
	Earl of Douglas
	Sir Richard Vernon
	Archbishop
	Sir Michael

What about Falstaff and all those tavern people? They're not serious contenders for power—in fact, they represent an alternate existence away from the court—so we place them somewhere else on the board, in a separate row or circle with the heading "tavern world." One of the first things students notice is the confusing surplus of Henrys. There are four Henrys and only one crown. Shakespeare is showing us just how competitive—and brutal—this political world is. The tag line from the movie *Highlander*—"there can only be one"—fits perfectly, even if no one gets beheaded in *1 Henry IV*.

As a matter of fact, no one gets beheaded in a presidential race, either, but thinking about the characters as politicians is useful because politics today is still aggressive and often nasty. Students are quite aware of this, and so we begin the play with an analysis of the play's current "president," Henry IV, and his opening—and lengthy—speech (1.1.1–29). I ask students to read it out loud: it's a halting and painful process. When we get to the end, I ask them: does this guy sound like someone you would want as president? They all say "no." Why not? They say it's because he speaks in the third person (that's creepy) and goes on and on about *something*. So here's my opportunity to bring up the royal "we" and then examine the speech with them to figure out what the *something* might be. In order to do so, I ask students to circle words that seem important or that catch their attention.

What can we tell about Henry IV from the speech? Even if we do not understand what he is saying, there are some notable words: "care," "time," "peace," "soil," "blood," "heaven," "shock," "butchery," "war," "friends," "Christ," "power," "purpose." In a way, these words convey what the play is about: Henry IV is "shaken" (i.e., worn out), and desires "peace" after "war," as well as reconciliation with "heaven" and "Christ" (we go over the history of Henry IV's accession after this exercise). The play, ultimately, dramatizes the threat of more "blood," "shock," and "butchery" in England's "soil" as those who oppose the king's "purpose" challenge his authority. Basically, we have a play about an aging king whose position is threatened (like that of a president trying to win a second term). As always, the key political issues include war, national identity, and religious convictions.

1 Henry IV is thus relevant to the political realities of our day, but students cannot realize this unless they engage closely with the text. Circling words in a speech encourages students to think about word choice and meaning without risking a wrong answer. Such an exercise also gives students the opportunity to discover that knowing every word is not important, since they can still extract meaning from a text if they focus on the way words are used to evoke mood and image. For example: why is "butchery" preceded by "civil" (1.1.13)? What do we associate with these words? The word *civil*, of course, means "occurring in a society or community," but a related word, *civility*, means "politeness, courtesy, consideration" ("Civil"; "Civility"). Shouldn't a society or community be founded on civility? When it's not, then you get the "intestine shock," the pain of a body not functioning properly (the lines suggest such shock is "furious," implying a body inwardly fighting violently against itself). We can go over many more words that students pick: "thirsty" and "lips" (5–6) serve as a starting conversation on the personification of England as a woman; "meteors" (10) on Elizabethan superstitions; and "pagans" (24) on the Crusades and English views of non-Christians. Once again, we can tie many of these issues—the persistence of gender stereotypes, the division over social issues, the othering of those who think and behave differently from us—to politics today.

Since *1 Henry IV* opens with a weary, older king who worries about the future, the play immediately invites us to think about who the future political candidates might be. The first candidate we see is Prince Hal, the king's son, in an unlikely place: a tavern. I ask students how they'd feel about a presidential candidate who spends all his time in a bar. Some students applaud; most have reservations about it (thankfully). I then give them another scenario for close reading: if we had a hidden camera in the tavern, and heard the following conversation, what would we say is the primary focus of Prince Hal's life?

> PRINCE HARRY. Why, what a pox have I to do with my Hostess of the
> tavern?
> FALSTAFF. Well, thou hast called her to a reckoning many a time and oft.
> PRINCE HARRY. Did I ever call for thee to pay thy part?
> FALSTAFF. No; I'll give thee thy due, thou hast paid all there.
> PRINCE HARRY. Yea, and elsewhere, so far as my coin would stretch; and
> where it would not, I have used my credit.   (1.2.41–48)

Almost immediately, someone says "money." I ask them to underline money-related words, and there are several: "reckoning," "pay," "due," "paid," "coin," and "credit." Why so many references to paying and getting one's due? In Hal and Falstaff's conversation, the subject of not paying back takes center stage. Falstaff uses the word *reckoning*, suggesting the dread of such a possibility. Hal jokes about it, yet somberly suggests that Falstaff will not be able to escape such a reckoning when replying to Falstaff's "Do not thou when thou art king hang a thief" with "No, thou shalt" and "thou shalt have the hanging of thieves" (53–54, 55, 57–58). Hal, it seems, is quite aware of the concept of paying for one's actions. If this is the case, why does he behave the way he does?

To understand how Hal's language reflects a keen awareness of the ways in which public opinion, timing, and image can all be manipulated for maximum political effectiveness, I ask students to read Hal's soliloquy (at the end of act 1, scene 2) and then write "Hal, the Unauthorized Interview," a script in modern-day English in which Hal explains himself using the same reasoning—and the same images—we see in the soliloquy:

> So, when this loose behavior I throw off
> And *pay the debt* I never promised,

By how much better than *my word* I am,
By so much shall I *falsify* men's hopes;
And like bright metal on a sullen ground,
My reformation, glittering o'er my fault,
Shall show more goodly and attract more eyes
Than that which hath no foil to set it off.
I'll so offend, to make offence a skill;
Redeeming time when men think least I will.   (184–92)

The italicized words or phrases are ones students have to incorporate into their scripts. After students get a chance to read their scripts, we discuss what we think about Hal. How do we feel about someone who expresses himself primarily through images related to the attractiveness of money? How do we relate to someone who thinks bad behavior is a kind of interest he can pay off and profit from? The exercise provides students with the sobering realization that financial language and logic seep into the political agenda even if monetary gain is not the immediate aim. Hal will benefit greatly from paying a debt he never incurred (*promised*, tellingly, is a word also used for monetary agreements and exchanges such as promissory notes). Images of metal (gold and money) are so prominent in the speech that it would not be an exaggeration to claim that Hal thinks primarily in terms of accruing interest, paying, and timing the market. Timing, or "time," is his most important asset in the play, since it's like an investment he can "redeem" in the future. His greatest "skill," ironically, is in being a "falsifier" of his own nature. Since counterfeit money has no value, however, Hal promises to eventually pay with authentic (and eye-dazzling) "bright metal" (his true self). His words reveal his views, and most students—even the students who admire his coolness and strategic vision—say they probably wouldn't like him as a person.

Who else could be president besides Hal? Hotspur—one of the other Henrys—who is Hal's foil and whose language reflects his hotheaded nature and impulsive tendencies. In act 1, scene 3, students have a chance to contrast Hal's language with Hotspur's. I ask them to find examples of exclamations, hyperbole, and personification in the following speech:

By heaven, methinks it were an easy leap
To pluck bright honour from the pale-faced moon,
Or dive into the bottom of the deep,
Where fathom-line could never touch the ground,
And pluck up drownèd honour by the locks,
So he that doth redeem her thence might wear
Without corrival, all her dignities.   (200–06)

The exercise shows that Hotspur is passionate ("by heaven"), thinks in extremes (the moon, the bottom of the ocean), and views honor not through interest but through heroism. An unauthorized interview with Hotspur would be useless, since he always says what he thinks. He is an open book: impulsive, brave, and passionate about his views. Upon having the class read the speech out loud, we see that it's much more exciting than Henry IV's and much more hurried than Hal's. If Hotspur had any political ads on TV, they'd be short and intense.

The final exercise students have to complete, before having a chance to vote for Hal or Hotspur, is a compare-and-contrast list summarizing the ways in which the two candidates talk about honor (one of the central issues in the play, like family values or the economy in today's political debates). While there is some variation between students' lists, the items generally fall under the following categories (see 1.3.193–97, 200–06, 120–92):

Hotspur	Hal
Imaginative, heroic, exciting	Exchange, calculation, duty
Expressed creatively	Expressed as a transaction
Emotional or uncontrolled	Controlled
Tangible (personified)	Tangible (debt and money)
Associated with the moon	Associated with the sun

So for whom would you vote? At the end of act 1, we count the ballots and see who won. The language of the play has already told us everything we need to know about the characters—whether history has favored our chosen candidate is another matter.

Over the years, results have varied greatly. Many students have been torn between Hotspur's frank nature and Hal's cool one. The play does, indeed, ask us to consider what we value in leaders—and, perhaps of equal importance, how leaders express what they value.

"I Know Thee Not, Old Man": Using Film and Television to Teach 1 and 2 *Henry IV*

Maya Mathur

While history plays were immensely popular in early modern England, their appeal is often lost on twenty-first-century readers, who are unused to their intricate plots, wide-ranging cast of characters, and hybridity of genres. I often face this issue in my undergraduate courses on Shakespeare, where students who respond enthusiastically to the comedies and tragedies are at sea when reading the histories. This task is complicated by the nature of the course I offer—a survey of early plays—which rarely affords the time or space to teach more than one or two histories a semester. As a result, the plays that I do teach are designed to provide a thorough overview of and generate an abiding interest in the genre. Teaching 1 and 2 *Henry IV* fulfills these goals nicely, since the plays invite us to examine the monarch's attitude toward his subjects as well as the effect that commoners might have on matters of state.

I place these debates at the center of my classes on 1 and 2 *Henry IV*, where we focus on the variety of guises that prince Hal adopts on his path to the throne. Of course, as my students soon discover, Hal's journey is not without obstacles. He has to deal with a disappointed father, a fabled military rival, and the comic knight Sir John Falstaff, who questions his fitness to be king. The encounters between Hal and Falstaff are particularly interesting in this regard since they help the prince test his wit and explore the ways in which he will deal with his more rebellious subjects when he is king. In class, I focus on how these issues come to a head in act 2, scene 5 from *1 Henry IV* and act 5, scene 5 from *2 Henry IV*. In the first scene, Hal and Falstaff take turns playing the king in an impromptu performance that ends with the knight's mock-banishment. In the second, the tables turn decidedly against Falstaff and his Eastcheap cohorts as the newly anointed Henry V makes good on his earlier promise and expels his former companions from his presence. These scenes allow us to ask whether Hal is sincere in the affection he initially shows Falstaff or if Falstaff simply serves as an instrument to test his mastery over the commons. Equally important, they invite inquiry into whether Falstaff is sincere in his affection for Hal or if he is parasitically awaiting the wealth and favors that he will enjoy upon Hal's coronation. Focusing on these scenes thus helps to open up a conversation about the conflicts that shape Hal's relationship with Falstaff and the extent to which these conflicts are resolved upon Hal's ascension to the throne.

Film and television versions of the scenes prove instructive in this regard, since a director tasked with representing the relationship between Hal and Falstaff can use blocking to heighten or reduce the level of intimacy between them, close-up shots to investigate whether they are affectionate or disdainful toward each other, and music to signal whether a scene should be read as comic or tragic by the audience. When available, students can also watch multiple adaptations of a scene, and they can do so more than once. Watching more than one version not only provides students with insight into how different directors might interpret the text but can also help enhance, qualify, or change their understanding of the plays.

Luckily, teachers of Shakespeare's histories can now use two television series —PBS's *Shakespeare Uncovered: Henry IV and V* (2013) and the BBC's *The Hollow Crown: Henry IV, Parts 1 and 2* (2013)—to supplement class discussion of the plays. In the PBS episode, its host, Jeremy Irons, examines the *Henry IV* plays with the help of key players in the film adaptation: its director, Richard Eyre, and chief actors, Tom Hiddleston and Simon Russel Beale. In class, I use *Shakespeare Uncovered* to help students visualize the historical context for the plays and the motives that drive its main characters. We then compare the plays' critical commentary with their interpretation on film. While *The Hollow Crown* provides an excellent study of the shift from page to screen, the possibilities for interpretation can be expanded if we examine the BBC adaptation in tandem with two films that are loosely based on the Henriad, Orson Welles's *Chimes at Midnight* (1965) and Gus Van Sant's *My Own Private Idaho* (1991). In class, I use this collection of films to provide students with multiple avenues for exploring the connection between Hal's sojourn in Eastcheap and his assumption of the throne.

Playing the King

In keeping with this framework, I begin my class on *1 Henry IV* by screening the opening segment from the PBS episode on the histories, which explores the opposition between the king's failure to control his son's behavior, on the one hand, and Falstaff's influence over him, on the other. The PBS episode provides an excellent point of entry for discussing the competition between true and false fathers that shapes Hal's development in the early parts of the tetralogy. After screening approximately ten minutes of the episode, I ask students to write a brief paragraph on what they learned about the history play from the segment. While the episode introduces students to the genre, it has limitations as a teaching tool, since it does not provide lengthy excerpts from or offer close analysis of any one scene. Film and television adaptations of the play come in handy here because they enable students to visualize plot and character with greater ease.

I prepare students to watch act 2, scene 5 from *The Hollow Crown* and *Chimes at Midnight* by asking them to consider whether Hal is serious when he threatens to banish Falstaff and his companions or whether he simply expands on the jesting persona he has developed in the tavern. On a related note, I invite them to examine whether Falstaff is eventually silenced by Hal's pronouncement of mock banishment or whether he maintains his resilience in spite of it. I pair these broad questions with a set of written prompts in which I ask students to observe how the placement of the actors in each shot, shifts in expression or tone, and the use of music or other sounds to indicate changes in the action influence their understanding of the Hal-Falstaff exchange. I also pause between the first clip and the second so that students can complete their observations. Once they have finished watching both scenes, I give students a few minutes to share these observations with two or three classmates, after which I ask members of the small groups to share their perspective with the class.

When asked what they had noticed in *The Hollow Crown*'s representation of act 2, scene 5, which focuses on Hal and Falstaff's rival attempts to play the king and secure the audience's support for their performance, the students point out that the camera magnifies Falstaff's girth and diminishes Hal's size in relation to him. Once Falstaff takes on the role of Henry IV, they note that the camera points up at him so that both Hal and the audience are forced to acknowledge his elevation over them. In contrast, when Hal takes on his father's role, students observe that the camera is kept at eye level, thereby reducing the social divisions between them. However, these low angle shots do not establish Falstaff's superiority over Hal. Instead, they isolate the knight by making him and not Hal the outsider in the Boar's Head. Falstaff's isolation helps to cement Hal's popularity in the tavern, and students note that he is awarded the greater share of the audience's applause as a result. Hal's populist portrait is assisted by his emotional response when he announces Falstaff's banishment. Students repeatedly discuss how Hal appears to fight back tears and show remorse for his decision even in the process of making it. *The Hollow Crown* employs such humanizing gestures in order to display both the prince's fondness for his tavern companions and his sorrow as he anticipates parting from them.

My students are also quick to distinguish between *The Hollow Crown's* portrayal and the path that Keith Baxter and Orson Welles stake out for Hal and Falstaff in *Chimes at Midnight*. In the film, their impromptu performance is shot in black and white before a much smaller audience than in *The Hollow Crown*, and their relationship is rendered more intimate as a result. Instead of performing for an audience, Hal and Falstaff appear to be speaking primarily to each other. The intimacy between them is sustained by the use of camera angles that place the actors in the same frame and thereby level the distinctions between them. As one student commented, Baxter plays the part of the jester throughout the scene and sustains his mockery of Falstaff even as he calls for Falstaff's expulsion. Baxter's lack of visible emotion suggests that he may engage in temporary banter with Falstaff but has no problem anticipating a future without him. However, as others noted, the leveling effect of the camera and Falstaff's ebullience in the face of Hal's insults also allow him to participate in the joke instead of being marginalized by it. In *Chimes at Midnight*, Falstaff's comic persona destabilizes Hal's authority instead of humanizing him.

As these student observations indicate, film adaptations can often reduce or heighten sympathy for the characters. Once they have seen *The Hollow Crown*, students who initially pitied Falstaff might revisit their claims and suggest that his disruptive presence has no place in Henry's reformed state. Conversely, upon watching *Chimes at Midnight*, students who thought that Falstaff's banishment was justified may revise their original stance and contend that his expulsion was cruel or unnecessary. Exposure to the film adaptations can thus prompt students to reexamine their views on the text based on what they have witnessed on screen.

Losing the Common Touch

In the class that concludes our discussion of *2 Henry IV*, I connect Falstaff's mock expulsion in the earlier play with his eventual banishment by screening segments of act 5, scene 5 from *The Hollow Crown*, *Chimes at Midnight*, and, on occasion, *My Own Private Idaho*. Before they watch these films, I ask students to meditate on whether Falstaff's expulsion is a sign of political leadership, a gesture of cruelty, or both. I also ask them to think about whether Falstaff deserves to be banished and how his banishment might affect Hal's life at court. I prepare them to answer these questions by asking them to note how the actors are positioned on screen, the manner in which they are attired, their tone of voice and expression, and the way in which diegetic and nondiegetic sound complements their exchange. If time permits, I divide the class into groups of three or four and give individual groups the responsibility for reporting on a specific adaptation. I also provide each group with some time to exchange notes and arrive at a set of conclusions that they can share with the class after the screening. Finally, I create columns on the board for each film and write down the groups' observations so that the students can see the many ways in which the same scene might be interpreted.

In their reports on *The Hollow Crown*'s representation of act 5, scene 5, students tend to focus on Hal's heightened authority in the narrative. The scene, which is set in the aftermath of his coronation, begins with Falstaff's interruption of the king in the midst of Henry's triumphal procession from the abbey. In the ensuing discussion, the students immediately point to the contrast between Falstaff's tattered appearance and Henry's glittering robes. They also observe that the film continues to humanize the king even as he repudiates Falstaff. In *The Hollow Crown*, the two figures stand shoulder-to-shoulder as they engage in their final conversation, and the heightened intimacy of their exchange tempers the brutality of Henry's rejection, as does his promise to provide for Falstaff and his companions. The film thus enables Henry to maintain his populist guise even as he disavows his youthful behavior and suggests that he is just as capable of winning over his audience as he was when he played the king in Eastcheap.

Chimes at Midnight offers an effective contrast to this portrait in its depiction of act 5, scene 5. As my students indicate, in this version, Falstaff interrupts the king's procession to the throne rather than his departure from it, which suggests both his potential to disrupt Henry's reign and his failure to do so. In addition, they notice that Welles heightens the king's power over his former friend by equipping the soldiers following him with long staves that diminish Falstaff's stature. The social and political divisions between the king and the knight are reiterated by the use of alternating camera angles, which shift between the two characters, so that they are never pictured in the same frame. Thus, Henry is depicted as standing majestically above the audience as he demands Falstaff's reformation, while Falstaff is pictured on his knees as he pleads for the king's favor. Finally, in discussion my students frequently point out that Henry's words are addressed to the audience rather than Falstaff, negating any hint of intimacy between them. The film reverses the power dynamic it offered the audience in act 2, scene 5 by generating sympathy for Falstaff's plight even as it magnifies Henry's power over him.

Including a segment from *My Own Private Idaho* alongside more traditional representations of the text can further complicate the debate about Henry's rejection of Falstaff. The film consists of two related strands: the tale of Mike Waters, a narcoleptic male prostitute played by River Phoenix, and that of Scott Favor, the son of Portland's mayor and Mike's occasional lover, who is played by Keanu Reeves. Like Hal, Scott eschews his political destiny for the company of Portland's disaffected young men and their mentor, Bob Pigeon, the film's embodiment of Falstaff. Although the film replicates several moments from the Henriad, including that of Falstaff's banishment, it departs from Shakespeare's text by focusing on Bob's death and his funeral, which it situates alongside the memorial service for Scott's father. The funerals are a study in contrasts, with

Favor's service portrayed as a sober affair that is attended by Portland's most wealthy and powerful citizens and Pigeon's service depicted as a boisterous celebration populated by the city's down-and-out. The differences between the ceremonies help to distinguish between Scott's current respectability, on the one hand, and his dissolute youth, on the other. In class, I ask students what Van Sant's inclusion of the two funerals adds to their understanding of Shakespeare's text. While some students consider Bob's funeral as a sign of Scott's triumph over his youthful indiscretions, others see the scene as a reminder of all that he has lost by rejecting his friends.

Taken together, these productions demonstrate how film adaptations can heighten or reduce sympathy for Hal and Falstaff respectively. Thus, *The Hollow Crown* invites the audience to commiserate with the difficult decision that Hal must make as he comes closer to gaining the throne, while *Chimes at Midnight* presents Hal's expulsion of Falstaff as a politically effective but unsympathetic gesture toward his former companion. *My Own Private Idaho* offers a third possibility for understanding the plays by imagining both the repercussions of Scott's actions on his friends and the social alienation that he may experience as a result of his decision. Instead of privileging one reading of the scene over another, these narratives help uncover the range of interpretive possibilities that are embedded in the texts of *1* and *2 Henry IV*.

Adaptations enhance the learning process by providing students with several avenues for uncovering why characters act in certain ways and how their actions influence the plot. This is especially important in the case of Shakespeare's history plays, which students are less familiar with when compared to the comedies and tragedies. Although these plays can be taught effectively without a performance to accompany them, watching segments from the histories can help students invest in the plays' plots and characters with greater ease as well as gain a stronger understanding of the genre.

Hustling Masculinity: Teaching *1 Henry IV* with *My Own Private Idaho*

Lisa Siefker Bailey

I teach an upper-level special topics course titled Conversations with Shakespeare, which is an interdisciplinary and intertextual study of Shakespeare's work and its influence up to the present day. Students compare Shakespeare texts with latter-day novels, plays, poems, and films that allude to or incorporate some aspect of Shakespeare's art. Our study of the reenvisioned work then becomes a foundation for new ways of reading Shakespeare's plays. Our history play in this class is *1 Henry IV*, which I pair with Gus Van Sant's *My Own Private Idaho* (1991). Students ultimately see Van Sant's film as an interpretation of Shakespeare's work and as a commentary on the ongoing pressures for men to be accepted by one another and to fill the roles assigned to them by fate and choice, society, and self. When we come to *1 Henry IV*, Friedrich Nietzsche's ideas about Apollonian and Dionysian forces help students articulate their own notions about honor, friendship, duty, and identity without oversimplifying or unfairly categorizing characters' choices as morally good or bad. They explore ways Van Sant uses Shakespeare in combination with two film genres, new queer cinema and the road movie.

I teach *1 Henry IV* in the middle of our semester, so my students have read and studied several plays, and they have become accustomed to my performance-based pedagogy. In approximately one-fourth to one-third of our class sessions, students work in groups examining various scenes using theatrical rehearsal techniques that I introduce with specific information and support with online video clips of those scenes' productions. I am convinced that this active, student-centered dimension of my course transforms my classroom into a zone that is both creative and analytical, a place where students feel safe to take risks in thinking and expression. Like Edward L. Rocklin, I find in these approaches the same "rich potential" he finds in uniting "the most attentive reading of the text as a design with reading the text through the body" (64).

At the onset of the semester, I explain how traditional Shakespeare scholars read plays and study sources in order to make interpretations and connect Shakespeare's art to universal themes and provocative ideas; but in this course we take a reverse approach, basing our study of the plays on selected texts that have been influenced by them. Ideally, I have my students attend one of our plays in live performance, and I strive to address a variety of spin-offs. From *YouTube* and *Bard Box* to films such as *Rosencrantz and Guildenstern Are Dead* (1990), *She's the Man* (2006), *Shakespeare in Love* (1999), *My Own Private Idaho* (1991), *10 Things I Hate about You* (1999), *Forbidden Planet* (1956), Julie Taymor's *The Tempest* (2010), and others, students see a variety of ways Shakespeare's work has been borrowed, revised, and rethought in American culture. I have also selected one or two novels per semester, such as Jane Smiley's *A Thousand Acres*, David Wroblewski's *The Story of Edgar Sawtelle: A Novel*, Christopher Moore's *Fool: A Novel*, Annette Fortier's *Juliet: A Novel*, or John Updike's *Gertrude and Claudius*. Neil Gaiman's graphic novel *The Sandman Vol. 3: Dream Country* and the *Manga Shakespeare* series, as well as a number of short stories and poems, are also featured. My goal is to have students study one major contemporary partner text alongside each play we read. By ensuring that students realize this course is an intense survey that requires rapid reading as well as viewing several films outside class, I have been able to manage up to nine plays and a wide variety of spin-offs each term.

In order to prepare students to work professionally with ideas they may find controversial in the course, my syllabus includes expectations on classroom etiquette that I have adjusted from our departmental guidelines. Even after setting expectations, I have had some students disappear from discussion of gay film or complain about the graphic sexual images in our unit on *My Own Private Idaho*. To mitigate such anxiety, I use Nietzsche's theory of Apollonian and Dionysian duality (33) to set up a paradigm for thinking about ways opposing forces compete for control and interplay on the stage. *My Own Private Idaho* offers a chance for particularly interesting discussion because the film presents quite a bit of paraphrasing and quoting of scenes from *1 Henry IV* and then moves into its own world focusing on street life, love stories, and road movie themes that take Scott and Mike to Rome and back to Portland.

Before screening the film, I provide students with a summary of the larger Henry plot and several handouts of Shakespeare's dialogue from other plays that Van Sant works into the film. Students need a section of *Henry V* act 2, scene 3 in order to have Mistress Quickly's report of Falstaff's death. They also benefit greatly from reading *Henry V* act 5, scene 5, which displays Hal's rejection of Falstaff. Students appreciate a preliminary discussion of *1 Henry IV* 2.4.460–81, which reveals Hal's plan to reject his companions. After discussing Van Sant's appropriation of Prince Hal's plan to shock his family and peers with his change in character and of his reworking of the tavern scenes into the underground world of Bob Pigeon and the street hustlers, students engage in lively discussion building on these ideas and on other ways *1 Henry IV* remains important today.

Robert Lang's "*My Own Private Idaho* and the New Queer Road Movies" can offer students background on the new queer cinema and the road movie genre. This article also addresses the ending and the film's debt to and deviation from *The Wizard of Oz*, the archetypal American road movie. After discussion of new queer cinema, I like to point out Matt Bergbusch's reading of the porn magazine scene in *My Own Private Idaho* as "self-reflexively ironic" about Shakespeare's authority, and I emphasize his statement that the "subtitles rely on their impact upon a simultaneous reinstalling and subversion of Shakespeare's cultural authority"—the titles "'out' the rumoured 'gay' Shakespeare" (216). While the opening scenes of the film are often shocking to many students, they are less so after we discuss some of new queer cinema's conventions. Most useful to our study is what Daniel Mudie Cunningham identifies as a consistent feature of new queer cinema: "queerness is continually represented in terms of 'movement'. Queerness is always 'on the go.'" He points out that queer's "movability" can often be seen "through the recurring motif of the road." Mike is "constantly asleep at the proverbial wheel of life." We consider ways Mike's narcolepsy might be overcome despite his traumatic family history and whether or not Scott can succeed in his role of authority in Portland.

The production designer David Brisbin describes the film's aesthetic as "Denny's Meets Shakespeare" (Loud 36), and I use this kitschy idea to frame discussion as a verbal scavenger hunt for Shakespearean images. Students can find echoes of medieval costumes on some of the street gang, Falstaff beer ads and bottles, and, of course, the titles on the covers of the porn magazines. They seek direct parallels to the characters, and we can all agree that Scott is Prince Hal and his father, the mayor of Portland, is king. Students want to see Mike as Poins, and that may work. I offer an alternative reading by pointing to the opening scene where Mike wears a uniform with the name "Bob" on the chest and suggest that Mike may represent a younger Falstaff, as argued by Hugh H. Davis, who sees Mike in the role of the knight (117).

Van Sant's use of Shakespeare invokes both Shakespeare's plays and Orson Welles's film *Chimes at Midnight*, which opens with an echo of the Gadshill episode.[1] In her essay comparing and contrasting the two films, Kathy M. Howlett makes a sound argument to illustrate how Van Sant "revises Welles's utopian experience as an expression of anxiety over the conditions of our modern and material existence" (179). My summaries of the Henriad plot and of the speeches from *2 Henry IV* and *Henry V* give students enough context to analyze the film and return to their work on *1 Henry IV*. Instructors who have more time, or would like to build in additional film study, might also use *2 Henry IV* act 3, scene 2, which includes the line, "We have heard the chimes at midnight, Master Shallow" (196–97), from which Orson Welles takes the title of his film.

After viewing the film, I ask students to continue considering honor, friendship, duty, and identity in *1 Henry IV* and *My Own Private Idaho* in a homework assignment for the next session. In a brief response essay, students select one quotation from *1 Henry IV*, which they heard recapitulated somehow in *My Own Private Idaho*, and do a close reading of it. In addition, students list popular representations of young (traditional college-aged) men in contemporary media. Lastly, students are required to locate, in print magazines or Internet sites, one or more representations they have listed and to bring those images to class.

When we reconvene, we use the responses to compare and contrast the pressures Hal faces with those today's young men face. Most of the images students bring illustrate society's pressures on young men to be hypermasculine in order to gain positions of power. Such recognition provides a relatable theme that helps students go beyond conventional discussions of the play. I have students select an identifying word or phrase for each image, and I have them write these identifiers on sticky notes. While students are welcome to use language from their homework lists, most of them forge new language inspired by the class work. I then ask students to put these notes on the whiteboard and, as a class, organize them into categories. In my most recent use of this exercise, students identified the following categories and identifiers: "hero," which encompassed only the noun identifiers of soldier, savior, and battler; "intellectual," which included only adjectives: sensitive, artsy, caring, and understanding; "nerd," which hosted only adjectives: smart, funny, goofy; "patriarch," which included both nouns and adjectives: stable, provider, leader, father, husband, successful, godfather; "jock," which included muscles, sports, athletes; "jester" or "joker"; and "jerk," which encompassed using people and things for pleasure. "Jester," "joker," and "jerk" had a wide variety in its list, with tropes of types and large phrases to suggest activities, such as "sex, drugs, rock-and-roll" and "picker, grinner, lover, sinner, smoker, midnight toker."

Students' categories have perennially fit into a mix of two basic types: the stereotypical jocks or jerks who are into alcohol, drugs, and casual sex, and who act uncaring, unintellectual, and basically too cool for school or other responsibilities; and the nerdy or effeminate guys whose qualities are polar opposites of the first type. It doesn't take much for students to infer ways Scott Favor and Mike Waters represent the two categories. Even the characters' names evoke the paradigms. "Favor" can connote the old boys' club in which male bonding comes with certain privileges, and "Waters" evokes landscape images often associated with the female body and invites consideration of sexual identity's fluid nature. Van Sant repeatedly uses images of salmon swimming upstream, grainy home movie memories of his mother, and a weathered old farmhouse to present Mike's memories, illusions, and visions of his family life.

I also want students to consider the import of Mike's mother, which works in building the Dionysian side of our discussion. In discussing Mike's confession of desire for Scott, I use Matthew Tinkcom's point that Scott's insistence that he "only has sex with other men for money . . . implies a kind of maternal love that remains between these men, as Scott holds Mike in a Pietà-like embrace of comfort and consolation" (243–44). The lines of stereotyping masculine images blur when we discuss ways Scott is connected to Mike, especially in this scene and at the end of the film.

My students have questioned ways their generation might view what appears to be a necessary sowing of wild oats and movement through a rite of passage into the responsibilities of marriage or fatherhood, which parallels the responsibilities Hal must face as he rejects Falstaff and steps up to his duty to take the crown.[2] Emboldening students to confront these issues helps them to grapple with notions of poverty, homelessness, and marginalized behaviors set forth in the Mike Waters plot, which fills the nonlinear Dionysian side of the film. Van Sant's jarring jump shots and gritty scenes add to this effect.

Ultimately, we conclude that the end of *My Own Private Idaho* makes sense only in the context of Van Sant's use of Shakespeare's *Henry IV* plays and the road movie genre. Without understanding how important the road is to these characters' identity and without realizing the centrality of pastiche to the new queer cinema, the film remains a failed experiment in using Shakespeare, as many of its reviewers found. Even with the foundation of the road movie genre in our reading of the film, the ending leaves the viewer wanting more. As Matthew Sini reminds us, "The road movie's promises of liberation are very rarely kept, or at least they are rarely sustained." Mike, in the tradition of the road movie, continues his journey with his symbolic death and new companion. Scott's rejection of Bob and Mike and of the hustling life only makes sense in terms of his Prince Hal legacy, as he steps up to take over the crown of Portland power left to him at his coming of age and his father's death.

The film is over two decades old, but it still feels fresh and generates strong reactions from students. Perhaps this quality can be attributed to what David Handelman calls "Van Sant's dry wit, painter's eye, musician's ear" along with his "openness to improvisation and anything-goes sensibility." However we close their unit on this challenging film, discussing Van Sant's personalized reworking of Shakespeare's characters, selected plot, and specific dialogue inspires my students to seek and to find new ways of making Shakespeare's plays say something important to them, and perhaps even *for* them.

NOTES

[1] For an in-depth discussion of Welles's use of the plays, see Pilkington's chapter on *Chimes at Midnight* (*Screening Shakespeare* 130–55).

[2] To investigate the Marxist approach further, see Andrew Barnaby, who argues that "the division between Scott and the homeless drifters marks the gap in American class structure itself" and that "the power-differential between Scott and his companions is caused by the discrepancy between those who are culturally advantaged and those who are disenfranchised or marginalized" (38–39). See also Naomi C. Liebler, who points out that the characters' "homosexual activity is a tactic for economic survival in a debased and dangerous urban subculture, not a joyful expression of natural inclination" (36).

Looking for Richard
in the Graphic Archives

Catherine E. Thomas

What can the archives of popular artwork from the seventeenth to twenty-first centuries teach our students about Shakespeare? What do early cartoons, caricatures, and comic strips tell us about Shakespeare's roles as an actor-playwright and national poet, the popularity and resonance of particular plays, and the cultural influences spreading through public discourse? The impetus for these questions and my pursuit of incorporating popular visual artwork into my Shakespeare courses began several years ago while sifting through folders and archival boxes in the Folger Shakespeare Library. As soon as I came across *Midsummer Night's Dream* cartoons cut out of *Punch Magazine* and pasted into scrapbooks and playing cards depicting characters from *Richard III*, I knew I wanted to bring this material to my students. Not only are such artifacts creatively fascinating, but they raise important questions about the relationship of Shakespeare to history and provide another way to talk with our students about the histories embedded in his works. They insistently remind us that adaptation is something that has a history in and of itself.

Fortunately, many libraries, such as the Folger, the Library of Congress, the British Cartoon Archive, and the National Art Library of England, are taking steps to bring just these kinds of texts into circulation via freely accessible on-line databases and catalogs. This move opens up new doors for interdisciplinary pedagogy. I would like to share a few thoughts about the value of incorporating the popular visual arts into the Shakespeare classroom, the critical and cultural stakes of doing so, and a few examples of how I've been working with my students toward a more nuanced and critical assessment of these pieces of Shakespeareana. I focus on their use in evaluating the history plays, as these works aptly illustrate how texts layer history and insist on intertextual analysis. The images often are both humorous and political in nature, engaging subjects repeatedly raised in Shakespeare's histories: the nature of governance, the boundaries of power, the dangers and intrigues of ambition, and the costs of war, just to name a few.

Two issues to consider are how we should assess popular visual texts like caricatures and cartoons and where we should place them in Shakespeare studies at large. What do they help us achieve in studying Shakespeare and training students in research, critical thinking, and writing? Adaptation theory provides a useful vocabulary and framework. Linda Hutcheon famously remarks that adaptations are inherently "palimpsestous" in that they cannot ever escape the presence of the texts they are based on (6). For example, William Heath's 1814 cartoon sketch of actor Edmund Kean as Richard III, "The Rival Richards or Sheakspear [sic] in Danger," illustrates Kean's popular rivalry with another actor, Charles Mayne Young, as a tug-of-war on the body of a very flustered Shakespeare, who cries "Murder!" (W. Heath). An 1817 etching published by S. W. Fores by the title "The Rival Richards!!!" takes the premise of its predecessor—Kean's rivalry with another actor (this time, Junius Brutus Booth)—and elaborates on it, adding satirical illustrations of other famous Shakespearean actors of the time. These are accompanied by various quotes from *3 Henry VI* and *Richard III*.

Both cartoons directly satirize Kean's domineering and competitive nature; however, indirectly, through the use of visual and verbal quotation, they engage us in thinking about how various play lines mean in multiple ways when applied in different settings. We are encouraged to compare Richard Gloucester's rapacious ambition and political competition with his brothers and Richmond to Kean's thirst for fame and his infamous conflicts with other actors. In both situations, viewers must consider the men's strategies for manipulating public opinion and their own image—as well as their failures when their deeds exceed the bounds of civility. Through these images, we are invited to understand, artistically and historically, how Shakespeare's words and characters were interpreted and appropriated in and out of their original context.

From a disciplinary perspective, we can find additional reasons for pursuing this kind of study. Peter Donaldson persuasively argues that our definitions and understandings of what constitutes a Shakespearean text have fundamentally changed: "In a decisive shift of meaning, what used to be thought of as criticism, editorial work, production history, adaptation, reception, or *Nachleben* (afterlife) is now thought of not as part of penumbra, periphery, or later history of a play, but as part of its text" (181). Popular cartoons, comics, and other graphic formats that engage Shakespeare's plays are not simply adaptive works but part of the network of meanings and responses that construct each drama's text in cultural history.

Beyond the conceptual benefits of including popular visual media in the Shakespeare classroom, there are other pragmatic outcomes. With many institutions encouraging interdisciplinary study, pairing Shakespeare play texts with comic art makes a lot of sense. Students are interested in the material because, at least in part, it gives them another creative outlet to examine besides film. Further, these artworks are recognizable predecessors of television cartoons and modern graphic novels. Students generally feel comfortable engaging "the popular." The key is to harness this initial consideration into the service of historically sound literary and visual analysis. Studying Shakespeare's history plays alongside their visual adaptations requires a host of important research and critical thinking skills.

The research project I am going to discuss, which I've titled Contextual Analysis of a Shakespeare Cartoon, was taught in similar versions in a first-year seminar called Shakespeare and the Comic Arts (for nonmajors and a general first-year student population) and a senior major capstone seminar titled Shakespeare and Popular Culture at the College of Charleston. The project easily could be adapted for lower- or upper-level Shakespeare surveys as well. In both cases, this analysis was the first major assignment of the semester. Students first picked a popular cartoon or caricature sketch from the nineteenth century or later. I had a selection of ten photographed images prearranged and uploaded on our course management site (a *Desire2Learn* platform). These were cartoons that used characters, scenes, or quotes from the particular plays we were covering that semester. Students could choose from that group or they could use the databases we would explore to find their own. Then they were instructed to research and analyze the references to Shakespeare in the image, the historical and cultural allusions (people, places, events), and basic information about the illustrator and publication in which the text was found.

The project goals included improvement of electronic data literacy through effective use of image and scholarly research databases; practicing close reading of textual (verbal and visual) evidence; drawing comparative links between the citation of Shakespeare and the contemporary subject matter illustrated; and generating supported conclusions about the cultural values represented and the means of adapting Shakespeare toward the cartoon's overall claim. Some images' arguments and contexts were elusive. We encountered incomplete catalog information, missing authorial inscriptions, and ambiguous cultural allusions. These problems also were a lesson for the students, for researchers often face dead ends and unanswered questions. A scaffolded approach to skill building is certainly advisable with this assignment, particularly if an instructor's students have less experience with the research process.

Because of some of these challenges, the grading stakes, as a whole, were fairly low—fifteen percent of the total course grade. I allotted about a week and a half to two weeks of class time to preparing students for the task and provided them with in-class opportunities to work on their projects. This also gave me the chance to have mini-conferences with students as the projects developed. In the first-year seminar, I had students work in pairs, while in the senior seminar, students worked alone. My logic behind this was that the first year students would be newer to the academic research process and therefore could benefit from a division of labor and ongoing collaborative discussion of their chosen text. The final products of these projects were presentations (oral for first years, digitized on *VoiceThread* software for seniors), a detailed outline or narrative of the presentation content, and an annotated bibliography of secondary and primary sources. Most of the assessment focused on the quality and organization of research rather than on an extended, polished writing product. I was chiefly interested in ensuring that students invest in responsible historical and literary research rather than stress about their writing skills.

One of the first steps was to get students thinking about the ways that popular graphic texts cite Shakespeare—whether the man or characters, scenes, and lines from the plays. To those ends, we spent some time looking at various image databases (primarily the Folger's *LUNA*, Library of Congress's *Prints and Photographs Online Catalog*, and the British Cartoon Archive online courtesy of the University of Kent). We discussed how a close reading and contextual study of an early cartoon or comic gives us a sense of how Shakespeare's work was understood beyond the literal: what scenes held special significance to a cultural moment, what issues matched a nation's anxieties, what characters from which plays seemed most popular because they spoke to the time. We also thought about how later visual texts talk back to the dramas, revising or lampooning them for particular political and social purposes. It is worth reiterating to students that adaptation is hardly a new concept but rather a steady cultural activity. Shakespeare did it to his Roman predecessors' plays in the Renaissance, Nahum Tate did it to Shakespeare's in the Restoration, and so on, up to and including our current film and graphic novel renditions.

A number of students selected cartoons that cited figures from the history plays (e.g., Richard III, Cardinal Wolsey, Henry V). They especially were interested in how particular speeches and scenes reflected contemporary politics. Richard III's dream haunting in act 5, scene 5 became the stage for John Tenniel's 1853 "Ghosts of the Session" cartoon in *Punch*, paralleling the tyrannical king's parade of ghostly victims to controversial domestic legislation. Another image, from the 6 February 1901 cover of *Puck* magazine, featured Richard Croker, an Irish immigrant to New York who rose to power and led Tammany Hall, a political organization infamous for controlling Democratic Party nominations in the city (Dalrymple). Wolsey's quote from *All is True (Henry VIII)* 3.2.224–28, which captures the cardinal's fall from grace, comments on Croker's struggles in the corruption scandal around the "Tammany Tigers" operation. The students' knowledge of Shakespeare, gained through study of the plays, appeared immediately applicable as they investigated and assessed the visual adaptations' use of these references in different historical contexts.

The next challenge was getting students comfortable with using not only the image catalogs and databases containing information about their artworks but also the various research databases that might hold valuable contextual material (e.g., periodical repositories, *Oxford Dictionary of National Biography*). Seth Cayley's account of the ideal outcomes of this stage of research is amusingly astute:

> One of the key goals of teaching undergraduate humanities students is to turn them from learners in need of a good reading list into scholars capable of researching a dissertation independently—or, as I like to put it, turn Harry Potter from innocent cherub into hardened wizard. Digital resources offer the key to the metaphorical Hogwarts. These resources transform learning because they allow students to engage with primary sources much earlier, and in greater depth, than was previously possible. Primary sources make the past tangible.   (211)

Historically, one of the barriers to having students work with archival materials was access. With the advent of openly available digitized texts, students no longer face these obstacles and can work with many of the same materials their professors are privileged to access. Being able to use archives from around the world multiplies the range and number of documents we can expose our students to and allows us to craft yet more creative ways to instruct them in the kinds of questions and techniques that make up humanistic studies as a whole. While we should celebrate the greater ease with which we can access texts, it remains important to ensure students understand that digital archives are not always complete or inclusive. They all have their strengths and limitations, as well as different search engines and wildcard terms.

As a result, there is an additional set of skills we need to teach them—a methodological history of seeking knowledge about history (literary or otherwise). Engaging primary sources is not simply about finding them, but finding out about them. We spent ample time in class learning, therefore, how to use different catalogs: what terms to look for, how to generate possible searches, what questions to ask to find out the information needed. Jim Mussell and other scholars working with the digital humanities remind us that while students may live in a highly technological, visually oriented age, we should not take their online research skills as a given. Rather, we should take responsibility for not only pointing students toward appropriate databases but also teaching them relevant digital and information literacy skills, particularly through collaborations with librarians and information technology staff (206).

For example, one of our technology resource staff, Jennifer Smith, was incredibly helpful in giving my upper-level students instruction on the basics of the *VoiceThread* software their projects were to be launched on. For those unfamiliar with this tool, *VoiceThread* may be best described as a cross between a wiki and a Web-based narrated slide interface. It is subscription-oriented, and institutions can purchase site licenses and embed *VoiceThread* in their learning management systems. We spent two class periods in a computer lab, and she and I were able to offer assistance as students practiced with the software and began to craft their presentations. It was, to be sure, not a seamless process. Students universally said the learning curve was pretty steep, although they enjoyed experimenting with a new report delivery system. They also appreciated their ability to annotate and comment on each other's presentations (which was part of the assignment). The final presentations of the first project for ENGL 460 Shakespeare and Popular Culture were mixed in terms of quality, but in my estimation, most of the learning goals were met. Their research and reasoning held together well, demonstrating a concentrated effort to find reliable resources and construct a plausible argument based on that evidence.

We should recognize that the technology of digital archives and databases allows students to manipulate and understand texts in new and helpful ways. Think about the utility of zoom functions for parsing out handwriting or studying details on an image, or the important abilities to save or print copies of the texts for notetaking, investigation, and comparison (Norcia 96). Analyzing archival artworks while studying Shakespeare (whether Shakespeare's history plays or his plays' place in history) requires students to learn new transferrable skills. Finally, it promotes a student-centered classroom, where all participants are engaged actively in knowledge production. As Bianca Falbo remarks, "It transforms the traditional pedagogical model in which the teacher owns and disseminates information the students 'lack'" (33). Therefore, incorporating popular artworks into the Shakespeare curriculum is not just an appealing activity but also sound and advisable pedagogical practice. We can explore the plays in new and different ways, teach ourselves and our students to be more versatile readers of visual texts and historical contexts, demonstrate the value of intertextuality, and help them acquire a new skill set in information and digital literacy.

Re-membering Falstaff with Digital Tools

Christy Desmet

One difficulty in teaching Shakespeare's plays devoted to the youth and reign of Henry V is negotiating between their status as histories and Falstaff's physical and verbal dominance. C. L. Barber identifies Falstaff as a lord of misrule, whose evocation of a primitive past through comic counterfeiting provides the social release and reconciliation of carnival; that release and clarification becomes impossible in *2 Henry IV*, Barber argues, as Falstaff's diseased corpus becomes merely symptomatic of England's ills. By *Henry V*, Falstaff has dwindled into a ghost of nostalgia, a mere memory of a lost festive English prehistory. Jonathan Baldo has argued that the project of Shakespeare's second tetralogy is precisely the selective forgetting on which nation building depends. To extend Baldo's argument, Falstaff is not only an agent of subversion, disrupting the project of national history with comic episodes of misrule, but also in himself an emblem of historical erasure, his origins in printed history as Sir John Oldcastle being denied in the plays and gradually deleted from the early printed texts.

The pedagogical unit that I describe in this essay uses digital texts and search functions to explore historical memory and forgetting in Shakespeare's Henry IV plays (*1 Henry IV*, *2 Henry IV*, and *Henry V*) through the figure of Falstaff as Oldcastle. Digital tools developed in the past two decades can help us "re-member" Falstaff's prior history in two ways: first, by providing convenient access to Oldcastle's story in digital archives, and second, by allowing us to re-member, or reconstruct, the historical record through searching, sampling, and collecting pieces of text from those archives. I originally developed this approach to the Henry IV plays for an upper-division course in Shakespeare and digital media, but the unit works equally well in a more traditional course focused on Shakespeare's histories and their cultural context. The simpler word searches in modern and facsimile digitized texts could be used also in lower-division classes that incorporate *1 Henry IV* and in which nonspecialist students would benefit from digital aids for negotiating difficult texts. The three exercises described below are organized in order of difficulty; it's quite possible to use the first two in isolation, but I have found that the final one, which involves sustained engagement with large and complex archives, needs to be built on the earlier exercises.

Finding Traces of Oldcastle in Shakespearean Quartos

For the first exercise, students are introduced to modern digital editions and digitized facsimiles of the early printed plays. We begin with simple, directed searches for traces of Sir John Oldcastle in *1* and *2 Henry IV*. I introduce them to the *Internet Shakespeare Editions* text of *1 Henry IV*, edited by Rosemary Gaby, where they can conduct a search in the modern text for the prince's reference to Falstaff as "my old lad of the castle" (*1H4* 1.2.156), a pun that makes no sense for a character named Falstaff, but does for one named Oldcastle.[1] Another trace of Oldcastle's presence in Shakespeare's imagination occurs in the First Quarto of *2 Henry IV* (Q1; 1600). A good way to see and appreciate this variant or printer's blunder is through a search of the British Library's site, *Treasures in Full: Shakespeare in Quarto*. Browsing through Q1 leads readers, through a series of clicks, to act 1, scene 2, where in Falstaff's interview with the Chief Justice, we find the erroneous speech prefix identifying Falstaff as "*Old.*" or Oldcastle.[2]

Working with both facsimile and modern digital editions of Shakespeare gives students a sense of early printed Shakespearean texts as evolving material artifacts that can offer up testimony of earlier words and intentions in the plays' transmission from stage to page. In advanced classes, we would conclude by talking more fully about the processes through which an early modern play is printed and distributed.

What's in a Word? Searching Digital Texts for Falstaff's "Honor"

Once students have encountered through targeted searches the evidence about Falstaff's original identity, they are ready for more large-scale searching of particular words in the plays. For this second exercise, in keeping with the theme of historical memorialization, I focus on *honor* as a rich concept for understanding both Falstaff's character and processes of writing history. Philip Sidney's *Apology for Poetry* praises poetry over the historian's "mouseaten records" on the basis that poetry not only records events but also depicts the larger-than-life actors whose heroic ethos gives those events meaning (Alexander 14). Thomas Nashe's *Pierce Penniless* cites Shakespeare's *1 Henry VI* as rescuing the heroic figure of Talbot from oblivion (128–29), and in the Saint Crispin's Day Speech, Shakespeare's Henry V offers his common soldiers an equal chance to be inscribed in historical memory through valorous deeds. Falstaff, famously, rejects the chance to achieve heroic memorialization, for to him the honor that is the hero's characteristic quality is no more than a word. While Hotspur pursues honor with all his being, Falstaff is no hero, and thus, no fit subject for national history.

Students can track evocations of *honor* in *1 Henry IV* through two useful online texts: *Shakespeare's Words* and *Folger Digital Texts*. *Shakespeare's Words* (Crystal and Crystal) is most useful for placing a particular word in the broadest possible Shakespearean context, while *Folger Digital Texts* are best for following instances of a word in a single play. Searching in all the plays and poems with *Shakespeare's Words*, we find a substantial 668 instances of the word *honour*.[3] *All's Well That Ends Well* alone offers thirty-eight, *Measure for Measure* forty occurrences of the word. In the plays considered in this essay, there are twenty-two instances of *honour* in *1 Henry IV*, fifteen in *2 Henry IV*, and eighteen in *Henry V*. In this case, we might conclude that while the history plays are concerned particularly with honor, so are the problem comedies, which might lead to a broader discussion of the concept across Shakespeare's plays and career.

The *Folger Digital Texts* site offers many of the same search capabilities as *Shakespeare's Words* and has the advantage of a particularly clean interface that lets readers scroll through the list of references (on the right) but simultaneously refer to those words in dramatic context (on the left). Searching for *honor* in *1 Henry IV*, students can discover for themselves that Hotspur covets honor, the king mourns the prince's dishonorable behavior, and Falstaff prefers life over honor; a topic that I used to lecture on becomes an opportunity for active learning. (It bears noting that this kind of activity can be adapted easily to different words and plays.) Again, I end the exercise with discussion of how readers, both contemporary and early modern, navigate texts, whether through a search engine, table of contents, or rubrics and other marginal markers discussed by historians of the book.

The Corpus of Sir John Oldcastle (The Holinshed Project *and* Unabridged Acts and Monuments Online)

Having re-membered Falstaff as Oldcastle through searches of digitized Shakespearean texts, the unit moves on to track Falstaff's historical avatar, Sir John Oldcastle, in two sources that have recently become available, with advanced searching features, in digitized form: Holinshed's *Chronicles* and John Foxe's *Acts and Monuments*. In this way, like Sidney's poet, we search Shakespeare's sources to restore Oldcastle to historical memory. Holinshed and Foxe offer two very different assessments of Oldcastle's character and historical import. Thomas Freeman and Susannah Monta argue that Holinshed's handling of the Oldcastle material subtly challenges Foxe's overtly hagiographical account, presenting Oldcastle as less a religious dissident than a political "rebel without a cause . . . an isolated troublemaker" (225). For Foxe, he is a proto-Protestant martyr.

In Holinshed, the history of Sir John Oldcastle (be sure to spell the name "Oldcastell") appears in the chapter on Henry V (beginning at 6:544, modern page numbering).[4] For the most part, I limit my discussion of Oldcastle's Lollardy to a brief account (Paul Strohm's 1997 essay is useful) that lays out the basic issues and focuses primarily on the delicate rhetorical maneuvering accusers and accused perform in the investigation of his religious views. In Holinshed, Oldcastle is introduced in the context of Henry V's first year of rule, when this "valiant capteine and a hardie gentleman" is accused of heresy. Holinshed's *Chronicle* is notable for its circumspect treatment of both the king's and Oldcastle's behavior (6:543; *Holinshed Project*, 1587 edition, vol. 6, sec. 14); it also temporizes on the question of Oldcastle's theological position and omits altogether his striking, and characteristic, vituperation against the pope. By contrast, Foxe shapes Oldcastle's narrative according to his rhetoric of Protestant martyrology. (A good, brief introduction to Foxe and his book can be found in the introduction to John King's Oxford World Classics edition of selected narratives.) *Acts and Monuments Online* provides transcribed copies of the 1563, 1570, 1576, and 1583 editions and allows readers to compare versions. I stick to the 1563 edition because the *ISE* edition of *1 Henry IV* reproduces parts of it and because it is the shortest and least digressive of all Foxe's versions. Reading Falstaff through Oldcastle's biography and Foxe's rituals of martyrdom, I focus on three key symbols that are evoked by Shakespeare in the plays featuring Falstaff: an imaginative prop (the gallows), a word (*abomination*), and an event (the examination scene).

The Gallows

The haunting image of the gallows figures strongly in *1 Henry IV* and particularly in that scene where the Prince refers to Falstaff as "my old lad of the castle" and Falstaff inquires, "I prithee, sweet wag, shall there be gallows standing in England when thou art king?" (1.2.62–63; FTLN 0169–70). The word surfaces again in the Gadshill episode (2.1). These references can be found easily by searching the Folger Digital Text of *1 Henry IV*. *Shakespeare's Words* confirms that the word is used more frequently than usual in the second Henriad; five out of twenty-two instances in the Shakespearean corpus come from *1* and *2 Henry IV* plus *Henry V*. Oldcastle's death, which is described with Foxe's usual attention to gruesome detail, features the typical tropes of gallows, chains, and fire:

> Than was he laid vpon an hardle as though he had bene a mooste hainous traitor to the crowne, and so drawne forth into saint Giles field, where as they had set vp a newe paire of Galowes. As he was comen to the place of execution, and was taken from the hardle, he fel down deuoutly vpon his knees, desiring almightye God to forgeue his ennemyes. . . . Than was he hanged vp there by the middle in chaines of yron, and so consumed aliue in the fyre, praising the name of God, so long as his life lasted. In the end, he commended his soule into the handes of God, and so departed hence most christēly, his body resolued into ashes.   (2: 328 [1563])

Searching on *Galowes* in the 1563 text (spelling is important, but the search is not case sensitive) will take readers directly to Oldcastle's narrative and to the woodcut that introduces it (2: 329). While the image of Oldcastle writhing in the flames is striking, an earlier woodcut that shows a group of supposed Lollards hanging from the gallows by the chains around their waists and waiting patiently for the application of fire brings home even more clearly the visual relation of the gallows used to martyr Lollards with those used more commonly to hang thieves.[5] The woodcuts from *Acts and Monuments* also resonate across media and time with an extradiegetic scene from Kenneth Branagh's popular film of *Henry V*, in which we see Bardolph carried in on a cart (as Oldcastle is carried in on a hardle) and then hanged as a particularly blasphemous thief who has, during the wars in France, stolen a pyx that contains the consecrated host.

Abomination

In the scene where Falstaff and Hal examine one another on the particulars of Hal's life, the prince, impersonating his royal father, memorably names "That villainous *abominable* misleader / of youth, Falstaff, that old white-bearded Satan" (*1H4* 2.4.279–80; FTLN 1467–68; my emphasis). Searching *Acts and Monuments Online* shows that the word *abominable* is used frequently by Foxe, usually in an accusation of blasphemy and sometimes in specific reference to the Book of Daniel. In the snippet from Foxe transcribed by Gaby for the *ISE*, we find the nominal form *abomination* in Oldcastle's hardline declaration to Henry V during their early meeting in the examination process:

> "You, most worthy prince," saith he, "I am always prompt and willing to obey, forasmuch as I know you a Christian king, and the appointed minister of God, bearing the sword to the punishment of ill doers and for safeguard of them that be virtuous. Unto you, next my eternal God, owe I my whole obedience and submit me thereunto, as I have done ever, . . . But as touching the Pope & his spiritualty, truly I owe them neither suit nor service, forsomuch as I know him by the scriptures to be the great Antichrist, the son of perdition, the open adversary of God, and the *abomination* standing in the holy place." (my emphasis)

The noun *abomination* appears only twice in the Shakespearean corpus, according to *Shakespeare's Words*, both in Lucrece's vituperations against Tarquin. Searching on the adjective *abominable* in *Shakespeare's Words* confirms that five of fifteen results come from the first and second Henriad, suggesting that Foxe and his account of Oldcastle, in particular, may function as an intertext for plays in the second tetralogy, and most strongly for *1 Henry IV*.

Dramas of Examination

The *Internet Shakespeare Edition* of *1 Henry IV* omits most of the portions of Foxe in which Oldcastle is examined on or gives testimony about his faith.[6] There are five instances: 1) Accused of heresy, Oldcastle pledges to Henry V his loyalty to the English king but denounces the pope as an Antichrist and abomination (2: 314). 2) The Archbishop of Canterbury sends for Oldcastle to administer a stricter examination, to which Oldcastle, in a written statement, articulates his Christian belief through the Apostles' Creed (2: 315). 3) After Henry refuses the testament and refers the case to church authorities, there follows Oldcastle's first oral examination, where he affirms his belief in the sacraments and the real presence of Christ (2: 316–18). 4) In the second examination, Oldcastle counters charges of heresy with a free confession of his sins and a denial of breaking God's law, distinguishing between his law and traditions of the church (2: 318). Arundel pushes him again on the question of transubstantiation, at which point Oldcastle temporizes by defining the host as Christ's body in the "form" of bread, meaning that it is "hidden" *under* the bread, an apparent statement of belief in consubstantiation rather than transubstantiation (2: 319). Oldcastle is condemned and committed to the Tower of London (2: 322, 325), escapes to Wales, and is, after some space of time, apprehended again and accused of participating in a Welsh uprising. 5) The final accusation, condemnation, and death of Oldcastle occur at 2: 328.

The various testimonies and examinations of Sir John Oldcastle are evoked but not realized in any concrete way in *1 Henry IV*, beyond the scene in which the prince urges Falstaff, "Do thou stand for my father and *examine* me / upon the particulars of my life" (2.4.387–99; FTLN 1375–1487; my emphasis). However, the 1563 marginalia in Foxe, characterizing the whole action against Oldcastle as a replaying of Jesus's betrayal at the hands of Judas and Caiaphas, resonates with the sense that Hal has betrayed Falstaff and the paradoxical denial of any virtue in fat Jack in *2 Henry IV*'s epilogue: "Oldcastle died a martyr, and this is not the man" (34; FTLN 3431). But what can we make of the allusive web of imagery linking Falstaff to the martyr Oldcastle? In recasting Oldcastle the proto-Protestant martyr as Falstaff the lord of misrule, Shakespeare renders comic not only the man himself but the whole apparatus of religious martyrology. Re-membering the texts from which the Falstaff/Oldcastle character is derived exposes the thin line separating thieves and martyrs when that record is restored.

The first two exercises I have described are each accomplished easily in a single class meeting; I usually combine one search exercise with a broader discussion or lecture for a total of two days. The third exercise takes two class periods. I do the final exercise only with upper-division classes, in part because of the skill required to navigate these two massive archives and take full advantage of their affordances, in part because the texts are complex, and in part because drawing conclusions from the searches requires a certain interpretive sophistication. Depending on whether my course emphasizes Shakespearean historiography or Shakespeare and digital media, I conclude the unit in one of two ways. The first is to meditate on the historical, textual, and dramatic erasure of Oldcastle from Shakespeare's plays as a symptom of the importance of forgetting in writing national history, which is interrupted and contested by the textual residue of alternative histories in Shakespeare's plays and their sources. The second is to use the students' experience with digitized versions of early modern texts to think about habits of reading in the period. Digital searching encourages discontinuous reading, a sampling of whole texts to find and scrutinize particular bits. To read with a search engine is, in an important sense, similar to the "ingenious reading machine" of Agostino Ramelli—a large wheel on which juxtaposed texts are rotated as the reader samples from them and compares them—that is discussed and reproduced in Robert Miola's book on *Shakespeare's Reading*. Thus, in using digital tools to track Shakespeare's historical lexicon and narrative patterns, we may be reading in a way that is at least analogous to how the early moderns read, drawing us bodily into the drama of remembering and forgetting that was early modern historiography.

NOTES

[1] Gaby's "Textual Introduction" offers a good account of the issues surrounding Q1 and directs readers to specific TLN numbers to track remnants of the old names.

[2] You may find the same line in act 1, scene 2 of the modern version or act 1, scene 2 of the quarto version of the *ISE* edition of *2 Henry IV* (TLN 389), which might provide a reading aid for students unaccustomed to the printed facsimiles. The *ISE* edition of *2 Henry IV* also offers a facsimile of the First Quarto, but I find the British Library site easier to navigate.

[3] Search for *honour*, as the Penguin texts employed by the site use British spelling.

[4] In this essay, all pages from Holinshed given are the modern page numbers, which is important to know when searching.

[5] Go to Critical Apparatus, Commentary on the Woodcuts, book 5, which is where the image of Oldcastle is located in the 1570 edition and after.

[6] In the 1563 edition, the relevant text is found in book 2, 313–28.

The King beyond the Clouds: Visualizing Statecraft in Shakespeare's History Plays

Vimala C. Pasupathi

As a scholar whose research on early modern literature is primarily historicist in nature, I have spent many years thinking about methods for making Shakespeare's history plays accessible to undergraduates without naturalizing these works' depictions of monarchy. Although summaries and genealogies could ameliorate the confusion posed by the sheer number of characters and events depicted through them, I struggled to engage students with the plays' broader concerns of statecraft without tacitly inviting them to make broad—and frankly, sometimes boring—assessments about politics and government. For instance, I typically found that if I began by teaching my students about the divine right theory of kingship, many of them would then project simplistic motives and perspectives onto characters, rather than carefully consider these characters' status along with the language and style of their speeches. Additionally, if I assigned excerpts from Hall or Holinshed, some students would conclude too readily that the playwright had simply repackaged the same events in a more stylized manner. While I could see that my students enjoyed reading the plays as character studies of people in power, too many were content to read Shakespeare's linguistic choices as mere ornamentation or embellishments for stories that had already been told.

It has been a relief then, if also something of a surprise, to see the transformative effect of digital tools and archives in our examination of the plays' key speeches on sovereignty and associated concepts. Complementing, rather than replacing, students' own independent close reading, digital tools made my students more interested and more informed close readers of the history plays' ideological underpinnings than they had been in prior semesters. They left my course better attuned to the complex ways that specific diction and images contribute to cultural perceptions of dynastic politics and political leadership more broadly.

In addition to being drawn in by new work on topic modeling and "distant reading,"[1] I was inspired to try digital tools in my courses after seeing the media coverage of American electoral politics leading up to the election in 2008 and, in particular, *The New York Times Data Visualization Lab*, a newly launched (but now defunct) blog on the *Times* Web site (Frons).[2] In a post on the Democratic and Republican National Conventions leading up to the election, the editors took the nomination acceptance speeches given by candidates of each party and ran them through a word cloud generator, reconfiguring them as a constellation of words that were resized according to the relative frequency with which they appeared in the speech (Ericson). By throwing key terms into sharp relief, these visualizations helped to highlight the main thrust of one candidate's platform as well as the recurrent themes that underpinned campaign rhetoric across the speeches. Although I was initially concerned that such clouds might encourage a decontextualized and reductive way of thinking about governance, I was ultimately won over by their potential for reaching students who were strong readers but who struggled with early modern syntax and by their capacity to facilitate examinations of language across multiple texts in a single visualization.

I was also swayed by the ease and speed at which they produced images for analysis in response to student-led queries that emerged in class. Most online tools that create text visualizations have simple interfaces, typically an open field into which users can enter text or a button that allows them to upload whole files. From the corpus users enter, they conjure pictures that, in the manner of the *Times Lab*'s visualizations, enlarge words that appear with the greatest frequency and omit articles and other common words. Some simple cloud generators also let users change some aspects of the cloud's appearance and content, allowing them to organize the cloud horizontally or vertically (or some variation between), to change the color and font of the text displayed, and to reorder the words in the passage so that they appear in alphabetical order. This feature is especially crucial—necessary, in fact—in the case of applications that cannot identify different forms of a word or that conflate them in its count. By organizing its display alphabetically, for instance, the rendering of King Henry's speech to Hal in act 3, scene 2 of *1 Henry IV* (29–91) by the generator at *Wordle* allows us to see quickly that Henry makes reference to an "eye" as well as "eyes" and "eyelids"; this ordering also conveys that Henry's disdain for what is too "common" applies as well to the "common-hackney'd" (fig. 1).

To say these visualizations enable students' recognition of such aspects is not to suggest that undergraduates are incapable of identifying features of prosody on their own. Strong readers don't need word clouds to tell them that Prince Hal is afforded few lines in the opening exchange with his father, nor that Hal's speeches are, like his final speech in act 1, scene 2 of *1 Henry IV*, in verse rather than in prose. In fact, visualization alone cannot help them fully understand the social implications of Shakespeare's choices in either case. Still, the word clouds help illuminate significant facets from the king's speeches that even very good students are less inclined to notice if they are simply reading the speech as it appears in their textbooks. For instance, in every instantiation of my in-class exercises on their conversation, word clouds elicited recognition of the king's repetition of possessive and subject pronouns, providing the impetus for specific questions about what might otherwise seem like insignificant parts of speech. What are those pronouns doing and what do they suggest about the dynamic between father and son, king and heir apparent? What nouns followed those possessives? What behaviors, aspects of character, or unique attributes did Henry attach to the future king? How were these behaviors and traits in violation of (or perhaps a slightly different version of) the principles that Henry himself described as integral to his attainment of the throne?

Fig. 1. *1 Henry IV* 3.2.1–91, as generated by *Wordle*.

In addition to contemplating the role that those parts of speech play in Henry's condemnation of his son's actions, the visualization of the exchange reveals that the king defines sovereignty primarily in relation to his son and Richard II's respective approaches, and, more specifically, it assists students in observing how those comparisons hinge on words associated with the physical presence and visibility of the royal person and the act of seeing it. From the recognition of those words' prominence, rich conversations can develop about Henry's tacit accusation that Hal has been seen too often and has made himself too common. In fact, that recognition led to my students' understanding that Henry IV's constructions of royalty are predicated on the sense that the monarch should be—in the descriptive phrase our word cloud created in the bottom right corner—"seldom seen."

Although these insights are apparent to any student who reads carefully, I found that the word cloud consistently helped my classes reach these insights with relative unity and greater speed. From a point of common understanding, we could then move quickly among multiple clouds, comparing, for example, Henry's notion of the "seldom" present monarch to Hal's assertion that holidays and princes are more desirable "when they seldom come" (1.3.184). While Henry's first long speech to Hal encourages audiences to see the two as enacting distinct behaviors toward the same goal, the word clouds of that speech and Hal's speech in act 1, scene 2 helped us see a connection between the approaches to statecraft articulated by the king and his heir.

Other fruitful observations emerged from comparisons with Henry's second long speech in act 3, scene 2, whose visualizations showed us that the conversation shifts from how seldom a king should be present to Hal's less praiseworthy absence on the battlefield. Among the most prominent words in the cloud generated from lines 93 to 128 is the verb "art," which contrasts with "hath," the other enlarged verb indicating past action. After closer inspection of these verbs in their textbook, students described their role in setting up contrasts between Hal and Douglas and Percy, whose names in the cloud are also significantly larger than other words. After noting that both of Hal's foils are renowned for their prowess in "arms" (another enlarged word in the cloud), students examined the speech and discussed Henry's constructions of each man through epic-style adjectives and epithets. In chastising what Hal is now and what he's not yet done, the king adds new dimensions to his sharp critiques of his heir by shifting his frame of reference from the easily deposed Richard to his currently formidable rivals.

This visible shift allowed my students to appreciate the implications of Hal's response to his father in the same scene, which features no central motifs about perception and instead centers on his promise to take swift action. As scholars of the play would expect, the visualization of this speech highlights Hal's intent to perform "glorious" actions and "deeds" and also projects a sense of futurity in its resizing of the words "good" and "time." My classes made note of these words as well as another revelation from the same cloud, Hal's repetition of "shame." They wondered whose shame Hal was invoking there, and they leapt back into the play to see how each instance worked in context.

Additionally, because of its proximity in the cloud to "good," "God," and "glorious," students also noticed "garment," a word that, for some sharp readers, recalled the image conjured by Hal's promise to "throw off" his "loose behavior" (1.2.186). Hal's promise to "wear a garment all of blood" (3.2.135) in the third act not only seemed to anticipate his glittering suit of armor in act 4 but also encouraged several of my students to return to King Henry's claim that he "dressed [him]self in . . . humility" (51), a metaphorical cloak that renders his "presence like a robe pontifical" (56). Excited by their ability to recall this phrase, I asked them to examine a scene in 2 Henry IV in which Hal assures an old nemesis that "this new and gorgeous garment, majesty, / Sits not so easy on me as you think" (5.2.44–45). In a genuinely collaborative manner, then, we relied on visualizations not just to mine the text but also to reaffirm our own knowledge and memory of the plays.

Over the course of several semesters, I found that the more I used word clouds to introduce the concepts of sovereignty, the more I could pique students' curiosity about other works and whether the history plays assigned in my course were representative or unique in their style and depictions of political authority. Students' interest in knowing more about plays that were not on our syllabus led me to develop similar exercises with Richard II, a play whose constructions of sovereignty are even more tightly bound up in material objects. For this endeavor, we used Voyant Tools, a Web-based suite that generates word clouds as well as many additional types of visualizations. With Voyant, users can isolate collocations and provide the precise context in which a given word appears, and they can control how to count and display forms of the same word; they can also group together words representing associated objects—such as *crown, sword,* and *balm*—in order to display trends in that group's raw and relative frequencies (fig. 2). Because sites like *Voyant* can handle large corpora, the language of sovereignty can be measured over the course of a single history play or across multiple history plays and in relation to plays in other genres. For instance, a class might examine a particular set of objects or sartorial diction from the first tetralogy to the second in order to determine whether the items that Richard lays down during his deposition in act 4, scene 1 are as integral to defining royalty in other history plays as they are in *Richard II.* Students might also expand their inquiries to include plays that are not histories but nonetheless focus intently on the lives of monarchs, or they might compare the histories with plays representing republican governance.

Furthermore, rather than simply generate clouds in advance of class meetings, instructors can include students in discussions about which parts of these scenes should be part of the corpus we chose for visual analysis. For example, in deciding whether our visualizations should include stage directions, students must contemplate the extent to which Richard's own speeches do the labor of representing kingship and the extent to which the concept is aided by the number and variety of ceremonial objects and physical actions. Soliciting student participation in making such decisions necessarily involves them in a conversation about evidence and methodology and also enables discussions of how to integrate both in written arguments about literary texts.

With the increasing accessibility of digitized corpora, it is easier than ever to share these tools with our classes. In January 2015, the Early English Books Online Text Creation Partnership fulfilled its promise to release digital files for 25,000 texts for public use. That corpus and additional archives for visualization are also available on public sites such as *Early Print, The Holinshed Project,* and

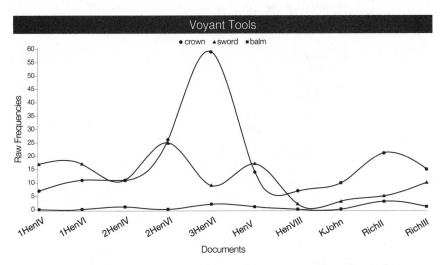

Fig. 2. References to three key objects in ten history plays, as generated by *Voyant Tools.*

the *Online Corpora of Early English Correspondence*. King Henry's mandate to be "seldom seen" notwithstanding, the rarity of the monarchical presence is indubitably a thing of the past. With unprecedented access to texts from the period and an ever-growing set of tools with which to explore them, we can see Shakespeare's monarchs and kingship more clearly than ever before, and the clouds are only the beginning.

NOTES

[1] Moretti, *Graphs*; and Moretti, *Distant Reading* are often credited as landmark studies in the field. However, blog posts tend to offer the most practical advice for the pedagogical use of these methods: see, for instance, Jason B. Jones; Underwood. For work on early modern drama and Shakespeare, see Michael Witmore and Jonathan Hope's *Wine Dark Sea* (winedarksea.org/); Heather Froehlich's research blog (hfroehlich.wordpress .com); and *Shakespeare Quarterly* vol. 61, no. 3, 2010 (mcpress.media-commons.org/ ShakespeareQuarterly_NewMedia/), an open-review issue on "Shakespeare and New Media." For additional guidance, see work by Moretti and others on the *Stanford Literary Lab* (litlab.stanford.edu/). My use of digital tools in the classroom has been significantly enhanced by conversations with Stephen Wittek and other members of the 2013 Shakespeare Association of America Workshop, Curating the Digital Folio of Renaissance Drama.

[2] *The New York Times* no longer maintains the lab as a distinct entity. The kinds of visualizations that used to appear there now are integrated into all sections of the paper's online presence.

Shakespeare's English Histories: Mirrors for Princes, Primers for Pedagogues

Caroline McManus

To "profess" Shakespeare is, inevitably, to engage in teacher training. The Common Core State Standards for English Language Arts (CCSS) require study of Shakespeare's work (along with "classic myths and stories from around the world, foundational U.S. documents, [and] seminal works of American literature"),[1] and future secondary instructors learn from us not only content but also pedagogical methodologies. Not surprisingly, the Shakespearean "exemplar texts" identified for grades 9 through 11 are *Macbeth* and *Hamlet*, plays I love to teach, but they, along with *Romeo and Juliet* and *Julius Caesar*, have come to constitute an ossified, Bradley-esque curriculum that may limit high school students' awareness of Shakespeare's generic range and, more important, his contemporary relevance.[2] I argue here that Shakespeare's English histories, frequently assumed to be arcane and inaccessible to students, may be, paradoxically, even more likely to engage them than the tragedies. The English histories simultaneously expose the intimate workings not only of courts and battlefields but also of domestic realms. Youthful characters come of age as they are pressured to conform to ill-suited familial identities or social roles (Henry VI), victimized by corrupt elders (Arthur, the Princes in the Tower), chastised when they flout their aged mentors (Richard II and John of Gaunt; Hotspur and Northumberland, Worcester, and Glyndŵr), or disillusioned when betrayed by trusted intimates or, often, themselves (Henry V, Wolsey). Students discover, as did the actors in a recent production of *The Life and Death of King*

John, that these "four-hundred-year-old play[s] contain . . . scenes that wouldn't seem out of place on the ten o'clock news" (Stone-Fewings 50).

Yet the history plays present notorious pedagogical challenges—how does one teach them without resorting to tedious genealogical charts and convoluted narratives in which the characters all seem to be named Henry, Edward, Richard, or Elizabeth? In what follows I describe some strategies I use in Teaching Shakespeare's Plays, a course for single-subject credential students and, occasionally, current high school teachers. The course assignments address individual College and Career Readiness Anchor Standards (reading, writing, speaking and listening, using language), but they are primarily designed to elicit the informed, critical, and creative student responses typical of a humanities education. I scaffold the exercises, building on students' existing knowledge and interests, both thematically (focusing on representations of friendship, families, war, politics, and education) and methodologically (using film and online media), even as I challenge them to deepen their knowledge, broaden their learning modalities, and practice increasingly complex cognitive tasks. Less concerned with information delivery (students can read Marjorie Garber's *Shakespeare After All* for erudite coverage of the plays) than with student analysis of that information, I advocate a type of flipped classroom whose activities could be linked to multiple educational paradigms (see, for example, Gardner; Costa and Kallick; Pink; Wagner; and Jacobs). Whatever the theory invoked, however, interdisciplinary pedagogical practices (already implemented by many Shakespeareans) render the history plays dynamic classroom curricula.

Nel Noddings, former dean of education at Stanford, has argued that we have an ethical and civic responsibility to teach adolescents about war's psychological and economic impact (5, 36–63), and Shakespeare's English histories are ideally suited to this task, especially when studied in conjunction with United States history and contemporary global conflicts. Falstaff's conscription methods in the *Henry IV* plays; the objections raised by Bates, Court, and Williams in *Henry V* act 4, scene 1; and the civil war tragedy of impressed sons and fathers killing one another in act 2, scene 5 of *3 Henry VI* can be compared to other military recruitment practices, past and present. A discussion of Montjoy's repeated offers to negotiate Henry's ransom could be linked to the nature and representation of Prince William's and Prince Harry's international military duties; Henry V's description of a diverse "band of brothers" being "gentled" (4.3.60, 63) and Williams's anticipation of Gower's elevation to knighthood raise real questions about the varying motivations, educational backgrounds, and future careers of those in the armed forces.[3] The Boy's presence in *Henry V* heightens awareness of the deployment of child soldiers, and not only the roles of Joan la Pucelle and Margaret of Anjou but also cross-gender casting (a female Talbot or governor of Harfleur, for example) provoke reflection on women's military experience, glass ceilings, and sexual assault (practiced overtly as a strategy of war or covertly in a military unit). Conflicting descriptions of veterans in *Henry V* (Gower's in act 3, scene 6; Henry's in act 4, scene 3; and Pistol's in act 5, scene 1) can be juxtaposed with journalistic accounts of veterans currently suffering from PTSD and other disabilities as they attempt to rejoin civilian society. Similarly, Fluellen's evocation of the Roman disciplines of war can historicize debates about contemporary munitions, such as the use of drones, and in weighing Henry's command to kill the French prisoners (and his troops' response to that command in various productions), students might also assess other wartime atrocities deemed "necessary." Such ethical dilemmas must be engaged by all global citizens, who are collectively responsible for influencing governmental decisions through informed debate.

Shakespeare's histories can function as proleptic commentaries on the "foundational U.S. documents" so central to the CCSS, exposing the moral ambiguities individuals confront as they negotiate complex political systems and discourses. Students might usefully compare and contrast Henry V's Saint Crispin's Day Speech with Abraham Lincoln's "Gettysburg Address" or Richard III's "I am myself alone" monologue (*3H6* 5.6) with an oration on human interdependency by Martin Luther King, Jr. We thus use the American familiar to (partially) decode the Shakespearean unfamiliar and then use the unfamiliar to estrange the familiar. To prevent students from seeing only presentist American concerns in Shakespeare's texts, however, we must also encourage them to engage the material and ideological worlds evoked by the histories. As Louise Rosenblatt suggests, students' questions about historical context will arise organically (115–16). One might unsettle complacent, ahistorical assumptions about the relative degrees of conformity and dissent practiced by political subjects in Shakespeare's day and our own by juxtaposing, as Warren Chernaik suggests, contemporary film versions of compliant soldiers obeying Henry V's "once more unto the breach" command with Shakespeare's stagecraft, which foregrounds resistance through the soldiers' lack of movement (144). Asking of each play, "Whose history is being told? Who leads, who follows, who refuses to follow, and why?" encourages students to challenge cultural scripts that promote war and conformity through, ironically, the valorization of individuals (heroes, rulers, named "characters") and to consider alternative constructions of identity and agency by focusing on working class characters and communal networks of service.

Students practice historiography by asking, "Who is writing this narrative, what's included or omitted, and why?" Biographical accounts of Richard II (a *Wikipedia* blurb or an introduction to Chaucer's life and times) or of Richard III (Holinshed's *Chronicles* or a history essay in an academic journal) invite claims about intended audience and rhetorical purpose. A discussion of what—and how—Elizabethans and Jacobeans were taught about English history puts the plays in dialogue with broadside ballads, Machiavelli, Edward Hall, and Samuel Daniel; Constance's lament in *King John* act 3, scene 4 ("Grief fills the room up of my absent child" [93]) generates questions about college textbooks' constructions of affect. Can rulers have friends? Francis Bacon's "Of Friendship" (1625) and journalistic accounts of presidential golf or basketball games prompt reflection on the reciprocal support, exploitation, and threat characteristic of inner circles (Bushy, Bagot, and Green; Cambridge, Scrope, and Grey). How do recent performances of Bardolph's execution in *Henry V*, for example, represent Henry as a friend? Tom Hiddleston's Henry merely encounters the body of the already executed Bardolph, Kenneth Branagh's reluctantly signals his assent, and Adrian Lester's shoots Bardolph in the head (directed by Sharrock, Branagh, and Hytner, respectively). At what point in the play's action might students "unfriend" Henry, and on what grounds? How, in other words, might they choose to tell his story, and why?

English teachers are now largely responsible for students' visual literacy, and increasingly Shakespeareans, especially those using performance pedagogies, expect students to identify the rhetorical or artistic choices made in a variety of media and to assess the significance of those choices. How, one might ask, did Shakespeare's histories function as a form of "social media" in early modern England? To what extent are the prophesying figures in *Richard III* analogous to today's journalists? How do the plots hatched by Margaret and Suffolk resemble the political machinations in contemporary entertainments, such as *House of Cards*? Shakespearean performances referencing politicians' use of technology (television, cell phones, *Twitter*) to acquire and maintain power or affect public opinion are accessible to media-savvy, *YouTube*-viewing adolescents. For example, Nicholas Hytner's 2003 production of *Henry V* used an onstage television screen that "symbolically masked the actual war zone" (Smallwood 19). The public relations strategies of Henry IV and Prince Hal (limiting versus freely granting access, respectively) resemble the contemporary practices of providing a nationally known newscaster with an exclusive interview and of posting informal selfies on *Facebook*—all are calculated to achieve maximum impact. How, why, and by whom are political images disseminated? Students could assess political cartoons and campaign images of a contemporary political figure and then design their own official and unofficial images of a Shakespearean politician, writing text-based rationales for their choices (media, composition, colors or hues, and other graphic elements). Alternatively, students might compile pertinent quotations from the plays as narration for a compilation of *YouTube* clips of world leaders (brutal, charming, beleaguered, sanctimonious, etc.), forming a neo-Machiavellian "How to rule / How not to rule" manual. Finally, students might apply current gender theories to representations of politically powerful women or compare the diplomatic strategies of Isabel of France, Madeleine Albright, and Hillary Clinton.

Precisely because the histories are simultaneously familiar ("Oh, yeah— Shakespeare") and unfamiliar ("*The Life and Death of King* who?"), these plays warrant students' careful scrutiny and promise opportunities for genuine discovery (which makes grading more interesting for us as well). I introduce each play by projecting, one at a time, seminal quotations, which the class, reading chorally when cued, intersperses with my barebones plot synopsis (adapted from Gibson 95–98); students could create their own ten-quotation reduced versions after studying the play. This prereading exercise provides an initial shared framework, akin to the basic historical awareness Shakespeare's audience probably brought to his plays, and reassures students that they can understand his language if they read contextually and slowly in brief syntactical or semantic units. My explication handout quotes Robert Scholes: "begin reading not looking for something between or behind the lines but focusing on the lines themselves. . . . The meaning in poetry is not hidden mysteriously but can be got at just by paying attention" (41, 67). A fail-proof strategy for engaging students in eager perusal of textual details (and teaching them to construct nuanced analytical claims) is the "take a stand" exercise: I read aloud an unqualified or imprecise or provocative claim ("Henry V is a wonderful king," "Catherine capitulates quickly to Henry's wooing in act 5," "The demonization of Joan in *1 Henry VI* has less to do with gender than with religion and politics," etc.), after which each student stands in the classroom space designated as "agree" or "disagree." They then discuss their stances with classmates who are similarly positioned, finding quotations to substantiate their individual takes on my controversial claim. Each group then briefly shares its rationale; class members are free to resituate themselves at any point if persuaded to do so. Such an exercise further demystifies Shakespeare's language and illustrates the communal construction of critical interpretation. I also use children's prose adaptations (by Charles Lamb and Mary Lamb and Leon Garfield, typically), not necessarily to assist students' comprehension but rather to deepen their critical awareness of the aesthetic and ideological implications of these seemingly objective accounts' scene selections, characterization techniques, and respective styles. Garfield employs vivid language: when Falstaff asks, "Do I not bate? Do I not dwindle?" he examines his face "in the diminishing bowl of a spoon"; Richard III's "velvet gown . . . flowed after him like a sea of blood" (*Shakespeare Stories* 155; *Shakespeare Stories II* 221). Yet Garfield's diction and extratextual figures of speech (plus Michael Foreman's illustrations) make specific choices about blocking, props, and costuming that the early modern scripts leave open. Students thus realize why familiarity with early modern editions of the plays is essential.

Comprehension of literal meaning, poetic figures, and performance potentialities are the three reading proficiencies I expect from students, and the class applies each protocol to a monologue (usually from 1.1 but sometimes from a later scene—Wolsey's "Farewell . . . to all my greatness" [*Henry VIII* 3.2.351–73] works well) when we commence discussion of a play. Individual monologue preparation demands all three modes of reading (students write a detailed explication prior to their in-class performances) and renders students responsible for the class's comprehension of their designated speeches. (Russ McDonald and Patsy Rodenburg provide models of detailed explication techniques in *Shakespeare and the Arts of Language* and *Speaking Shakespeare*, respectively, and Simon Palfrey and Tiffany Stern demonstrate the significance of Richard III's metrics, particularly his medial shifts, in *Shakespeare in Parts* [358–71].) Monologue performance requires prospective teachers to apply basic grammatical knowledge when emphasizing a speaker's subject, verb, and object or when conveying the dramatic significance of the character's mood (indicative, subjunctive, or imperative). *OED* exercises alert students to the layered meanings of familiar words ("How might Richard III be considered a 'politician'?" or "Why does Pistol refer to Henry as 'the lovely bully'?") and thus address CCSS literacy goals pertaining to vocabulary acquisition and use of "specialized reference materials." Prior to their performances, students meet individually with me to explain how their selected monologue's structure signals shifts in audience, purpose, and tone (yet another CCSS). Declaiming Shakespeare has long been part of the American educational tradition, and these performances are designed to enhance public speaking skills not only in civic settings but also in classrooms, as future teachers practice oral interpretation techniques.

The assessment measures most applicable to my focus here involve students independently planning and teaching a twenty-minute lesson to their classmates (active learning methods only—no lecturing) or, in groups of approximately five, collaboratively preparing a performance. (Each assignment fulfills a CCSS for speaking and listening.) Early in the term I model the use of various prompts, such as imagining at least five potential performance choices making use of a particular historical detail (Henry V's stepmother, Joan of Navarre, being left in charge of England, for example) or critical argument (Diana E. Henderson's call for "seeing more money changing hands" in *Henry V* [236]). Students might explain where they would perform a given play (at the presidential inaugural festivities in Washington, DC? on the steps of their local city hall or veterans' home? in a history or English department lecture hall?) and why (setting *1 Henry VI*'s rose-plucking scene in the Folger Shakespeare Library's garden, given its proximity to the Capitol, evokes parallels between allegiances to "red" and "blue" states as well as Lancastrian red and Yorkist white roses). How might students creatively use the empty state (throne) that functions as a reminder "of the King's all-seeing control" (Dillon 113), or how might crowns (or other costume elements) of various sizes, designs, and materials symbolically convey the power and characters of their owners?

Gradually I remove the scaffolding and pose more open-ended questions, such as "How might your production comment on early modern English and contemporary American educational philosophies and practices?" Students might stage pageant-like montages featuring Jack Cade's disdain for, and Lord Saye's promotion of, education in *2 Henry VI* (4.7.28–39) or the multiple scenes of instruction in *Henry V*. The latter play's curriculum ranges from lessons in public speaking ("*Il faut que j'apprenne à parler*" [3.4.4–5]) to history ("This story shall the good man teach his son" [4.3.56]) to economics, diplomacy, even sex education ("Teach you our princess English?" [5.2.261–62]). Its pedagogies are similarly varied, as Alice coaches Catherine through guided practice, Fluellen attempts "community-based" group work, and Henry reproduces the witty linguistic performances and lengthy lectures of his mentors, Falstaff and Henry IV. Significantly, the play foregrounds three particularly resistant learners—the Boy, Williams, and Pistol—who, in their skeptical awareness of their would-be teachers' fallibility, remind us to be genuine and to practice humility in our teaching. Awareness of national standards can inform, even enhance, our instructional practices, as long as we continue to be taught by the plays themselves and work to bring them to life for our own students and those whom they will someday teach.

NOTES

[1] See "English Language Arts Standards" and "Common Core State Standards."
[2] The plays most frequently taught in American high schools, according to a recent Folger Shakespeare Library survey, are *Romeo and Juliet, Macbeth, Hamlet, Julius Caesar, A Midsummer Night's Dream, Othello, The Taming of the Shrew, Much Ado about Nothing, Twelfth Night*, and *The Tempest* (LoMonico).
[3] See "Military Recruitment 2010."

Teaching Shakespeare's History Plays in the Composition Classroom

Diane K. Jakacki

Undergraduate students often engage with Shakespeare's history plays in literature-oriented humanities learning environments. Students also find them on the syllabi of political and social sciences courses. But what can teaching Shakespeare's history plays offer in the context of a first-year composition course? How does an instructor use these plays to impress on students best practices in critical thinking and strategies for effective communication? As an instructor in the Writing and Communication Program at the Georgia Institute of Technology, I was presented with these challenges; I faced them by offering a composition and research course that used Shakespeare's Henriad to teach effective strategies for mastering multimodal communication. In the process I created a course in which students developed a strong understanding of how Elizabethan history plays shaped—and were shaped by—important political, religious, and societal trends and events while providing a constructive forum for students to develop sophisticated writing skills. In this essay I will relate the experience of teaching *1* and *2 Henry IV* and *Henry V* as part of an overarching communication and research agenda. I will relate how digital assignments gave students confidence in engaging with the plays and how Shakespeare's history plays provided students with a complex and sophisticated approach to developing strong communication skills in written, oral, electronic, and visual registers.

At Georgia Tech all students must take two required communication courses. These courses are offered by the Writing and Communication Program within the School of Literature, Media, and Communication. For most students, these courses constitute their only university experience in the humanities. The second of these courses, English 1102, "develops communication skills in networked electronic environments, emphasizes interpretation and evaluation of cultural texts, and incorporates research methods in print and on the Internet" ("Courses"). English 1102 is designed to give students "opportunities to practice and hone their multimedia strategies in relation to issues and concerns in science and technology" ("Composition Courses"). These goals speak to the standardized objectives and outcomes set by the Georgia State Board of Regents, which oversees the writing and communication programs of Georgia's public universities.

As an instructor I was expected to incorporate my own research interests into course design, employing my expertise to help students learn how to think critically, engage in research, and communicate effectively, thereby establishing a pedagogical framework that would strengthen course objectives and outcomes. For the three sections of English 1102 that I taught in fall 2012 I chose as my subject Shakespeare's (English) history. Teaching the history plays allowed me to engage students in questions about Shakespeare's role in Elizabethan theatrical development and his reliance on published chronicles and contemporary theater to craft his history plays, to introduce students to concepts relating to the mediation of history for political and cultural purposes, and to help them assess their engagement with—and ability to—interpret edited texts.

I designed the course to help these non-liberal-arts students move past their preconceptions of Shakespeare's works and better consider ways in which we understand history. I emphasized the cultural and political importance of these plays as artifacts that assist us as we evaluate the relation between Elizabethan and medieval societies. I focused on the history plays because I thought Georgia Tech students, whose academic study is overwhelmingly in engineering and the sciences, might connect more with these plays in terms of political and military history and concepts of good government. In addition to the plays and attendant introductory matter, we examined the source materials Shakespeare used in writing them. Students were assigned research projects in which they compared sixteenth-century chronicle sources with modern scholarly considerations of medieval and early modern English history. Finally, we looked at *The Famous Victories of Henry the Fifth*, the Queen's Men play that provided much of the inspiration for the Henriad.

For the course I assigned the Penguin print editions of all three plays, the online *Internet Shakespeare Edition (ISE)* of *Henry V*, the facsimile of the section in Holinshed's 1587 *Chronicles* about the battle of Agincourt, and the Malone Society facsimile edition of *Famous Victories*. I decided on a hybrid examination of the editions to reinforce the importance of editorial process in different publishing environments in strengthening student understanding of the fluidity of these texts and to help them better comprehend the benefits and challenges afforded by digital editions. In particular, the side-by-side examination of the Penguin and *ISE* editions of *Henry V* enhanced students' recognition of the role the editor plays in negotiating a text on behalf of an audience or audiences.

In class, students watched the BBC *Hollow Crown* productions of *Henry IV, Part 1*; *Henry IV, Part 2*; and *Henry V* and Kenneth Branagh's *Henry V*. We engaged in a close reading exercise on the Harfleur scene in each production. Students wrote response papers considering how Tom Hiddleston and Kenneth Branagh (the actors who portrayed Henry in the respective productions) interpreted Henry's behavior in the siege sequence and Harfleur's surrender. In addition, we analyzed a mash-up of the Saint Crispin's Day Speech from the BBC, Branagh, and Laurence Olivier adaptations. All of this helped to strengthen student understanding of the texts and to introduce the idea of adaptation and how directorial intention is reflective of temporal cultural and political perspectives.

As defined by the Writing and Communication Program, students were expected to build proficiency in several writing genres, public speaking, and visual rhetoric. The instructors teaching English 1102 experiment with concepts associated with digital pedagogy approaches, creating assignments that require students to write in electronic environments and produce multimodal digital artifacts. For this course I designed all assignments to be electronic in nature, focusing on three major scaffolded writing intensive assignments. Students contributed to a semester-long blog designed to encourage examination and analysis of specific themes, characters, and scenes in the Henry plays. Students gave in-class presentations as part of a collaborative "knowledge base" research project involving historical, political, cultural, and societal topics. These presentations also included the publication of an abstract on the course Web site. The final class project was a collaborative digital edition of *The Famous Victories*, for which students worked alone and in groups to transcribe, gloss, and publish their own edited text.

Blog

Prior experience with having students work in collaborative online, semester-long writing environments had convinced me that regular, public-facing writing reinforces the importance of process, emphasizes consideration of audience, and results in a heightened sense of development for the writer. Additionally, students begin to appreciate modes of publication and best practices for the visual presentation of information. In this case, the blog challenged students to reflect on characters and themes in the plays, and helped track their developing understanding of the subject matter.

Each student was required to write five posts of three hundred words each, submitted every other week. I gave a prompt for each post and defined a rubric based on rhetorical appeal, structure, and design for medium. Students were required to state a thesis, defend it with evidence from the plays, and include at least one evocative image, all while presenting work that best reflected online writing. Each prompt showed our developing analysis of the plays. Early posts focused on character development and themes such as good government, corruption, and shifting identity. Later posts emphasized the students' transition from engaged readers to active editors, challenging them to consider their experiences working on the digital edition of *Famous Victories*. Here I wanted them to examine their experience transcribing the play and participating in collaborative work, the comparison between the Queen's Men play and Shakespeare's version, and the temporality of historical representation through a dialogic reading of the plays.

Short Research Project

I designed the research assignment to reinforce contemporary cultural relevance of the plays through traditional scholarly research. Students developed a broader contextual understanding of the subject matter in the Henriad while gaining perspective on the political and cultural events occurring in England and Europe in the 1580s and 1590s. I worked with our embedded subject librarian to create a research guide designed to educate the students about the difference between reliable and unreliable sources. The librarian and I created a list of subjects—people, events, issues—that resonated in the plays and would have been important to a sixteenth-century audience. Each student chose a subject and was required to publish on the course Web site a 250-word abstract and bibliography of their research. The abstract identified a research question that they then focused on in their five-minute in-class presentation. This presentation demonstrated the student's ability to synthesize that argument with compelling evidence augmented by audiovisual aids. This assignment also involved a peer-review component: at the end of each presentation other students provided instant feedback through in-line comments appended to the posted abstract.

Final Project

Working individually and in groups, students transcribed the Malone Society facsimile of the 1598 edition of *Famous Victories*. They glossed the text, updated and standardized spelling and punctuation, and incorporated contextual information about the Middle Ages, the Elizabethan era, and the textual relation between the Henriad and *Famous Victories*. I chose *Famous Victories* as a complementary text to the Henriad to reinforce the course's focus on source material and adaptation. I also wanted to emphasize how cultural expression of historical themes and events can change from author to author, even in a relatively short span of time. Through the experience of editing the play, I urged students to reflect on how the texts they read are universally edited in some way and that they—as readers and writers—need to become more discerning about the material with which they engage. The print and electronic editions we read in class and a variety of other materials gave students a better understanding of how the material in an edition is presented and why it is important. We discussed at length how a digital edition might allow for more fluid and dynamic integration of text and context—and how reading a text in electronic form changes our relationship with the work.

Method

My commitment to teaching this course in this way required significant planning and preparation. I built the Writing and Communication Program learning objectives and outcomes into every assignment to establish a balance between subject matter and developing communication competencies. The addition of complex digital assignments predicated on process and collaboration dictated that I had to incorporate significant in- and out-of-class time to skill development and experimentation with tools and platforms. Taking into account the maxim that if technology can fail it will, I had to be flexible and transparent with students about course adjustment related to unexpected complications.

While this overt commitment to digital pedagogy was challenging, I found that it helped me to establish a sound course structure with a stronger sense of scope and expectation than other literature and composition courses I had previously taught. More important, it forced me to make sure that the plays and historical context did not become incidental and that the digital focus on engagement and research skills didn't overwhelm the subject matter. This concern to keep the Henriad central to the course experience was ongoing for me throughout the semester; I believe that I maintained that crucial balance and ensured that these predominantly science and engineering students came away with a sophisticated experience of analyzing and contextualizing early modern drama.

In order to ensure sufficient time for students to master the necessary digital tools and platforms, as well as to provide time for the scaffolded group work in the digital edition assignment, I set aside one of each week's three class sessions as a technology lab day. Students brought their laptops to class and used the lab time to work collaboratively on assignments: Mondays were devoted to lecture about the plays and historical context, Wednesdays involved student-led discussion about specific assigned topics, and Fridays were lab and work days. To ensure that this structure reinforced learning objectives, reading assignments were keyed to the first half of the week and analytical and reflective writing assignments were usually associated with the latter part of the week.

Evaluation

The centrality of Shakespeare's history plays in my English composition course was a success for three reasons: first, reading and analyzing the Henry plays in a writing-intensive course challenged nonhumanities students to engage critically with the plays; second, presenting the plays in a comparative historical context reinforced the importance of literature and art as crucial components of cultural identity; and third, engaging students as producers of edited texts established an opportunity for them to better understand the collaborative and intentional nature of knowledge production. My approach to the course was ambitious and not without its pitfalls. By creating an interreliance on close-read literature, composition and communication, and digital humanities approaches, I set for myself and my students a learning experience that involved high risks but ultimately delivered equal reward. Certainly my confidence that students would have adequate access to technology (both hardware and software) allowed me to design digitally intensive classroom experiences and sophisticated assignments. The Writing and Communication Program's course structure required me to be deliberate about how students would engage with and analyze texts at a level and in ways that I might not have thought to pursue in a more traditional course. Perhaps most important was the need for me to thoroughly prepare for introducing students not only to the history plays but to Shakespeare more generally. These were all high-achieving, intelligent students, but because of their academic focus on sciences, math, and engineering I could not assume that they would exhibit much interest in Shakespeare's plays. Therefore, I had to plan carefully and focus on fewer plays over longer periods than I might otherwise have done.

The experience and results were transformative to my growth as an educator. This course represented my most ambitious development of a technology-centric syllabus, and I exposed myself to high pedagogical and intellectual risks. By incorporating an unfamiliar text as the culminating learning experience, I chanced losing the focus on how these history plays affect students' understanding of Elizabethan society. These factors forced me to reconsider my own assumptions about how to communicate this importance. Knowing my audience and recognizing the parameters for the course required that I present the Henry plays and English literature and history as unknown quantities while at the same time not limiting or minimizing their cultural importance. In essence I had to approach the course as I would design an intellectual puzzle and then work with students as they solved it. Certainly the course design and implementation have altered the way in which I will teach these plays in the future.

Teaching Shakespeare's history plays in a composition course offered a challenge that I would encourage other instructors to accept. Relying on the Henriad as a core text provided opportunities to incorporate adaptations and other associated works that might not otherwise have been so readily accessible— specifically the availability of filmed and televised productions to augment readings. The incorporation of digital-humanities-enriched assignments added a higher level of complexity that could have ended unsuccessfully for students without ready access to technology. As it turned out, the digital components created a bridge to the interests of my Georgia Tech students. The ongoing response writing in the blog helped students to strengthen their connections to the characters and themes in the plays while reinforcing the importance of process in good writing. More important still, the production of the *Famous Victories* digital edition provided a platform from which students could reevaluate the contextual importance of the history genre to an Elizabethan audience while reconsidering the importance of critical and informed reading. I believe that the opportunity for composition students to consider and collaborate on these plays in a public-facing manner offered them invaluable insights into the works and their contexts while achieving the goals and objectives of the composition course.

Turning to the Stranger in Shakespeare's *Henry V*

Ruben Espinosa

While *Henry V* appears to extol a communal desire for English nationalism, the actions of the English in the play—leaders and thieves alike—are certainly rendered suspect. Stephen Greenblatt sees the nuances "of royal hypocrisy, ruthlessness, and bad faith" veiled in "the context of a celebration, a collective panegyric to 'This star of England', the charismatic leader who purges the commonwealth of its incorrigibles and forges the martial national State" ("Invisible Bullets" 56). However, we know that those "incorrigibles" are never purged from the commonwealth but rather from the presence of the eponymous monarch. In the aftermath of war, Pistol vows to return to the streets of England to pimp, thieve, and deceive (5.1.76–78). *Henry V*, then, explores ambivalent attitudes about English identity. Indeed, when the Chorus states, "O England—model to thy inward greatness," it immediately qualifies that "greatness" by exclaiming, "What mightst thou do, that hounour would thee do, / Were all thy children kind and natural?" (2.0.16–19). "Were," of course, is the hypothetical hope behind that promise. Of more importance, to my mind, is the way that the phrase "kind and natural" not only evokes the idea of geniality but also underscores the desire for legitimate (natural) kinship (kind) among the English.

The play's consideration of "kind and natural" Englishness inevitably draws attention to the value of those who are deemed unworthy and dissimilar in the play—that is, the Scots, Irish, Welsh, and foreigners imagined as "pilfering borderers," "coursing snatchers," "giddy neighbor[s]," and "dog[s]" who inhabit "th'ill neighbourhood" (1.2.142, 143, 145, 218, 154) surrounding England.[1] It is precisely this aspect of the play—the imagined borders evocative of inclusion, exclusion, and assimilation—that I examine in this essay. With a twenty-first-century American student demographic in mind, this essay interrogates how the negotiation of alterity in the play registers Shakespeare's keen attention to the role of the immigrant-alien-stranger-other in its nation-building enterprise and also how that negotiation reveals the play's rich cultural currency for today's underrepresented students, whose own epistemological standpoints are often informed by issues of immigration, xenophobia, and the imagined value of homogeneity.[2]

Attention to the role and value of the strangers in *Henry V* allows us and our students to scrutinize the nuances of this play in a novel way, and it opens the door to varied discussions about national identity, ethnicity, gender, and social inequities, both then and now. In our current sociopolitical climate, where debates about immigration and English-only initiatives often shape views of insiders and outsiders, I believe that the stranger's perspective—in both the play and our academic communities—is valuable in understanding how language and intercultural influences bear on national identity. These issues impact both our worldview and our view of Shakespeare. Addressing the advantages of cross-historical studies, Peter Erickson argues that, while our own interests are influenced by "the perspectives we bring from our early modern involvements," we also have much to gain from "the methodological value of the present" (172). This approach, he says, "enables us to see early modern formations with new eyes—to loosen the iconographical blinders, to change the interpretive filters, to look again" (173). In other words, as early modern scholars, we need not only engage the historical past but also allow the historical present to influence, in meaningful ways, how we see the formation of that past. "To look again" at *Henry V* with mindful attention to the stranger—in both the play and our world—allows for a fresh understanding of the stranger in, and the strangeness of, Shakespeare for our students.[3]

Bastard Normans

To arrive at the stranger, I first consider that which strangeness is set against in *Henry V*. As I mention above, England's neighbors are disparaged early in the play, but Henry is imagined as "a true lover of the holy Church" (1.1.24), "[r]ipe for exploits and mighty enterprises" (1.2.121), and "the mirror of all Christian kings" (2.0.6). The play leads its audience to see Henry as a valiant emblem of English kingship. Moreover, the Bishop of Ely encourages Henry to draw on his kind—that is, his royal ancestry—to garner strength: "Awake remembrance of those valiant dead," Ely says to Henry, "The blood and courage that renownèd them / Runs in your veins" (1.2.115–18). Here, Ely aligns the martial campaign with the larger narrative of English kinship. In a play that imagines its country's own history, the emphasis on this historical kindness is telling.

The truth, as the monarch's musings reveal, is that Henry's legitimacy, like the legitimacy of the war, is hardly clear-cut. When Henry does awake "remembrance of those valiant dead," what he recalls is his father's usurpation of Richard II: "O not today, think not upon the fault / My father made in compassing the crown" (4.1.275–76). What it means to be "kind and natural," then, is rather nebulous. In this vein, we should encourage our students to scrutinize Henry and the construction of English identity and to tease out the implications therein.

The manifold views of Englishness from without complicate the engendering of national identity, and to unpack this facet of the play through our teaching is to draw attention to the power of the making of King Henry V for our students. Close reading, small-group exercises allow students to analyze specific moments where similitude and strangeness are explored in *Henry V*. More often than not, these exercises produce class discussions that center on issues of legitimacy and the influence of strangers in both the world of the play and our own society. In small-group settings, students tend to offer candid views about the deliberate exclusion and denigration of strangers in the play, and they are quick to draw connections to the way this applies to immigrants, and a host of underrepresented groups, in America.

The play constructs its national hero, and asking students to examine and discuss specific moments that undermine that construction leads to the recognition that the strangers in the play have a role in that creation. One such moment that I have asked students to consider is when the Constable impresses on King Charles that they must fight to keep the "barbarous" English from taking French vineyards. The Dauphin's response is particularly striking:

> *O Dieu vivant!* Shall a few sprays of us,
> The emptying of our fathers' luxury,
> Our scions, put in wild and savage stock,
> Spirt up so suddenly into the clouds
> And overlook the grafters?   (3.5.5–9)

On the heels of the Dauphin's suggestion that the English are mere offshoots of French sexual desire, the Duke of Bourbon says about the English: "Normans, but Bastard Normans, Norman bastards!" (10). This French insult is expected, but the move to undermine English identity is interesting in a play seeking to establish that identity. Whatever is being born, the French suggest, is neither kind nor natural.

Through this view of English bastardy, the play attends to apparatuses that shape national and cultural identity, and in the process it underscores the tenuous nature of kindness and legitimacy. Given the urgency of the present-day immigration debate in America, the idea of who is deemed a legitimate insider is a significant entry point to discussions about identity politics for our students. As I mention above, my students at the University of Texas, El Paso—students living in one of the largest binational communities in the world and who experience the fluid, intercultural nature of the border on a daily basis—often draw connections between tensions surrounding the construction of national identity in *Henry V* and the tensions surrounding the citizenship and status of Latino/as in America. The play's attention to the unfixed nature of national, ethnic, and cultural identity clearly holds currency for our twenty-first-century students, and it has allowed my students to discuss how views of national identity are often wrought and reinforced.

Broken English

While the Chorus and Henry's entourage work as propagandistic machinery for the king, the play also offers competing viewpoints on Henry's heroism. French antagonism is expected, but sentiments closer to home offer insight into the way that national, ethnic, and cultural identities are anything but stable. Amid this instability, the play allows for the interrogation of both the imagined parameters that define national identity and the value of assimilation.

Scrutinizing how national identity is often shaped along the lines of linguistic similitude and against intercultural influences is key, as these issues inform views of insiders and outsiders in our own society. As Carola Suárez-Orozco and Marcelo Suárez-Orozco argue, language is "a marker of identity and instrument of power" that politicizes the issue of English in America. These authors write, "Where one language is clearly a higher-status language, native speakers of the lower-status language often have trouble mastering and will indeed resist using the higher-status language" (135). For some Mexican American students— the group these authors discuss—Shakespeare exists as an iconic marker of that "higher-status language."[4] For this reason, asking students to consider how present-day tensions surrounding language and cultural identity are politicized before asking them to attend to the way *Henry V* interrogates language as an "instrument of power" is key to drawing out the play's rich, contemporary, cultural relevance. Turning to the stranger, both in our world and in *Henry V*, allows us to mine the play for moments that explicitly engage linguistic and cultural difference.

One such moment involves the influence of foreigners in the unifying enterprise of war. While the sentiment behind Henry's "band of brothers" (4.3.60) speech espouses kinship for all men fighting for England, all men are clearly not alike. The Scot Jamy, the Irish MacMorris, and the Welsh Fluellen all represent cultural otherness, and we can foster the importance of this when we encourage students to interrogate how the language and cultural identity of the stranger impacts the construction of Henry and of English identity.[5] When Henry historicizes the English victory by connecting it to Saint Crispin's Day, for example, Fluellen reminds him of Edward the Black Prince's victory in France and the role of the Welsh therein. He explains how this victory was and is commemorated:

> If your majesties is remembered of it, the Welshmen did good service in a garden where leeks did grow, wearing leeks in their Monmouth caps, which your majesty know to this hour is an honourable badge of the service. And I do believe your majesty takes no scorn to wear the leeks upon Saint Tavy's day.   (4.7.89–94)

This practice to commemorate the feast of Saint David (the patron saint of Wales) was observed not only by Henry in this play but also by Queen Elizabeth I (Craik 318). Fluellen infuses Henry's historicizing moment with an alternative and equally significant cultural tradition. Because the Welsh register an "otherness" for the English, this move is rather keen.[6]

The play goes on to connect Henry with Welsh tradition. Responding to the leek-wearing custom, Henry says, "I wear it for a memorable honour, / For I am Welsh, you know, good countryman" (4.7.95–96). Henry's Welsh connection is tenuous (Ivic 86–87), but Fluellen responds in kind: "All the water in the Wye cannot wash your majesty's Welsh plood out of your pody" (4.7.97–98). "There is no desire to assimilate with the English here," as I argue elsewhere, "but instead a clear desire on the part of Fluellen to honor Wales and the Welsh" ("Fluellen's Foreign Influence" 82). Fluellen goes on to say, "By Jeshu, I am your majesty's countryman. I care not who know it. . . . I need not to be ashamed of your majesty, praised be God, so long as your majesty is an honest man" (4.7.101–05). Not only is Henry's Englishness diluted, but Fluellen also establishes himself as the one worthy of accepting the English other as his Welsh countryman, so long as Henry is honest. However, Henry's honesty—his legitimacy and kindness— is fairly fluid.

To attend to this undermining of the dominant culture's identity in *Henry V* is to encourage our students to scrutinize structures that govern notions of national identity and legitimacy. The play deploys Fluellen's confidence in his cultural identity to speak to England's own emerging self-perception, and it questions that ethnocentrism. When, in an offstage moment, the knavish Englishman Pistol ridicules Fluellen in a public space, Fluellen demands to be treated with dignity. He force-feeds Pistol a leek, beats him, and says, "If you can mock a leek, you can eat a leek" (5.1.34). The bloody scene is so striking that Gower says to Fluellen: "Enough, captain, you have astonished him" (35). While the violence is sobering, Gower sides with the foreigner standing up for himself by saying to Pistol, after Fluellen departs:

> Will you mock at an ancient tradition, begun upon an honourable valour, and dare not avouch in your deeds any of your words? . . . You thought, because he could not speak English in the native garb, he could not therefore handle an English cudgel. You find it otherwise. And henceforth let a Welsh correction teach you a good English condition.   (62–70)

Gower calls for respect of the stranger's cultural traditions and personhood and also for dignified behavior on the part of the host society. This critical moment allows our students to see how language discrepancies—as Fluellen cannot speak English in the "native garb"—and cultural identity, issues vividly relevant to our society today, infuse a play that imagines an inclusive brotherhood while demonstrating how that inclusion is always just out of reach for the stranger. Despite Henry's hollow promise of kinship, the *other* kind in the play offers something edifying by demonstrating an impressive level of self-respect.

This attention to language, intercultural encounters, and the resistance of assimilation proves important throughout *Henry V*. When students explore ideas like this through reflection papers, small-group discussions, and performance projects, they inevitably begin to find other dramatic moments that engage these energies. While my focus here has been on Fluellen as a springboard to discussions about these issues, other meaningful characters and moments in the play allow students to interrogate how *Henry V* explores national identity, ethnicity, gender, citizenship, and social inequities. Once we establish the relevance of the stranger to the forming of nation, we can consider the defensive posturing of MacMorris (3.3.59–72), the incredulity of Williams (4.1), and—perhaps most important—Catherine's role in England's imagined future and the security of empire that the English accord with France affords.

As the play draws to a conclusion, the language barriers between Henry and Catherine offer insight into the intercultural implications behind England's growth. Henry understands French (5.2.244–46), yet he is determined to woo Catherine in English: "O fair Catherine, if you will love me soundly with your French heart, I will be glad to hear you confess it brokenly with your English tongue. Do you like me, Kate?" She responds, "*Pardonnez-moi*, I cannot tell vat is 'like me'" (104–07).[7] Catherine not only fails to understand what "like me" means but also suggests that she cannot tell what is *like* her—that is, what is akin to her. Certainly, it is not Henry who is akin to her, as he is the foe to her country and culture. But his intent is certainly to make her like him, both in love and in identity: "Shall not thou and I, between Saint Denis and Saint George, compound a boy, half-French half-English, that shall go to Constantinople and take the Turk by the beard?" (193–96). The shared identity he imagines is anchored both in Christianity (invoked through the patron saints of France and England) and in a common disdain for the further removed religious and cultural other—the Turk, who, in the English imagination, is certainly not kind or natural.

To approach *Henry V* with the stranger in mind—with the understanding that in the unfamiliar we find unique epistemological standpoints—is to open up this play, and Shakespeare's other histories, to ample possibilities. Even through lesser-taught histories, we stand to benefit by considering the stranger—the blackened women of *Henry VIII*, for example, or the illegitimacy and cross-cultural connections in *King John*.[8] Always, when there is a stranger, a valuable perspective is tendered. To capitalize on this is our imperative, because our own underrepresented students will undoubtedly be the ongoing makers of Shakespeare for generations to come. To witness the making of Shakespeare in this vein, then, is to adapt our "interpretive filters" and look at the stranger Shakespeare with new eyes.

NOTES

[1] In regard to 1.2.154, the folio version of *Henry V* reads, "th'ill neighbourhood," while the quarto reads, "the bruit hereof." *Norton Shakespeare* reads, "the bruit thereof," but I include the folio version here, as it explicitly addresses the uneasiness surrounding England's neighbors. For attention to this difference, see Craik's edition of the play (141). In regard to "foreigner," Lloyd E. Kermode writes that "the term 'foreigner' referred to persons from outside the city or region. . . . Continental aliens were usually 'foreigners' too, then, in so far as they rarely gained the freedom of the city and became 'citizens'" (2). I follow Kermode's lead here.

[2] I approach this essay from my experiences teaching at the University of Texas, El Paso (UTEP), a Hispanic Serving Institution situated on the United States–Mexico border with a nearly eighty percent Hispanic student population.

[3] For sustained attention to the value of looking to the stranger when considering the contemporary relevance of Shakespeare, see my essay "Stranger Shakespeare."

[4] In my experience, when students at UTEP resist Shakespeare's language, it is typically for the same reason most college students resist Shakespeare—the strange nature of blank verse and its thorny syntax. On the whole, however, my students have been quite willing to engage Shakespeare without hesitation and seem to welcome the strangeness of his language.

[5] See, for example, my chapter in *Shakespeare and Immigration*.

[6] Welsh otherness is, of course, paradoxical, as Wales was often perceived to be the origin of English identity, and indeed a feature of Tudor identity itself. For this issue, see Davies; Hopkins; and Maley.

[7] I am indebted to Marjorie Rubright's keen reading of this line during a discussion in the "Brothers and Others: New Directions" seminar at the 2014 Annual Meeting of the Shakespeare Association of America.

[8] For a sharp reading of alterity in *Henry VIII*, see Andrea.

Teaching Shakespeare's Histories Using the Internet

Hugh Macrae Richmond

Shakespeare's English histories are well served by the Internet. It facilitates student appreciation and understanding of these plays by creation of a vivid historical context. Experience of the historical references behind the plays' themes, plot, and characters can be evoked visually for students to whom the material may be remote and alien. The plays' histories can be re-created by searching the Internet for stills of portraits of figures such as Richard II and Richard III from the National Portrait Gallery (United Kingdom); for pictures of historical locales such as Leeds Castle, used in the BBC video of *Henry VIII*; for displays of stage scenery and costuming in performances in historical or modern guise in Laurence Olivier's *Henry V* and Orson Welles's *Julius Caesar*; and for stills and clips from such classic films and tapes of live productions. These last can mostly be found by searching *YouTube*, not forgetting the rich documentation for the recent PBS/BBC series *The Hollow Crown*. Such excerpts serve as textual illustrations, following teaching procedures presented in such Web sites as *Shakespeare's Staging*.

As for scripts, texts of Shakespeare's collected works on the Internet are of varying value, from the British Museum authoritative collection *Shakespeare in Quartos* and the *Gutenberg Folio* to modern versions such as the MIT Shakespeare collection and those of *Open Source Shakespeare*. The problem with many modernized collections on the Web is that they date from the nineteenth century, because copyright laws deny use of current editions. Web collections are often deficient of the insights of modern scholarship. However, *Google Books* has dared to digitize partial versions (previews) of many excellent modern single play editions in such series as the Oxford, Cambridge, and Arden. These editions are also available on the Internet at minimal prices, from even $1 up, through *Amazon, Abe Books*, and other publishers.

Through searches for the plays and related historical people, places, and events, the Web also affords invaluable information about the plays' backgrounds and theatrical histories, such as Web reprints of published interpretations of the historical figures on which the plays are based, as in Paul Kendall's *Richard III*. Other data on how these contextual approaches were adapted comes from sources to the plays' dramatic counterparts, as seen in Geoffrey Bullough's *Narrative and Dramatic Sources of Shakespeare*; in bibliographies about how these plays were staged in Shakespeare's times and performed for later centuries, from sites such as *Shakespeare's Staging*; and by access to the scholarly and critical commentary excerpted in many entries of *Google Books*. Most of this material is available through *Google Books*, or on *Wikipedia, YouTube*, or *Flickr*. There are more specific sources provided by institutions such as the Folger Shakespeare Library, the Furness Shakespeare Collection, and the Victoria and Albert Theatre Collection.

For detail about Shakespeare's historical precedents, the much-censured *Wikipedia* provides a preliminary source and illustrations in entries that are made increasingly precise and reliable by providing professional authorities in their footnotes and bibliographies—but should not be left unvalidated by further research. *Wikipedia*'s visual materials are extended in its associated Yorck Project, which offers relevant illustrations with the advantage that this collection (unlike *Google Images*) certifies that its contents are legally out of copyright, at least by United States law about the public domain (operative in material antedating 1923). This free access is being accepted by United States collections, particularly libraries of academic institutions. Among these groups another helpful visual collection is that of San Jose State University's *WorldImages* photographic collection, which explores historical artifacts, many relating to Shakespearean figures, including classical ones in plays like *Julius Caesar* and *Troilus and Cressida*. The best source about English historical personalities is provided by the British National Portrait Gallery Web site, but its disadvantage is that copyright claims are enforced, as by other major art galleries like the Tate and commercial groups such as Getty Images and Bridgeman Art Library. *Flickr* also copyrights its images. However, this may not preclude momentary class use and use in student papers.

For performance history there are numerous collections, including the Cleveland Press collection at Cleveland State University, the University of Illinois collection of historical actors, the Furness Shakespeare collection, the Victoria and Albert Museum Theatre Collection, and the Shakespeare Centre's Royal Shakespeare Company (RSC) archives. Modern collections of still images and reviews are available from the University of Victoria (Canada), mostly

from modern, local productions, including background material about companies. Post-1960 British productions are covered by images and data in the Arts
and Humanities Data Service Performance collection. For videos of recorded
live performances, *YouTube* has clips from modern Shakespeare productions,
of variable quality; fragments of classic film and stage productions; and many
amateur ones, distilled by groups such as *Bardweb*. Material from *YouTube* is
not stable as copyright challenges often suspend access to excerpts from classic
films and videoed stagings.

For printed scholarship and criticism, the much-debated *Google Books* reprints provide access to partial selections from many significant books and fragments of others, but coverage is unpredictable. Intense searches, through local
library access to scholarly collections such as *JSTOR*, may provide full access
to some sources. College libraries may provide free Internet access to texts for
registered readers, as a result of contracts with groups purveying scholarly and
reference material such as Questia Media and Credo Reference.

The simplest procedure in using these Internet resources is to google the
title and names of the principal characters because, under the heading "Images"
in any such *Google* search, there is usually a sequence of images of the chosen
subject, including historical data: portraits such as the effigies of Richard II,
Henry IV, and Henry V's wife, Catherine, from Westminster Abbey; pictures of
major occasions featured in the plays, such as the coronation of Anne Boleyn re-
created in *Henry VIII*; and performance images of such settings. A similar series
of images can be called up from the Furness Shakespeare Library, the Victoria
and Albert Museum's Theatre collections, *Flickr*, the University of Illinois Actors collection, and the Yorck Project's picture gallery, to name a few. Though
search mechanisms of collections are available, such materials may remain un-
sorted and difficult for students to locate and control, so the best pedagogical approach may be for an instructor to list sources but preselect examples of relevant
images for a *PowerPoint* presentation. Then it will be easier for students to pick
their own selections for personal projects. In following up on the historical figures in *Wikipedia* entries, students will find that the better entries carry images
and notes about authoritative starting points for historical data and sources.

Having established what is generally available, we can trace these materials'
use through applications to specific plays, showing how the Internet elucidates
even neglected plays like *Henry VI, King John*, and *Henry VIII*, as well as *Richard III, Henry IV Part 1*, and *Henry V*.

Henry VI *through* Richard III

Texts and commentaries for *Henry VI* can be accessed completely (or excerpted)
by searching "Shakespeare" and a play title in *Google Books*. The most service-
able introductions to single play editions are from the Oxford, Cambridge, and
Arden series, which contain stage histories and bibliographies. There are two

memorable productions of *Henry VI* available in discontinuous fragments on *YouTube*, starting with the BBC recording of the famous fourth centennial production of the two tetralogies in historical sequence by the RSC, under the direction of Peter Hall and John Barton (1963–64). This version has the virtue and defect of revising the script drastically to enhance its coherence and speed. The fragments scattered through *YouTube* have to be reassembled, and it may be advisable simply to select key clips after their review. The same awkwardness of presentation on *YouTube* complicates use of the BBC's own production of *Henry VI* in its Shakespeare series, produced with Time/Warner: a more modest, open-stage production, designed for television. Currently the three parts are available on *YouTube*.

A bibliography relevant to such productions appears in the single play bibliography at *Shakespeare's Staging*, which also includes short extracts from *Henry VI* in its video gallery and still images from productions over the centuries in its performance galleries. The best use of this material is to focus on key scenes and characters, such as Joan la Pucelle (Joan of Arc), her enemy the English General Talbot, and Queen Margaret—brilliantly portrayed by Peggy Ashcroft in the RSC production.

Many of the Internet sources related to *Henry VI* also apply to its sequel, *Richard III*, which includes most of the earlier plays' characters and plot lines. However, the controversial character of Richard III, both historically and in art, gives him unique richness for source material. There are such sites as that of the Richard III Society and the memorable video documentary currently available on *YouTube* of the recently recovered skeleton of Richard in Leicester: *Richard III: The King in the Car Park*. There are also versions of the play on *YouTube*, of which Olivier's and Ian McKellen's are the most striking. The two versions of the opening scene are memorable in contrasting ways (as noted in the video gallery at *Shakespeare's Staging*) and provide themes for discussion of historical staging and modern dress production. One of the earliest films of *Richard III* is excerpted on *Shakespeare's Staging*.

Richard II, 1 *and* 2 Henry IV, *and* Henry V

In the second tetralogy, *Richard II* is the least covered play, but it too appears in the above-cited sources. Mark Rylance's comic rendering of Richard's last soliloquy at the restored Shakespeare's Globe Theatre at Bankside, London, is on *YouTube*—and equally effective is the audio of Richard Burton speaking Richard's rueful remarks in act 3, scene 2. King Richard's distinction as a proto-Hamlet is a fascinating topic illustrated by such Shakespeare clips.

All these dramatized historical figures have representation in such sources as the British National Portrait Gallery. This material can be located by *Google* search under the rulers' names, which not only provides a range of historical backgrounds in such systems as *Wikipedia*, but the *Google* heading "Images" offers collections of portraits and related historical material. While these sources reveal the characters of Henry VI and Richard III, Richard II is more vividly illustrated, since he and his court were notable for their artistic brilliance seen in visual materials such as the *Wilton Diptych* from the National Gallery in London. These images invite discussion of the oft-neglected talents and limitations of King Richard II in history and as he reappears in Shakespeare. Currently David Giles's direction of Derek Jacobi's memorable performance is available on *YouTube* as *"Richard II"* (1970), with John Gielgud as John of Gaunt, Jon Finch as Bolingbroke, and Wendy Hiller as Duchess of York.

Though there are *Google* images for King Henry in *Henry IV*, they are dull compared with the dominant figure in these two plays: Falstaff. While Falstaff derives indirectly from historical figures, the *Google* image bank devoted to him is rich in the number of productions he dominates. By far the best film clips featuring him on *YouTube* come from Orson Welles's *Chimes at Midnight*, in which he plays Falstaff—but there are other clips of varying quality dominated by Verdi's opera based on the lesser Falstaff in *Merry Wives of Windsor*. The place of Falstaff in the tradition of the braggart soldier is traced by a video in *Shakespeare's Staging*. This diversity of presentations provokes discussion and interpretation.

With *Henry V* the greatest Internet teaching resource is the juxtaposition of contrasting clips from Olivier's picturesque if bellicose film and Branagh's gloomier, pacifist one. The relevant *Google Images* collection includes historical data about Henry but even more memorable stills of the production history of this play, including both these films.

King John

This unpopular play frustrates modern expectations of John's involvement with the Magna Carta and Robin Hood—neither appears in the script. Among reprinted articles on King John on the Web, this issue is summarized in "Shakespeare's *King John*: Drama versus History" by J. M. Pressley. The *Wikipedia* article on the play is also compact but well documented, inviting further research ("John"). *Google* images of *King John* are useful, showing how the script fostered elaborate Victorian staging, also visible in stills in the Victorian Gallery of *Shakespeare's Staging* and in a clip of the first film of Shakespeare ending that site's video gallery. A *Google* search includes reviews of individual productions, including one of a bizarre RSC staging: "A Production of Many Colours: RSC's Glistering *King John*" (Martirosyan), and *YouTube* covers performance extracts in an "Interview with the Cast of King John / Royal Shakespeare Company."

Henry VIII

Despite a reputation undercut by a supposed divided authorship between Shakespeare and his successor, John Fletcher, as King's Men's scriptwriter, this play has a sustained history as one of the most brilliantly staged of all Shakespeare's plays, reflected in *Google* images of it. The BBC Television film, with Claire Bloom as Queen Katherine of Aragon, was held the best in the Time series by the Shakespeare Association of America. There are also recordings of the successful Shakespeare's Globe Theatre production. The numerous Internet references to the historical Henry VIII mislead about the play, which concerns the earlier, less controversial parts of Henry's reign. Though the play selectively covers the reign and is centered on the falls of Queen Katherine of Aragon and Cardinal Wolsey, it has usually been produced as its stage directions specify, with full historical detail, so historical images are relevant (the BBC version was shot in Leeds Castle, residence of queens such as Katherine). Most productions base their period costumes on Holbein court paintings and sketches, available in a *Google Images* search for "Henry VIII." Sets usually reflect precedents such as Leeds Castle and Hampton Court, pictures of which can be called up on the Internet. The *Google* images of both the historical Katherine of Aragon and Anne Boleyn are memorable and thought-provoking, as are shots of actresses in the roles.

A final word of caution requires a reminder that the Internet is unstable: clips on *YouTube* may be withdrawn by copyright owners—but duplicates and alternatives often exist under slightly different titles. Web sites may also not be sustained or updated by withdrawal of sponsors or creators. Seemingly apt search terms may not elicit the best examples: try variants. Nevertheless, the Internet offers a wealth of material, even if it requires sifting and preparation by instructors to achieve the impact denied earlier generations without electronic access.

APPENDIX: RESOURCES

Collected Works

Folger Shakespeare Library, www.folger.edu/
Internet Shakespeare Editions, internetshakespeare.uvic.ca
MIT Shakespeare Collection, shakespeare.mit.edu/
Open Source Shakespeare, www.opensourceshakespeare.org
Shakespeare in Quarto, www.bl.uk/treasures/shakespeare/homepage.html
Shakespeare Resource Center, www.bardweb.net
Shakespeare's First Folio, Project Gutenberg, www.gutenberg.org/ebooks/2270

Image and Picture Collections

Arts and Humanities Data Service, www.ahds.ac.uk
Cleveland Press Shakespeare Photographs, engagedscholarship.csuohio.edu/shakespeare
Furness Theatrical Image Collection, sceti.library.upenn.edu/sceti/furness/
National Portrait Gallery, www.npg.org.uk/collections.php

"Portraits of Actors, 1720–1920," U of Illinois, Urbana-Champaign, images.library.uiuc
.edu/projects/actors

Shakespeare's Staging, shakespearestaging.berkeley.edu

Tate Britain, www.tate.org.uk/visit/tate-britain

WorldImages, worldimages.sjsu.edu

Yorck Project, commons.wikimedia.org/wiki/Category:PD-Art_%28Yorck_Project%29

Performances and Video Clips

"Beerbohm Tree," *Shakespeare's Staging*, shakespearestaging.berkeley.edu

Henry VI, Part 3, BBC, www.youtube.com/watch?v=m9PaVDqZrHs

Henry VIII, Globe Theatre, www.youtube.com/watch?v=9kp9craIvoQ

The Hollow Crown, www-tc.pbs.org/wnet/gperf/files/2013/09/HollowCrown

"Interview with the Cast of King John," www.youtube.com/watch?v=Xuno6W0U1PQ

"Now Is the Winter of Our Discontent," Ian McKellen as Richard III, www.youtube
.com/watch?v=pjJEXkbeL-o

"Now Is the Winter of Our Discontent," Laurence Olivier as Richard III, www.youtube
.com/watch?v=px5hvNWoVLE

"Richard III: The Skeleton in the Car Park," www.youtube.com/watch?v=Uqyw
U9RQfl0

RSC Archives, www.rsc.org.uk/about-us/collections-and-archives

Shakespeare's Staging, shakespearestaging.berkeley.edu

"Theater and Performance," *Victoria and Albert Museum*, www.vam.ac.uk/page/t/
theatre-and-performance

The Wars of the Roses, RSC, www.youtube.com/watch?v=aXKKCDricTQ

NOTES ON CONTRIBUTORS

Ronda Arab, associate professor of English at Simon Fraser University, is the author of *Manly Mechanicals on the Early Modern English Stage* (2011), an examination of the gender status of working men in Shakespeare and his contemporaries. She is editor, with Michelle Dowd and Adam Zucker, of *Historical Affects and the Early Modern Theater* (2015).

M. G. Aune is professor of English at California University of Pennsylvania. His chapters, articles, and reviews have appeared in *Approaches to Teaching Shakespeare's The Taming of the Shrew, Shakespeare, Shakespeare Bulletin,* and *Early Modern Literary Studies*. His current project is a study of the performance of Shakespeare's plays at tourist destinations such as summer festivals.

Rebecca Ann Bach, professor of English at the University of Alabama, Birmingham, is the author of *Colonial Transformations: The Cultural Production of the New Atlantic World, 1580–1640* (2001) and *Shakespeare and Renaissance Literature before Heterosexuality* (2007). She is editor with Gwynne Kennedy of *Feminisms and Early Modern Texts: Essays for Phyllis Rackin* (2010). She has published many essays in journals and edited collections, including an essay in *Approaches to Teaching English Renaissance Drama*. Her new book, *Birds and Other Creatures in Renaissance Literature: Shakespeare, Descartes, and Animal Studies*, is forthcoming from Routledge.

Lisa Siefker Bailey is a senior lecturer at Indiana University–Purdue University, Columbus, where she also serves as director of the Literature in England Study Abroad Program. Her recent publications appeared in *Approaches to Teaching the Works of Anton Chekhov, Christianity and Literature, Civil Strife in a Complex and Changing World: Perspectives Far and Near,* and *Edward Albee: A Casebook.*

David J. Baker is Peter G. Phialas Professor in the Department of English and Comparative Literature at the University of North Carolina, Chapel Hill. He is the author of *On Demand: Writing for the Market in Early Modern England* (2010) and *Between Nations: Shakespeare, Spenser, Marvell and the Question of Britain* (1997). With Willy Maley, he is the editor of *British Identities and English Renaissance Literature* (2002).

Lynne Bruckner is professor of English at Chatham University, where she has been teaching ecocritical courses since 1996. Editor with Dan Brayton of *Ecocritical Shakespeare* (2011), Bruckner recently contributed chapters to *Ecofeminist Approaches to Early Modernity* (2011) and *Shakespeare and the Urgency of Now* (2013). She also is editor with Jen Munroe and Ed Geisweidt of *Ecological Approaches to Early Modern English Texts: A Field Guide to Reading and Teaching* (2015).

Joshua Calhoun is assistant professor of English at the University of Wisconsin, Madison. He is editor (with Lois Potter) of the collection *Images of Robin Hood: Medieval to Modern* (2008) and has published articles in such venues as *Shakespeare Studies, PMLA,* and *South Atlantic Review*. His current projects include a monograph titled "The Nature of the Page in Renaissance England: Ecology, Poetry, and Papermaking."

Paula Marantz Cohen is distinguished professor of English and dean of the Pennoni Honors College at Drexel University. She is the author of five nonfiction books and five best-selling novels. She has written for such publications as the *Times Literary Supplement*, *The Chronicle of Higher Education*, *The Yale Review*, *The Southwest Review*, and *The American Scholar* and is an editor of *JML: Journal of Modern Literature*. She also hosts the nationally distributed television talk show, *The Drexel InterView*.

Christy Desmet is Josiah Meigs Distinguished Teaching Professor at the University of Georgia. She is the author of *Reading Shakespeare's Characters: Rhetoric, Ethics, and Identity* (1992) and editor of *Shakespeare and Appropriation* (with Robert Sawyer, 1999), *Harold Bloom's Shakespeare* (with Robert Sawyer, 2001), *Shakespearean Gothic* (with Anne Williams, 2009), and *Helen Faucit* (2011). She is currently working on "Shakespeare 2.0."

Laurie Ellinghausen is associate professor of English at University of Missouri, Kansas City, and the author of *Labor and Writing in Early Modern England, 1567–1667* (2008). Her articles have appeared in such venues as *Approaches to Teaching Shakespeare's The Taming of the Shrew*; *Studies in English Literature, 1500–1900*; *Exemplaria*; and *Explorations in Renaissance Culture*. Her current project is a study of renegades in early modern English drama and popular print.

Ruben Espinosa, associate professor of English at the University of Texas, El Paso, is the author of *Masculinity and Marian Efficacy in Shakespeare's England* (2011) and editor (with David Ruiter) of *Shakespeare and Immigration* (2014). He has published essays in *Shakespeare Quarterly*, *Explorations in Renaissance Culture*, and *Literature Compass*. His current book project explores the intersections between Shakespeare and Mexican American culture.

Jonathan Hart—poet, historian, and literary scholar—is a core faculty member in comparative literature at Western University. He has held visiting appointments at Harvard, Cambridge, Princeton, the Sorbonne-Nouvelle, and elsewhere. He has published a number of books including, most recently, *Poetics of Otherness: War, Trauma, and Literature* (2015), *From Shakespeare to Obama: Language, Slavery, and Place* (2013), *Textual Imitation: Making and Seeing in Literature* (2013), *Fictional and Historical Worlds* (2013), and *Literature, Theory, History* (2011). Recently he became chair professor in the School of Foreign Languages at Shanghai Jiao Tong University.

Peter C. Herman is professor of English at San Diego State University. His most recent publications include a contextual edition of Thomas Deloney's *Jack of Newbury*, *A Short History of Early Modern England*, *Royal Poetrie: Monarchic Verse and the Political Imaginary of Early Modern England* (*Choice* Outstanding Academic Title, 2010), and, with Elizabeth Sauer, *The New Milton Criticism*. He has also edited Approaches volumes on *Paradise Lost* (second edition) and on Milton's shorter poetry and prose. He is currently working on the literature of terrorism, and has published essays on that topic in the *Journal for Cultural Research*, *Modern Philology*, and *Critical Terrorism Studies*.

Diane K. Jakacki is digital scholarship coordinator and an associated teaching faculty member in the Comparative Humanities Program at Bucknell University. Her research interests include early modern drama, literature and popular culture, and digital humanities and pedagogy. Her current research focuses on sixteenth-century English touring theater troupes. Publications include a digital edition of *King Henry VIII*, essays on *A Game at Chess* and *The Spanish Tragedy*, and research projects associated with the Records of Early English Drama and the Map of Early Modern London.

Yu Jin Ko is professor of English at Wellesley College. He is the author of *Mutability and Division on Shakespeare's Stage* (2004) and editor of *Shakespeare's Sense of Character: On the Page and from the Stage* (2012). His current projects include a book provisionally titled "From the Wooden O to the Cineplex: Shakespeare's Original Stage Conditions and Their Afterlives."

Joyce Green MacDonald is associate professor of English at the University of Kentucky. She is the author of *Women and Race in Early Modern Texts* (2002) and of several essays on race and performance in Renaissance drama. She is at work on two book manuscripts: "New World Shakespeares: Race, Nature, and Cultural Value" and "Black Women in the Early Modern Transatlantic: Memory, Miscegenation, Embodiment."

Patricia Marchesi is a faculty member in the English Department at LaGrange College. Previously she taught at Northern Arizona University, where in 2013 she was one of the nominees for a Liberal Studies Faculty Excellence Award. Her latest publications include the chapter " 'Limbs Mangled and Torn Asunder': Magic, Dismemberment, and the Blazon in Christopher Marlowe's *Doctor Faustus*" in *Staging the Blazon in Early Modern Drama* (2013).

Maya Mathur is associate professor of English at the University of Mary Washington. Her work has appeared in the *Journal for Early Modern Cultural Studies*, *Early Theatre*, and *Early Modern Literary Studies*. She is working on a book on comedy and popular politics in early modern England.

Caroline McManus is professor of English at California State University, Los Angeles, where she teaches courses in early modern English literature, pedagogy, and children's literature. Her publications include *Spenser's* Faerie Queene *and the Reading of Women* (2002) and several articles on Elizabethan and Jacobean literature and culture. She is currently writing a book on the reading and rereading of children's texts.

Mary Janell Metzger is professor of English at Western Washington University. She is the author of *Shakespeare without Fear: Teaching for Understanding* (2004) and several recently published articles on Shakespeare and pedagogy. Her current projects include a book of essays on Shakespeare and epistemological justice.

Howard Nenner, Roe/Straut Emeritus Professor in the Humanities and Emeritus Professor of History at Smith College, has published extensively in the field of seventeenth-century English constitutional history. His study, *The Right to Be King: The Succession to the Crown of England* (1995), was one of the cornerstones of Authority and Legitimacy in the Age of More and Shakespeare, the course he taught jointly with Bill Oram.

Glenn Odom is senior lecturer at the University of Roehampton. His recent articles appear in such venues as *Comparative Drama*, *Comparative Literature*, *Journal of Dramatic Theory and Criticism*, and *Studies in English Literature*. His *World Theories of Theatre* is forthcoming from Routledge in 2017.

William A. Oram is the Helen Means Professor at Smith College. He is the coordinating editor of the *Yale Edition of the Shorter Poems of Edmund Spenser* (1989) and the author of *Edmund Spenser* (1997) and of articles on Spenser, Milton, Shakespeare, and other (mostly Renaissance) writers.

Neema Parvini, lecturer in English at the University of Surrey, is the author of *Shakespeare and Contemporary Theory: New Historicism and Cultural Materialism* (2012), *Shakespeare's History Plays: Rethinking Historicism* (2012), *Shakespeare and Cognition: Thinking Fast and Slow through Character* (2015), and *Shakespeare and New Historicist Theory* (2017). He is currently working on a book called *Shakespeare's Moral Compass: Ethical Decision-Making in His Plays*.

Vimala C. Pasupathi is associate professor of English at Hofstra University. Her work on military affairs in early modern literature appears in *Shakespeare, Modern Philology, Early Theatre, Philological Quarterly, Yearbook of English Studies, ROMARD,* and *ELH,* as well as in a variety of essay collections. She has also written on Shakespeare and digital pedagogy for *The Journal of Interactive Technology and Pedagogy.* She is currently finishing a book on the militia in English history and drama.

Phyllis Rackin, professor of English emerita at the University of Pennsylvania, has published on Shakespeare and related subjects in such journals as *PMLA, Shakespeare Quarterly,* and *Shakespeare Jahrbuch.* She also has published *Shakespeare's Tragedies; Stages of History: Shakespeare's English Chronicles; Engendering a Nation: A Feminist Account of Shakespeare's English Histories,* written in collaboration with Jean E. Howard; *Shakespeare and Women;* and an anthology of essays on *The Merry Wives of Windsor,* edited with Evelyn Gajowski.

Hugh Macrae Richmond is professor of English emeritus, University of California, Berkeley, with degrees from Cambridge (BA) and Oxford (DPhil.) and diplomas from Florence and Munich. His books cover European love and landscape poetry; John Milton; performance histories of *Richard III* and *Henry VIII*; works titled *Shakespeare's Political Plays, Shakespeare's Sexual Comedy, Shakespeare's Tragedies Reviewed;* and editions of *1 Henry IV* and *Henry VIII.* He has created two Web sites: *Shakespeare's Staging* and *Milton Revealed.*

Barbara Sebek is professor of English at Colorado State University. She is editor (with Stephen Deng) of *Global Traffic: Discourses and Practices of Trade in English Literature and Culture from 1550 to 1700* (2008). Her articles on early modern literature and the global have appeared in such venues as *Shakespeare Studies, Journal X,* and numerous edited collections.

Kathleen Kalpin Smith is associate professor of English at the University of South Carolina, Aiken. She is the editor of the New Kittredge Shakespeare's *All's Well That Ends Well* (2012) and the author of articles appearing in *Literature Compass, Studies in English Literature,* and *Women's Studies.* She is currently working on a book titled "Gender, Speech, and Audience Reception in Early Modern England."

Matthew J. Smith is assistant professor of English at Azusa Pacific University. He is associate editor of *Christianity and Literature.* His recent publications appear in *English Literary Renaissance, Studies in English Literature, Medieval and Renaissance Drama in England,* and *The Return of Theory in Early Modern English Studies, Volume 2.*

Catherine E. Thomas is professor of English and associate dean for the School of Transitional Studies at Georgia Gwinnett College. She is editor (with Jennifer Feather) of the collection *Violent Masculinities: Male Aggression in Early Modern Texts and Culture* (2013), and her essays have appeared in journals such as *Studies in English Literature*, *The Journal of Popular Culture*, and *Upstart Crow*. Her current projects study Shakespeare and the early comic arts.

SURVEY PARTICIPANTS

Mara Amster, *Randolph College*
Sallie Anglin, *University of Mississippi*
Jean Arnold, *California State University, San Bernadino*
Dana E. Aspinall, *Alma College*
M. G. Aune, *California University of Pennsylvania*
Taye Ayowemi, *Redeemer's University, Ogun State, Nigeria*
Lisa Siefker Bailey, *University of Indiana–Purdue University, Columbus*
Ann Basso, *University of South Florida*
Bradley Bleck, *Spokane Falls Community College*
Todd Borlick, *Bloomsburg University*
Bruce Brandt, *South Dakota State University*
Katherine Steele Brokaw, *University of California, Merced*
Lynne Bruckner, *Chatham University*
Regina Buccola, *Roosevelt University*
Claire Busse, *LaSalle University*
Todd Butler, *Washington State University, Pullman*
Al Cacicedo, *Albright College*
Victor L. Cahn, *Skidmore College*
Thomas Canfield, *University of Missouri, Kansas City*
Brooke A. Carlson, *Hankuk University of Foreign Studies, Seoul, Korea*
Lisa Celovsky, *Suffolk University*
Stephanie Chamberlain, *Southeast Missouri State University*
Cindy Chopoidalo, *University of Alberta*
Tan Meng Chwen, *Sunway College, Malaysia*
Paula Marantz Cohen, *Drexel University*
Michael J. Collins, *Georgetown University*
Chuck Conaway, *University of Southern Indiana*
Jennifer Crowder, *Providence Reformed Collegiate*
Robert Darcy, *University of Nebraska, Omaha*
Marie-Hélène Davies, *Paris-X Nanterre*
Christy Desmet, *University of Georgia*
Mario A. DiCesare, *Binghamton University, State University of New York*
Cary DiPietro, *University of Toronto, Mississauga*
Lars Engel, *University of Tulsa*
William E. Engel, *University of the South*
Marcia Eppich-Harris, *Marian University*
Catherine R. Eskin, *Florida Southern College*
Ruben Espinosa, *University of Texas, El Paso*
Joe Falocco, *Texas State University*
Valerie M. Fazel, *Arizona State University*
Kavita Mudan Finn, *Nashua, New Hampshire*
Gregory Foran, *Nazareth College of Rochester*
Barry Gaines, *University of New Mexico*

William Germano, *Cooper Union*
Jonathan Goossen, *Ambrose University College*
Suzanne Gossett, *Loyola University Chicago*
Douglas E. Green, *Augsburg College*
Marissa Greenberg, *University of New Mexico*
Eric Griffin, *Millsaps College*
Jonathan Hart, *Western University*
Robert W. Haynes, *Texas A&M International University*
Mark Heberle, *University of Hawai'i, Manoa*
Pax Hehmeyer, *University of California, Santa Barbara*
Fran Helphinstine, *Morehead State University*
Roze Hentschell, *Colorado State University*
Peter C. Herman, *San Diego State University*
James Hirsh, *Georgia State University*
Robin Hizme, *Queen's College, City University of New York*
Jean Howard, *Columbia University*
Sujata Iyengar, *University of Georgia*
Lee Jacobus, *University of Connecticut*
Diane Jakacki, *Bucknell University*
Neil B. Johnston, *Louisiana College*
Susan Jones, *Palm Beach Atlantic University*
Sarah Kelen, *Nebraska Wesleyan University*
Deborah J. Knuth Klenck, *Colgate University*
Chikako D. Kumamoto, *College of DuPage*
Ian Lancashire, *University of Toronto*
Jasmine Lellock, *University of Maryland*
Linda Linzey, *Southeastern University*
Sandra Logan, *Michigan State University*
Robert Lynch, *New Jersey Institute of Technology*
Ellen MacKay, *Indiana University, Bloomington*
Gabrielle Malcolm, *Canterbury Christ Church University*
Patrick Maley, *Centenary College*
Patricia Marchesi, *LaGrange College*
James Mardock, *University of Nevada*
Maya Mathur, *University of Mary Washington*
Andrew Mattison, *University of Toledo*
Margaret Maurer, *Colgate University*
Caroline McManus, *California State University, Los Angeles*
Toni McNaron, *University of Minnesota*
Mary Janell Metzger, *Western Washington University*
Miklos Mezosi, *University of West Hungary*
Kathryn Moncrief, *Washington College*
Samantha Morgan-Curtis, *Tennessee State University*
Jessica C. Murphy, *University of Texas, Dallas*
M. Stephanie Murray, *Carnegie Mellon University*
Vin Nardizzi, *University of British Columbia*
Karen Newman, *Brown University*
Glenn Odom, *Rowan University*

Niamh O'Leary, *Xavier University*
Rebecca Olson, *Oregon State University*
William A. Oram, *Smith College*
Vimala C. Pasupathi, *Hofstra University*
Anthony Guy Patricia, *University of Nevada, Las Vegas*
Lesley Peterson, *University of North Alabama*
Douglas Pfeiffer, *Stony Brook University*
Joseph A. Porter, *Duke University*
Matthew Powers, *Herkimer County Community College*
Kevin Quarmby, *Oxford College of Emory University*
Phyllis R. Rackin, *University of Pennsylvania*
Ruth Rassool, *College of the Canyons*
Mala Renganathan, *North-Eastern Hill University, India*
Hugh Macrae Richmond, *University of California, Berkeley*
Peter Rudnytsky, *University of Florida*
Jeff Rufo, *Trinity University*
David Ruiter, *University of Texas, El Paso*
Sharon Schuman, *University of Oregon*
Carolyn F. Scott, *National Cheng Kung University, Taiwan*
Nancy Simpson-Younger, *University of Wisconsin, Madison*
Sarah Stafford Sims, *Campbellsville University*
Kathleen Kalpin Smith, *University of South Carolina, Aiken*
Matthew J. Smith, *Azusa Pacific University*
William Henry Spates, *Qatar University*
Goran Stanivukovic, *Saint Mary's University*
Robert Stark, *University of Exeter*
Emily Stockard, *Florida Atlantic University*
Virginia Strain, *Loyola University Chicago*
Richard Strier, *University of Chicago*
Joseph R. Teller, *College of the Sequoias*
Catherine E. Thomas, *Georgia Gwinnett College*
Janet Thormann, *College of Marin*
Bente Videbaek, *Stony Brook University*
Allyna E. Ward, *Booth University College*
Deborah Willis, *University of California, Riverside*
Sarah Wright, *Skidmore College*
Laura Lehua Yim, *San Francisco State University*
Karen Youngberg, *Augustana College*
Cybele Zufolo, *Borough of Manhattan Community College, City University of New York*

WORKS CITED

Abbott, E. A. "A Shakespearean Grammar." 1987. *Perseus Digital Library*, www
.perseus.tufts.edu/hopper/text?doc=Perseus%3Atext%3A1999.03.0080.

———. *A Shakespearean Grammar: An Attempt to Illustrate Some of the Differences
between Elizabethan and Modern English*. Dover Publications, 2003.

Alexander, Gavin, editor. *Sidney's* The Defence of Poesy *and Selected Renaissance
Literary Criticism*. Penguin Books, 2004.

Allmand, Christopher. *Henry V*. Yale UP, 2011. Yale English Monarchs.

Anderson, Benedict. *Imagined Communities: Reflections on the Origin and Spread of
Nationalism*. Rev. ed., Verso, 2006.

Anderson, Lorin W., and David R. Krathwohl, editors. *A Taxonomy for Learning,
Teaching, and Assessing: A Revision of Bloom's Taxonomy of Educational Objectives*. Allyn and Bacon, 2000.

Andrea, Bernadette. "'A Noble Troop of Strangers': Masques of Blackness in Shakespeare's *Henry VIII*." Espinosa and Ruiter, pp. 91–112.

Arab, Ronda. *Manly Mechanicals on the Early Modern English Stage*. Susquehanna
UP, 2011.

Archer, Harriet. "Holinshed and the Middle Ages." Kewes et al., *Oxford Handbook*,
pp. 171–86.

Aristotle. *The Art of Rhetoric: With an English Translation by John Henry Freese*.
William Heinemann, 1947.

———. *Poetics*. Translated by James Hutton, W. W. Norton, 1982.

Atkins, J. W. H. *English Literary Criticism: The Renascence*. 2nd ed., Methuen Publishing, 1951.

Augustine. *The Confessions*. Translated by Maria Boulding, edited by John E. Rotelle,
New City Press, 1997.

Bach, Rebecca Ann. "Manliness before Individualism: Masculinity, Effeminacy, and
Homoerotics in Shakespeare's History Plays." Dutton and Howard, pp. 220–45.

———. *Shakespeare and Renaissance Literature before Heterosexuality*. Palgrave,
2007.

Baker, David J., and Willy Maley, editors. *British Identities and English Renaissance
Literature*. Cambridge UP, 2002.

Baldo, Jonathan. *Memory in Shakespeare's Histories: Stages of Forgetting in Early
Modern England*. Routledge, 2012.

Baldwin, T. W. *William Shakespere's Petty School*. U of Illinois P, 1943.

———. *William Shakespere's Small Latin and Lesse Greeke*. 2 vols., U of Illinois P,
1944.

Baldwin, William. *A Myrroure for Magistrates*. London, 1559. *Early English Books
Online*, gateway.proquest.com/openurl?ctx_ver=Z39.88–2003&res_id=xri:eebo
&rft_id=xri:eebo:image:4738.

Bale, John. *King Johan*. Edited by Barry B. Adams, Huntington Library, 1969.

"The Ballad upon King Henry 5th's Victory over the French at the Battle of Agincourt." *English Broadside Ballad Archive*, U of California, Santa Barbara, ebba .english.ucsb.edu/ballad/31627/citation.

Barber, C. L. "Rule and Misrule in *Henry IV*." *Shakespeare's Festive Comedy: A Study of Dramatic Form and Its Relation to Social Custom.* Princeton UP, 1959, pp. 192–221.

Barker, Roberta. "Tragical-Comical-Historical Hotspur." *Shakespeare Quarterly*, vol. 54, no. 3, Fall 2003, pp. 288–307.

Barker, Simon. *War and Nation in the Theatre of Shakespeare and His Contemporaries.* Edinburgh UP, 2007.

Barnaby, Andrew. "Imitation as Originality in Gus Van Sant's *My Own Private Idaho.*" *Almost Shakespeare: Reinventing His Works for Cinema and Television*, edited by James R. Keller and Leslie Stratyner, McFarland, 2004, pp. 22–41.

Barnet, Sylvan, editor. *Histories*. Alfred A. Knopf, 1994.

Bartolovich, Crystal. "'Travailing' Theory: Global Flows of Labor and the Enclosure of the Subject." Singh, pp. 50–66.

Barton, John. *Playing Shakespeare.* Methuen Publishing, 1984.

Bateson, Gregory. *Steps to an Ecology of Mind.* Ballantine Books, 1972.

Bede. *Ecclesiastical History of the English People.* Edited by D. H. Farmer and Robert Latham, translated by Leo Sherley-Price, Penguin Books, 1991.

Beier, A. L. *Masterless Men: The Vagrancy Problem in England, 1560–1640.* Methuen Publishing, 1985.

Berg, James E. "'This Dear, Dear Land': Dearth and the Fantasy of Land-Grab in *Richard II* and *Henry IV*." *English Literary Renaissance*, vol. 29, no. 2, 1999, pp. 225–45.

Bergbusch, Matt. "Additional Dialogue: William Shakespeare, Queer Allegory, and *My Own Private Idaho.*" *Shakespeare without Class: Misappropriations of Cultural Capital*, edited by Donald Hedrick and Bryan Reynolds, Palgrave Macmillan, 2000, pp. 209–25.

Berger, Harry. "Harrying the Stage: *Henry V* in the Tetralogical Echo Chamber." *Harrying: Skills of Offense in Shakespeare's Henriad*, Fordham UP, 2015, pp. 155–64.

Berry, Edward I. *Patterns of Decay: Shakespeare's Early Histories.* U of Virginia P, 1975.

Bilgrami, Akeel. "Secularism: Its Content and Context." *Boundaries of Toleration*, edited by Alfred Stepan and Charles Taylor, Columbia UP, 2014, pp. 79–129.

Bolam, Robin. "*Richard II*: Shakespeare and the Languages of the Stage." Hattaway, pp. 141–57.

Bondanella, Peter. Introduction. *The Prince*, by Niccolò Machiavelli, Oxford UP, 1979, pp. iv–xvi.

Booth, Stephen. *The Book Called* Holinshed's Chronicles: *An Account of Its Inception, Purpose, Contributors, Contents, Publication, Revision, and Influence on William Shakespeare.* Book Club of California, 1968.

Boswell-Stone, Walter George. *Shakespeare's Holinshed: The Chronicle and the Plays Compared*. Dover Publications, 1968.

Bradley, A. C. "The Rejection of Falstaff." *Oxford Lectures on Poetry*, HardPress Publishing, 2012, pp. 247–78.

Bradshaw, Graham, et al., editors. *Shakespeare and Montaigne Revisited*. Ashgate Publishing, 2006.

Braunmuller, A. R. "*King John* and Historiography." *ELH*, vol. 55, no. 2, 1988, pp. 309–32.

Bray, Alan. *Homosexuality in Renaissance England*. Columbia UP, 1996.

Bray, Gerald, editor. *Documents of the English Reformation, 1526–1701*. James Clarke, 1994.

Bristol, Michael D. *Carnival and Theatre: Plebeian Culture and the Structure of Authority in Renaissance Britain*. Routledge, 1985.

Bromley, James M., and Will Stockton, editors. *Sex before Sex: Figuring the Act in Early Modern England*. U of Minnesota P, 2013.

Brotton, Jerry. *The Renaissance: A Short Introduction*. Oxford UP, 2006.

Bruckner, Lynne. "'Consuming Means, Soon Preys upon Itself': Political Expedience and Environmental Degradation in *Richard II*." *Shakespeare and the Urgency of Now: Criticism and Theory in the Twenty-First Century*, edited by Cary DiPietro and Hugh Grady, Palgrave Macmillan, 2013, pp. 223–37.

———. "Teaching Shakespeare in the Ecotone." Bruckner and Brayton, 223–37.

Bruckner, Lynne, and Dan Brayton, editors. *Ecocritical Shakespeare*. Ashgate Publishing, 2011.

Buchanan, George. *A Dialogue on the Law of Kingship among the Scots: A Critical Edition and Translation of George Buchanan's De Jure Regne Apud Scotos Dialogus*. Edited and translated by Roger A. Mason and Martin S. Smith, Scolar Press, 2004. St. Andrew's Studies in Reformation History.

Bullough, Geoffrey. *Narrative and Dramatic Sources of Shakespeare*. Columbia UP, 1957–75. 8 vols.

Burrow, Colin. *Shakespeare and Classical Antiquity*. Oxford UP, 2013.

Burt, Richard, and John Michael Archer, editors. *Enclosure Acts: Sexuality, Property, and Culture in Early Modern England*. Cornell UP, 1994.

Cahill, Patricia. *Unto the Breach: Martial Formations, Historical Trauma, and the Early Modern Stage*. Oxford UP, 2008.

Calderwood, James. *Metadrama in Shakespeare's Henriad*: Richard II *to* Henry V. U of California P, 1979.

Calhoun, Joshua, and Ethan Kay. *The RNB Hive*, rnbhive.joshuacalhoun.org/.

Campbell, Lily B. *Shakespeare's Histories: Mirrors of Elizabethan Policy*. Huntington Library, 1947.

Caravaggio. *The Betrayal of Christ*. 1602, National Gallery of Art, Dublin.

Carpenter, Christine. *The Wars of the Roses: Politics and the Constitution in England, c. 1437–1509*. Cambridge UP, 1997.

Carr, Virginia M. "Once More into the Henriad: A 'Two-Eyed' View." *The Journal of English and Germanic Philology*, vol. 77, no. 4, 1978, pp. 530–45.

Carroll, William B. *Fat King, Lean Beggar: Representations of Poverty in the Age of Shakespeare*. Cornell UP, 1996.

———. "Theories of Kingship in Shakespeare's England." Dutton and Howard, pp. 125–45.

Castiglione, Baldassare. *The Courtyer of Count Baldessar Castilio Divided into Foure Bookes. Very Necessary and Profitatable for Yonge Gentilmen and Gentilwomen Abiding in Court, Palaice or Place, Done into Englyshe by Thomas Hoby*. London, 1561.

Cayley, Seth. "Digitization in Teaching and Learning: The Publisher's View." *Victorian Periodicals Review*, vol. 45, no 2, Summer 2012, pp. 210–14.

Champion, Larry S. *The Noise of Threatening Drum: Dramatic Strategy and Political Ideology in Shakespeare and the English Chronicle Plays*. U of Delaware P, 1990.

———. *Perspective in Shakespeare's English Histories*. U of Georgia P, 1980.

Chernaik, Warren. *The Cambridge Introduction to Shakespeare's History Plays*. Cambridge UP, 2007.

Chimes at Midnight. Directed by Orson Welles, performance by Welles, Keith Baxter, Jeanne Moreau, and Margaret Rutherford, Mr. Bongo Films, 1965.

Chrétien de Troyes. *Arthurian Romances*. Translated by William W. Kibler and Carleton W. Carroll, Penguin Books, 1991.

Chrimes, S. B. *Henry VII*. Yale UP, 1999. Yale English Monarchs.

Christiansen, Nancy L. *Figuring Style: The Legacy of Renaissance Rhetoric*. U of South Carolina P, 2013.

Church of England. *The Booke of Common Praier, and Administration of the Sacramentes, and Other Rites and Ceremonies in the Churche of Englande*. London, 1559.

"Civil, *Adj.*" *Oxford English Dictionary Online*, June 2004, Oxford UP, www.oed.com .relay.lagrange.edu/view/Entry/33575?rskey=8plsJy&result=1.

"Civility, *N.*" *Oxford English Dictionary Online*, June 2004, Oxford UP, www.oed.com .relay.lagrange.edu/view/Entry/33581?redirectedFrom=civility&.

Cohen, Derek. "History and the Nation in *Richard II* and *Henry IV*." *SEL*, vol. 42, no. 2, Spring 2002, pp. 293–315.

Cohen, Jeffrey. *Prismatic Ecologies: Ecotheory beyond Green*. U of Minnesota P, 2014.

Cohen, Walter. *Drama of a Nation: Public Theater in Renaissance England and Spain*. Cornell UP, 1985.

"Common Core State Standards for English Language Arts and Literacy in History/Social Studies, Science, and Technical Subjects." *Common Core State Standard Initiatives*, 2016, www.corestandards.org/assets/Appendix_B.pdf.

The Complete Dramatic Works of William Shakespeare: Henry IV Part One. Directed by David Giles, British Broadcasting Corporation, 1979.

The Complete Works of William Shakespeare. MIT, 1993, shakespeare.mit.edu.

"Composition Courses." *Writing and Communication Program*, Georgia Institute of Technology, wcprogram.lmc.gatech.edu/courses/composition.

Costa, Arthur L., and Bena Kallick. *Discovering and Exploring Habits of Mind*. ASCD, 2000.

"Courses." *Writing and Communication Program*, Georgia Institute of Technology, wcprogram.lmc.gatech.edu/courses.

Crowl, Samuel. *Shakespeare and Film: A Norton Guide*. W. W. Norton, 2007.

Crystal, David, and Ben Crystal. *Shakespeare's Words: Glossary and Language Companion*. Penguin Books, 2002.

Cunningham, Daniel Mudie. "Driving the 'Dustless Highway' of Queer Cinema." *The Film Journal*, 2002, web.archive.org/web/20101226053022/http:/www.thefilm journal.com/issue5/highway.html.

Dalrymple, Louis. "His Finish." *Puck*, vol. 48, no. 1248, J. Ottman Lithography Company, 6 February 1901. *Library of Congress Prints and Photographs Online Catalog*, www.loc.gov/pictures/resource/ppmsca.25496/.

Daniel, Samuel. *The First Foure Bookes of the Civile Wars between the Two Houses of Lancaster and Yorke*. London, 1595. *Early English Books Online*, eebo.chadwyck.com/search/full_rec?SOURCE=pgimages.cfg&ACTION =ByID&ID=V9759.

Davies, John. *A History of Wales*. Penguin Books, 1990.

Davis, Hugh H. "'Shakespeare, He's in the Alley': *My Own Private Idaho* and Shakespeare in the Streets." *Literature/Film Quarterly*, vol. 29, no. 2, 2001, pp. 116–21.

DCNR Shale-Gas Monitoring Report. Pennsylvania Department of Conservation and Natural Resources, 16 Apr. 2014, www.dcnr.state.pa.us/cs/groups/public/ documents/document/dcnr_20029147.pdf.

De Grazia, Margreta, and Stanley Wells, editors. *The New Cambridge Companion to Shakespeare*. Cambridge UP, 2010.

De Somogyi, Nick. *Shakespeare's Theatre of War*. Ashgate Publishing, 1998.

Detrow, Scott. "Can Pennsylvania's State Forests Survive Additional Marcellus Shale Drilling?" *StateImpact*, 12 Sept. 2011, stateimpact.npr.org/pennsylvania/ 2011/09/12/can-pennsylvanias-state-forests-survive-additional-marcellus-shale -drilling/.

DiGangi, Mario. *The Homoerotics of Early Modern Drama*. Cambridge UP, 1997.

———. "Sex Matters." *Approaches to Teaching English Renaissance Drama*, edited by Karen Bamford and Alexander Leggatt, Modern Language Association of America, 2002, pp. 150–57.

———. *Sexual Types: Embodiment, Agency, and Dramatic Character from Shakespeare to Shirley*. U of Pennsylvania P, 2011.

Dillenberger, John, editor. *Martin Luther: Selections from His Writings*. Anchor Books, 1962.

Dillon, Janette. *Shakespeare and the Staging of English History*. Oxford UP, 2012.

DiPietro, Cary, and Hugh Grady. "Presentism, Anachronism and the Case of *Titus Andronicus*." *Shakespeare*, vol. 8, 2012, pp. 44–73.

"The Distressed Pilgrim, Who Being in Much Misery, He Serves the Lord most Faitfully: And Repenteth for the Things Are Past, And Prayes for a Heavenly Place at Last." 1678–88. *English Broadside Ballad Archive*, U of California, Santa Barbara, ebba.english.ucsb.edu/ballad/30392/image.

Djordjevic, Igor. *Holinshed's Nation: Ideals, Memory, and Practical Policy in the Chronicles*. Ashgate Publishing, 2010.

Dobree, Bonamy, and Geoffrey Web, editors. *The Complete Works of Sir John Vanbrugh*. Nonesuch Press, 1927. 4 vols.

Dobson, Michael, and Stanley Wells, editors. *The Oxford Companion to Shakespeare*. Oxford UP, 2009.

Dollimore, Jonathan, and Alan Sinfield, editors. *Political Shakespeare: New Essays in Cultural Materialism*. Manchester UP, 1985.

Donaldson, Peter S. "Digital Archive as Expanded Text: Shakespeare and Electronic Textuality." *Electronic Text: Investigations in Method and Theory*, edited by Kathryn Sutherland, Clarendon Press, 1997, pp. 173–97.

Dutton, Richard, and Jean E. Howard, editors. *A Companion to Shakespeare's Works: The Histories*. Wiley Blackwell, 2005.

Edwards, John. *Mary I: England's Catholic Queen*. Yale UP, 2011. Yale English Monarchs.

Eggert, Katherine. *Showing Like a Queen: Female Authority and Literary Experiment in Spenser, Shakespeare, and Milton*. U of Pennsylvania P, 2000.

Eliot, T. S. "The *Pensées* of Pascal." *Selected Prose*, edited by Frank Kermode, Faber and Faber, 1975.

Elizabeth I. "Queen Elizabeth's Armada Speech to the Troops at Tillbury." *Elizabeth I: Collected Works*, edited by Leah Marcus et al., U of Chicago P, 2000, pp. 325–26.

Ellis, Henry, editor. *Holinshed's Chronicles of England, Scotland and Ireland*. AMS Press, 1965. 6 vols.

Empson, William. "Falstaff." *Essays on Shakespeare*, edited by David B. Pirie, Cambridge UP, 1986, pp. 29–78.

"English Language Arts Standards." *Common Core State Standards Initiative*, 2016, www.corestandards.org/ELA-Literacy/.

Enterline, Lynn. *Shakespeare's Schoolroom: Rhetoric, Discipline, Emotion*. U of Pennsylvania P, 2012.

Erasmus. *The Education of a Christian Prince*. Edited by Lisa Jardine, Cambridge UP, 1997.

Erickson, Peter. "Race Words in *Othello*." Espinosa and Ruiter, pp. 159–76.

Ericson, Matthew, editor. "The Words They Used." *The New York Times*, 17 Apr. 2011, www.nytimes.com/interactive/2008/09/04/us/politics/20080905_WORDS_GRAPHIC.html?_r=0.

Erikson, Erik. *Childhood and Society*. W. W. Norton, 1950.

Espinosa, Ruben. "Fluellen's Foreign Influence and the Ill Neighborhood of *King Henry V*." Espinosa and Ruiter, pp. 73–90.

———. "Stranger Shakespeare." *Shakespeare Quarterly*, vol. 67, no. 1, 2016, pp. 51–67.

Espinosa, Ruben, and David Ruiter, editors. *Shakespeare and Immigration*. Ashgate Publishing, 2014.

Everitt, Alan. "Farm Labourers, 1500–1640." *Rural Society: Landowners, Peasants and Labourers, 1500–1750*, edited by Christopher Clay, Cambridge UP, 1990, pp. 161–230.

Fagan, Brian. *The Little Ice Age: How Climate Made History, 1300–1850*. Basic Books, 2000.

Falbo, Bianca. "Teaching from the Archives." *RBM*, vol. 1, no. 1, 2000, pp. 33–35.

The Famous Victories of Henry the Fifth. Edited by Mathew Martin and Karen Sawyer Marsalek. *Internet Shakespeare Editions*, 2014, qme.internetshakespeare.uvic .ca/Foyer/plays/FV.html. Queen's Men Editions.

The Famous Victories of Henry Fifth. London: Tudor Facsimile Texts, 1913. *Internet Archive*, archive.org/details/famousvictorieso00ameruoft.

Findlay, Alison. "New Directions: The Madcap and Politic Prince of Wales: Ceremony and Courtly Performance in *Henry IV*." *1 Henry IV: A Critical Guide*, edited by Stephen Longstaffe, Continuum International, 2011, pp. 86–98.

Fisher, Will. *Materializing Gender in Early Modern English Literature and Culture*. Cambridge UP, 2006.

Folger Shakespeare Library. *Shakespeare's Plays from Folger Digital Texts*. Edited by Barbara Mowat et al., 2016, www.folgerdigitaltexts.org.

Forrest, John. *The History of Morris Dancing, 1458–1750*. U of Toronto P, 1999.

Fortescue, John. *In Praise of the Laws of England. On the Laws and Governance of England*, edited by Shelley Lockwood, Cambridge UP, 1997, pp. 1–80.

Freeman, Thomas S., and Susannah Monta. "Holinshed and Foxe." Kewes et al., *Oxford Handbook*, pp. 217–34.

Freud, Sigmund. *Civilization and Its Discontents*. Edited and translated by James Strachey, W. W. Norton, 1961.

Froehlich, Heather. "Of Time, Numbers, and Due Course of Things." *Heather Froehlich*, 9 June 2014, hfroehlich.wordpress.com/2014/06/09/of-time of numbers -and-due-course of-things/.

Frons, Marc. "*The New York Times* Data Visualization Lab." *New York Times*, 27 Oct. 2008, open.blogs.nytimes.com/2008/10/27/the-new-york-times-data -visualization-lab/?_r=0.

Frye, Northrop. "The Argument of Comedy." *Shakespeare: An Anthology of Criticism and Theory*, edited by Russ McDonald, Blackwell Publishing, 2004, pp. 93–99.

Gajowski, Evelyn, editor. *Presentism, Gender, and Sexuality in Shakespeare*. Palgrave Macmillan, 2009.

Garber, Marjorie. *Shakespeare After All*. Anchor Books, 2004.

Gardner, Howard. *Intelligence Reframed: Multiple Intelligences for the Twenty-First Century*. Basic Books, 1999.

Garfield, Leon. *Shakespeare Stories*. Houghton Mifflin, 1985.

———. *Shakespeare Stories II*. Houghton Mifflin, 1994.

Ge, Nikolai. *Conscience, Judas*. 1891. Tretyakov Gallery, Moscow.

———. *The Last Supper*. 1863. Tretyakov Gallery, Moscow.

Gibson, Rex. *Teaching Shakespeare*. Cambridge UP, 1998.

Gillespie, Stuart. *Shakespeare's Books: A Dictionary of Shakespeare's Sources*. Athlone, 2001.

Gillies, John. *Shakespeare and the Geography of Difference*. Cambridge UP, 1994.

Glenza, Jessica. "Colorado Teachers Stage Mass Sick-Out to Protest US History Curriculum Changes." *The Guardian*, 30 Sept. 2014, www.theguardian.com/ education/2014/sep/29/colorado-teachers-us-history-sickout-protest-contracts -jefferson.

Goldberg, Jonathan. *James I and the Politics of Literature: Jonson, Shakespeare, Donne, and Their Contemporaries*. Johns Hopkins UP, 1983.

————. *Sodometries: Renaissance Texts, Modern Sexualities*. Fordham UP, 2010.

Goy-Blanquet, Dominique. *Shakespeare's Early History Plays: From Chronicle to Stage*. Oxford UP, 2003.

Grady, Hugh, and Terence Hawkes, editors. *Presentist Shakespeares*. Routledge, 2006.

Graff, Gerald, and Cathy Birkenstein. *They Say / I Say: The Moves That Matter in Academic Writing*. W. W. Norton, 2006.

Greenblatt, Stephen. "Invisible Bullets: Renaissance Authority and Its Subversion: *Henry IV* and *Henry V*." *Shakespearean Negotiations*, U of California P, 1988, pp. 21–65.

————. "Murdering Peasants: Status, Genre, and the Representation of Rebellion." *Representations*, vol. 1, Feb. 1983, pp. 1–29.

————. *Renaissance Self-Fashioning: From More to Shakespeare*. U of Chicago P, 1980.

————. *Shakespearean Negotiations*. U of California P, 1988.

Grene, Nicholas. *Shakespeare's Serial History Plays*. Cambridge UP, 2002.

Guttman, Selma. *The Foreign Sources of Shakespeare's Works: An Annotated Bibliography of the Commentary Written on This Subject between 1904 and 1940, Together with Lists of Certain Translations Available to Shakespeare*. Octagon Books, 1968.

Hagen, Uta. *A Challenge for the Actor*. Scribner, 1991.

Hall, Edward. *Hall's Chronicle; Containing the History of England, during the Reign of Henry the Fourth, and the Succeeding Monarchs, to the End of the Reign of Henry the Eighth, in Which Are Particularly Described the Manners and Customs of Those Periods. Carefully Collated with the Editions of 1548 and 1550*. Edited by Henry Ellis, AMS Press, 1965.

————. *The Union of the Two Noble and Illustre Familes of Lancastre and York*. Edited by Henry Ellis, J. Johnson et al., 1809.

Hall's Chronicle; Containing the History of England during the Reign of Henry the Fourth, and the Succeeding Monarchs, to the End of the Reign of Henry the Eighth, in Which Are Particularly Described the Manners and Customs of Those Periods. Carefully Collated with the Edition of 1548 and 1550. London, 1809.

"Hall's Chronicle (Selection)." *Internet Shakespeare Editions*, 2014, internet shakespeare.uvic.ca/doc/Hall_H5_M/complete//;jsessionid=4A13DFDBEDE0 C05D8673C4AFD19FB649.

Handelman, David. "Gus Van Sant's Northwest Passage." *Rolling Stone*, vol. 616, 31 Oct. 1991. *Academic Search Premier*, search.ebscohost.com.

Harris, Jonathan Gil. *Shakespeare and Literary Theory*. Oxford UP, 2010.

———. *Sick Economies: Drama, Mercantilism, and Disease in Shakespeare's England*. U of Pennsylvania P, 2004.

Harriss, Gerald. *Shaping the Nation: England, 1360–1461*. Oxford UP, 2007. New Oxford History of England.

Hart, Jonathan. *Columbus, Shakespeare, and the Interpretation of the New World*. Palgrave Macmillan, 2003.

———. *From Shakespeare to Obama: A Study in Language, Slavery, and Place*. Palgrave Macmillan, 2013.

———. *Shakespeare and His Contemporaries*. Palgrave Macmillan, 2011.

———. *Shakespeare: Poetry, History, and Culture*. Palgrave Macmillan, 2009.

———. *Theater and World: The Problematics of Shakespeare's History*. Northeastern UP, 1992.

Hattaway, Michael, editor. *The Cambridge Companion to Shakespeare's History Plays*. Cambridge UP, 2003.

Hayward, John. *The Life and Raigne of King Henrie IIII*. Edited by John J. Manning, Royal Historical Society, 1991.

Heal, Felicity, and Henry Summerson. "The Genesis of the Two Editions." Kewes et al., *Oxford Handbook*, pp. 3–20.

Heath, Michael J. *The Panegyric for Archduke Philip of Austria*. Edited and translated by Lisa Jardine, Cambridge UP, 1997.

Heath, William. *The Rival Richards or Sheakspear [sic] in Danger*. London, 1814. *Folger Digital Image Collection*, Folger Shakespeare Library, luna.folger.edu/luna/servlet/detail/FOLGERCM1~6~6~304492~123913:The-rival-Richards-or-Sheakspear—s.

Helgerson, Richard. *Forms of Nationhood: The Elizabethan Writing of England*. U of Chicago P, 1992.

———. "Writing Empire and Nation." *The Cambridge Companion to English Literature, 1500–1600*, edited by Arthur F. Kinney, Cambridge UP, 2000, pp. 310–29.

Henderson, Diana E. "Meditations in a Time of (Displaced) War: *Henry V*, Money, and the Ethics of Performing History." *Shakespeare and War*, edited by Paul J. C. M. Franssen and Ros King, Palgrave Macmillan, 2008, pp. 226–42.

"Henry IV, Part 1." Directed by Richard Eyre, performances by Jeremy Irons, Simon Russell Beale, Tom Hiddleston, Julie Walters, and Maxine Peake. *The Hollow Crown*, British Broadcasting Corporation, 2012.

"Henry IV, Part 2." Directed by Richard Eyre, performances by Jeremy Irons, Simon Russell Beale, Tom Hiddleston, Julie Walters, and Maxine Peake. *The Hollow Crown*, British Broadcasting Corporation, 2012.

Henry V. Directed by Kenneth Branagh, performance by Branagh, Derek Jacobi, Paul Scofield, Ian Holm, and Emma Thompson, MGM, 1989.

Henry V. Directed by Nicholas Hytner, 13 May 2003, National Theatre, London.

Henry V. Directed by Laurence Olivier, performance by Olivier, Leslie Banks, Robert Newton, Renee Asherson, and Leo Genn, Criterion, 1944.

"Henry V." Directed by Thea Sharrock, performances by Tom Hiddleston, John Hurt, Anton Lesser, Julie Walters, and Joseph Patterson. *The Hollow Crown*, British Broadcasting Corporation, 2012.

"Henry VI, Part 1." Directed by Dominic Cooke, performances by Hugh Bonneville, Sally Hawkins, Tom Sturridge, and Sophie Okonedo. *The Hollow Crown: The Wars of the Roses*, British Broadcasting Corporation, 2016.

"Henry VI, Part 2." Directed by Dominic Cooke, performances by Benedict Cumberbatch, Ben Daniels, Sophie Okonedo, and Tom Sturridge. *The Hollow Crown: The Wars of the Roses*, British Broadcasting Corporation, 2016.

Herman, Peter C. *A Short History of Early Modern England: British Literature in Context*. Wiley Blackwell, 2011.

Heywood, Thomas. *An Apology for Actors*. 1612. Scholars Facsimiles and Reprints, 1941.

Highlander. Directed by Russell Mulcahy, performance by Christopher Lambert, Roxanne Hart, Clancy Brown, Sean Connery, Thorn EMI Screen Entertainment, 1986.

Hill, Christopher. "The Industrious Sort of People." *Society and Puritanism in Pre-Revolutionary England*, Schocken Books, 1964, pp. 99–117.

Hiltner, Ken. *What Else Is Pastoral? Renaissance Literature and the Environment*. Cornell UP, 2011.

Hodgdon, Barbara. *The End Crowns All: Closure and Contradiction in Shakespeare's History*. Princeton UP, 1991.

———, editor. *The First Part of King Henry the Fourth: Texts and Contexts*. Bedford/St. Martin's, 1997.

Hoenslaars, Ton, editor. *Shakespeare's History Plays: Performance, Adaptation and Translation in Britain and Abroad*. Cambridge UP, 2007.

Holderness, Graham. *Shakespeare's History*. St. Martin's Press, 1985.

———, editor. *Shakespeare's History Plays*: Richard II *to* Henry V. St. Martin's Press, 1992.

The Holinshed Project. Oxford U, 2008–13, english.nsms.ox.ac.uk/holinshed.

Holinshed, Raphael. *The Chronicles of England, Scotland and Ireland*. London, 1587. Horace Howard Furness Memorial Shakespeare Library, Philadelphia. Folio.

———. *The Chronicles of England, Scotland and Ireland*. 1587. 2nd edition, London, 1807–08. 6 vols.

Holland, Peter, editor. *Shakespeare's English Histories and Their Afterlives*. Cambridge UP, 2010. Shakespeare Survey 63.

The Hollow Crown: The Complete Series. British Broadcasting Corporation, 2012.

Holy Bible. King James Version, Regency Publishing House, 1976.

"An Homily against Disobedience and Wylful Rebellion." 1570. *Divine Right and Democracy: An Anthology of Political Writing in Stuart England*, edited by David Wootton, Penguin Books, 1986, pp. 94–98.

Hope, Jonathan. *Shakespeare's Grammar*. Arden Shakespeare, 2003.

Hopkins, Lisa. *Shakespeare on the Edge: Border-Crossing in the Tragedies and the Henriad*. Ashgate Publishing, 2005.

Horace. *The Odes*. Translated by A. S. Kline, *Poetry in Translation*, www.poetryin translation.com/PITBR/Latin/HoraceOdesBkIII.htm#anchor_Toc40263846.

Hosley, Richard, editor. *Shakespeare's Holinshed: An Edition of* Holinshed's Chronicles, *1587: Sources of Shakespeare's History Plays*, King Lear, Cymbeline, *and* Macbeth. Capricorn Books, 1968.

Howard, Jean E., and Phyllis Rackin. *Engendering a Nation: A Feminist Account of Shakespeare's English Histories*. Routledge, 1997.

Howlett, Kathy M. "Utopian Revisioning of Falstaff's Tavern World: Orson Welles's *Chimes at Midnight* and Gus Van Sant's *My Own Private Idaho*." *The Reel Shakespeare: Alternative Cinema and Theory*, edited by Lisa S. Starks and Courtney Lehmann, Fairleigh Dickinson UP, 2002, pp. 165–88.

Humes, Edward. "Fractured Lives: Detritus of Pennsylvania's Shale Gas Boom." *Sierra Magazine*, July–Aug. 2012, vault.sierraclub.org/sierra/201207/pennsylvania -fracking-shale-gas-199.aspx.

Hunt, Maurice. *Shakespeare's Religious Allusiveness: Its Play and Tolerance*. Ashgate Publishing, 2003.

Hunter, Lynette, Lynne Magnusson, and Sylvia Adamson, editors. *Reading Shakespeare's Dramatic Language*. Arden Shakespeare, 2000.

Hutcheon, Linda. *A Theory of Adaptation*. Routledge, 2006.

Ivic, Christopher. "'Bastard Normans, Norman Bastards': Anomalous Identities in *The Life of Henry the Fift*." Schwyzer and Maley, pp. 75–90.

Jacobs, Heidi Hayes, editor. *Curriculum 21: Essential Education for a Changing World*. ASCD, 2010.

James VI and I. *Basilikon doron*. Edinburgh, 1599. *Early English Books Online*, gateway.proquest.com/openurl?ctx_ver=Z39.88–2003&res_id=xri:eebo&rft_ id=xri:eebo:image:1192.

———. "A Speech to the Lords and Commons of the Parliament at White-Hall." 1610. *Divine Right and Democracy: An Anthology of Political Writing in Stuart England*, edited by David Wootton, Hackett Publishing, 2003, pp. 107–09.

———. *The Trew Law of Free Monarchies; or, the Riciprock and Mutuall Dutie Betwixt a Free King and His Natural Subjects. The Political Works of James I*. Edited by Charles Howard McIlwain, Harvard UP, 1946.

———. *The True Law of Free Monarchies*. London, 1598. *Early English Books Online*, gateway.proquest.com/openurl?ctx_ver=Z39.88–2003&res_id=xri:eebo&rft_ id=xri:eebo:image:20049.

John Foxe's The Acts and Monuments Online. U of Sheffield, 2001, www.johnfoxe.org.

"John, King of England." *Wikipedia*, Wikimedia Foundation, en.wikipedia.org/wiki/ John,_King_of_England.

Jones, Emrys. *The Origins of Shakespeare*. Clarendon Press, 1977.

Jones, Jason B. "How to Read Three Victorian Novels in 2.5 Hours." *The Salt Box*, 27 March 2008, www.jbj.wordherders.net/2008/03/27/how-to-read- victorian -novels-in-25-hours/.

Jones, Robert C. *These Valiant Dead: Renewing the Past in Shakespeare's Histories*. U of Iowa P, 1991.

Joseph, Miriam. *Rhetoric in Shakespeare's Time: Literary Theory of Renaissance Europe*. Harcourt, Brace, and World, 1962.

Kahn, Coppélia. *Man's Estate: Masculine Identity in Shakespeare*. U of California P, 1981.

Kaiser, Walter. *Praisers of Folly: Erasmus, Rabelais, Shakespeare*. Harvard UP, 1963.

Kantorowicz, Ernst Hartwig. *The King's Two Bodies: A Study in Medieval Political Theology*. Princeton UP, 1957.

Kastan, David Scott. *A Companion to Shakespeare*. Wiley-Blackwell, 1999.

———. *Shakespeare after Theory*. Routledge, 1999.

———. *Shakespeare and the Shapes of Time*. UP of New England, 1982.

Kendall, Paul. *Richard III*. W. W. Norton, 1956.

Kermode, Lloyd E. *Aliens and Englishness in Elizabethan Drama*. Cambridge UP, 2009.

Kerridge, Richard. "An Ecocritic's *Macbeth*." Bruckner and Brayton, pp. 193–210.

Kewes, Paulina, et al., editors. *The Oxford Handbook of Holinshed's* Chronicles. Oxford UP, 2013.

Kewes, Paulina, et al. "The Making of the Chronicles." *The Holinshed Project*, Oxford U, 2008–13.

King, John, editor. *Foxe's* Book of Martyrs: *Select Narratives*. Oxford UP, 2009.

Klinck, Dennis R. "Shakespeare's Richard II as Landlord and Wasting Tenant." *College Literature*, vol. 25, no. 1, 1998, pp. 21–34.

Kott, Jan. *Shakespeare, Our Contemporary*. Translated by Boleslaw Taborski, Double- day, 1964.

Laing, R. D. *The Politics of the Family*. Vintage Books, 1972.

Lane, Robert. "'When Blood Is Their Argument': Class, Character, and Historymaking in Shakespeare's and Branagh's *Henry V*." *ELH*, vol. 61, no. 1, 1994, pp. 27–52.

Lang, Robert. "*My Own Private Idaho* and the New Queer Road Movies." *The Road Movie Book*, edited by Steven Cohan and Ina Rae Hark, Routledge, 1997, pp. 330–48.

Laroche, Rebecca, and Jen Munroe. "On a Bank of Rue: Ecofeminist Inquiry and the Garden of *Richard II*." *Shakespeare Studies*, vol. 42, 2014, pp. 42–50.

Leggatt, Alexander. *Shakespeare's Political Drama: The History Plays and the Roman Plays*. Routledge, 1988.

Lester, Adrian. "King Henry V." Smallwood, pp. 145–62.

Levin, Carol. *The Heart and Stomach of a King: Elizabeth I and the Politics of Sex and Power*. U of Pennsylvania P, 1994.

Levine, Nina S. *Women's Matters: Politics, Gender, and Nation in Shakespeare's Early History Plays*. U of Delaware P, 1998.

Levy, F. J. *Tudor Historical Thought*. Huntington Library, 1967.

Liebler, Naomi C. "Kings of the Road: 'My Own Private Idaho' and the Traversal of Welles, Shakespeare, and Liminality." *Post Script*, vol. 17, no. 2, 1997, pp. 26–38.

LoMonico, Mike. E-mail message to Caroline McManus. 13 Dec. 2012.

Longstaffe, Steven. *A Critical Edition of the Life and Death of Jack Straw, 1594*. Edwin Mellen Press, 2002.

Looking for Richard. Directed by Al Pacino, performance by Pacino, Harris Yulin, Kevin Spacey, Alec Baldwin, and Winona Ryder, Twentieth Century Fox, 1996.

Lordi, Robert Joseph. *Thomas Legge's* Richardus Tertius: *A Critical Edition with a Translation*. Garland Publications, 1979.

Loud, Lance. "Shakespeare in Black Leather." *American Film*, vol. 16, no. 9, 1991, pp. 32–37.

Low, Jennifer A. *Manhood and the Duel: Masculinity in Early Modern Drama and Culture*. Palgrave Macmillan, 2003.

Lucas, Scott. "Holinshed and Hall." Kewes et al., *Oxford Handbook*, pp. 203–16.

Lyne, Raphael. *Shakespeare, Rhetoric and Cognition*. Cambridge UP, 2011.

MacGregor, Neil, narrator. "England Goes Global." *Shakespeare's Restless World*, British Broadcasting Corporation Radio 4, 16 Apr. 2012, www.bbc.co.uk/podcasts/series/r4shakespeare/all.

———. *Shakespeare's Restless World: A Portrait of an Era in Twenty Objects*. Penguin Books, 2012.

Machiavelli, Niccolò. *The Prince*. Translated by Robert M. Adams, 2nd ed., W. W. Norton, 1992.

Mack, Peter. *Reading and Rhetoric in Montaigne and Shakespeare*. Bloomsbury Academic Publishing, 2010.

Maley, Willy. "'Let a Welsh Correction Teach You a Good English Condition': Shakespeare, Wales, and the Critics." Schwyzer and Maley, pp. 177–90.

Manheim, Michael. *The Weak King Dilemma in the Shakespearean History Play*. Syracuse UP, 1973.

Mann, Jenny C. *Outlaw Rhetoric: Figuring Vernacular Rhetoric in Shakespeare's England*. Cornell UP, 2012.

Manning, Roger B. *Village Revolts*. Clarendon Press, 1988.

Marie de France. *The Lais of Marie de France*. Edited by Glyn S. Burgess and Keith Busby, Penguin Books, 1999.

Marlowe, Christopher. *Edward II*. Edited by Martin Wiggins and Robert Lindsey, Methuen Drama, 2005.

Marlowe, Christopher, and George Chapman. *Hero and Leander: A Poem*. C. Whittingham, 1821, pp. 50–51. *Internet Archive*, archive.org/stream/heroand leandera00chapgoog#pag /10/mode/2up.

Martirosyan, Annie. "A Production of Many Colours: RSC's Glistering *King John*." *Sprint for Shakespeare*, 19 Oct. 2012, shakespeare.bodleian.ox.ac.uk/2012/10/19/a-production-of-many-colours-rscs-glistering-king-john/.

McDonald, Russ. "Politics and Religion: Early Modern Ideologies." *The Bedford Companion to Shakespeare: An Introduction with Documents*, 2nd ed., Bedford/St. Martin's, 2002, pp. 303–52.

———. *Shakespeare and the Arts of Language*. Oxford UP, 2001.

McKibben, Bill. "Why Not Frack?" *New York Review of Books*, 8 Mar. 2012, www.nybooks.com/articles/2012/03/08/why-not-frack/.

Menon, Madhavi, editor. *Shakesqueer: A Queer Companion to the Complete Works of Shakespeare*. Duke UP, 2011.

Metzger, Mary Janell. *Shakespeare without Fear: Teaching for Understanding*. Heinemann, 2004.

"Military Recruitment 2010." *National Priorities Project*, www.nationalpriorities.org/analysis/2011/military-recruitment-2010/.

Miola, Robert. *Shakespeare's Reading*. Oxford UP, 2000.

Montaigne, Michel. *The Complete Essays*. Penguin Books, 2003.

More, Thomas. The History of King Richard III *and Selections from the English and Latin Poems*. Edited by Richard S. Sylvester, Yale UP, 1976.

———. The History of King Richard III: *A Reading Edition*. Edited by George M. Logan, Indianapolis UP, 2005.

———. *Utopia*. Edited and translated by George M. Logan, 3rd ed., W. W. Norton, 2011.

Moretti, Franco. *Distant Reading*. Verso, 2013.

———. *Graphs, Maps, Trees: Abstract Models for Literary History*. Verso, 2007.

Moretti, Franco, et al. "Pamphlets." *Stanford Literary Lab*, litlab.stanford.edu/?page_id=255.

Morrow, David. "Local/Global *Pericles*: International Storytelling, Domestic Social Relations, Capitalism." Singh, pp. 355–77.

"A Mournefull Dittie, Entituled Elizabeths Losse, together with a Welcome for King James." 1603. *English Broadside Ballad Archive*, U of California, Santa Barbara, ebba.english.ucsb.edu/ballad/32231/xml.

Muir, Kenneth. *Shakespeare's Sources*. Methuen Publishing, 1957.

Munday, Anthony. *Sir John Oldcastle*. London, 1600. *Early English Books Online*, gateway.proquest.com/openurl?ctx_ver=Z39.88–2003&res_id=xri:eebo&rft_id=xri:eebo:image:6664.

Mussell, Jim. "Teaching Nineteenth-Century Periodicals Using Digital Resources: Myths and Methods." *Victorian Periodicals Review*, vol. 45, no. 2, Summer 2012, pp. 201–09.

My Own Private Idaho. Directed by Gus Van Sant, performance by River Phoenix, Keanu Reeves, William Richert, and Udo Kier, New Line Cinema, 1991.

Nardizzi, Vin. *Wooden Os: Shakespeare's Theatres and England's Trees*. U of Toronto P, 2013.

Nashe, Thomas. *Pierce Penilesse His Supplication to the Devil. Three Elizabethan Pamphlets*. Edited by George Richard Hibbard, Books for Libraries P, 1969, pp. 71–159.

Neill, Michael. "Broken English and Broken Irish: Language, Nation and the Optic of Power in Shakespeare's Histories." *Shakespeare Quarterly*, vol. 45, no. 1, 1994, pp. 1–32.

"A New Ballad Intituled, A Bell-man for England, Which Night and Day Doth Sta. Ring in All Mens Hearing, Gods Vengeance is at Hand." 1620. *English Broadside Ballad Archive*, U of California, Santa Barbara, ebba.english.ucsb.edu/ballad/20035/image.

Nicoll, Allardyce, and Josephine Nicoll, editors. *Holinshed's Chronicle as Used in Shakespeare's Plays*. J. M. Dent and Sons, 1927.

Nietzsche, Friedrich. *The Birth of Tragedy and the Case of Wagner*. Translated by Walter Kaufmann, Vintage Books, 1967.

Noddings, Nel. *Critical Lessons: What Our Schools Should Teach*. Cambridge UP, 2006.

Norcia, Megan A. "Out of the Ivory Tower Endlessly Rocking: Collaborating across Disciplines and Professions to Promote Student Learning in the Digital Archive." *Pedagogy*, vol. 8, no. 1, 2007, pp. 91–114.

Norwich, John Julius. *Shakespeare's Kings: The Great Plays and the History of England in the Middle Ages, 1337–1485*. Scribner, 1999.

O'Brien, Peggy, editor. *Shakespeare Set Free*. Folger Shakespeare Library, 2006. 3 vols.

O'Dair, Sharon. "Is It Ecocritical If It Isn't Presentist?" Bruckner and Brayton, pp. 71–85.

Ogborn, Miles. *Global Lives: Britain and the World, 1550–1800*. Cambridge UP, 2008.

Onions, C. T., and Robert D. Eagleson. *A Shakespeare Glossary*. 3rd ed., Oxford UP, 1986.

Open Source Shakespeare. George Mason U, 2003–14, www.opensourceshakespeare.org/.

Ormrod, W. Mark. *Edward III*. Yale UP, 2013. Yale English Monarchs.

Ornstein, Robert. *A Kingdom for a Stage: The Achievement of Shakespeare's English History Plays*. Harvard UP, 1972.

Palfrey, Simon. *Shakespeare's Possible Worlds*. Cambridge UP, 2014.

Palfrey, Simon, and Tiffany Stern. *Shakespeare in Parts*. Oxford UP, 2007.

Paré, Ambroise. *On Monsters and Marvels*. Translated by Janis L. Pallister, U of Chicago P, 1982.

Parvini, Neema. *Shakespeare's History Plays: Rethinking Historicism*. Edinburgh UP, 2012.

Paster, Gail Kern. "*Henry IV* and *Henry V* with Jeremy Irons." *Shakespeare Uncovered*, Public Broadcasting Corporation, 1 Feb. 2013.

Patterson, Annabel. *Censorship and Interpretation: The Conditions of Reading and Writing in Early Modern England*. U of Wisconsin P, 1984.

———. *Reading* Holinshed's Chronicles. U of Chicago P, 1994.

———. *Shakespeare and the Popular Voice*. Basil Blackwell, 1989.

Peacham, Henry. *The Garden of Eloquence*. Brigham Young U, humanities.byu.edu/rhetoric/Primary%20Texts/Peacham.htm.

Peck, Linda Levy. *Court Patronage and Corruption in Early Stuart England*. Taylor and Francis, 2003.

Pierce, Robert B. *Shakespeare's History Plays: The Family and the State*. Ohio State UP, 1971.

Pilkington, Ace G. "The BBC's Henriad." *Literature/Film Quarterly*, vol. 21, no. 1, 1993, pp. 25–32.

———. *Screening Shakespeare from* Richard II *to* Henry V. U of Delaware P, 1991.

Pink, Daniel. *A Whole New Mind: Why Right-Brainers Will Rule the Future*. Riverhead Books, 2005.

Pocock, J. G. A. *The Ancient Constitution and the Feudal Law: A Study of English Historical Thought in the Seventeenth Century*. W. W. Norton, 1967.

Pollard, A. J. *The Wars of the Roses*. St. Martin's Press, 1988.

Ponet, John. *A Short Treatise of Politique Power*. Strasbourg, 1556. *Early English Books Online*, gateway.proquest.com/openurl?ctx_ver=Z39.88–2003&res_id=xri:eebo&rft_id=xri:eebo:image:15453.

Popkin, Richard. *The History of Skepticism from Erasmus to Descartes*. Koninklijke Van Gorcum, 1960.

Porter, Joseph A. *The Drama of Speech Acts: Shakespeare's Lancastrian Tetralogy*. U of California P, 1979.

The Prayer-Book of Queen Elizabeth, 1559. Edited by William Benham, published by John Grant, 1911. *Internet Archive*, archive.org/stream/prayerbookof que00chur#page/18 mde/2up.

Pressley, J. M. "Shakespeare's *King John*: Drama versus History." *Shakespeare Resource Center*, www.bardweb.net/content/ac/kingjohn.html.

Prestwick, Michael. *Plantagenet England, 1225–1360*. Oxford UP, 2005. New Oxford History of England.

Prior, Moody E. *The Drama of Power: Studies in Shakespeare's History Plays*. Northwestern UP, 1973.

Private Libraries in Renaissance England. Folger Shakespeare Library, 2005, plre .folger.edu.

Proctor, Thomas. *Of the Knowledge and Conducte of Warre*. 1578. Da Capo Press, 1970.

Pugliatti, Paola. *Shakespeare and the Just War Tradition*. Ashgate Publishing, 2010.

———. *Shakespeare the Historian*. Palgrave Macmillan, 1996.

Puttenham, George. *The Arte of English Poesie*. *Internet Archive*, U of Virginia, etext .lib.virginia.edu/toc/modeng/public/PutPoes.html.

Pye, Christopher. *The Regal Phantasm: Shakespeare and the Politics of Spectacle*. Routledge, 1990.

Rabkin, Norman. "Rabbits, Ducks, and *Henry V*." *Shakespeare Quarterly*, vol. 28, no. 3, 1977, pp. 279–96.

Rackin, Phyllis. *Stages of History: Shakespeare's English Chronicles*. Cornell UP, 1990.

Rappaport, Steve. *Worlds within Worlds: Structures of Life in Sixteenth-Century London*. Cambridge UP, 1989.

Ribner, Irving. *The English History Play in the Age of Shakespeare*. Princeton UP, 1957.

Richard II. Directed by David Giles, performance by Derek Jacobi and John Gielgud, British Broadcasting Corporation, 1978.

Richard II. Directed by Rupert Goold, performance by Ben Whishaw, Rory Kinnear, David Suchet, and Patrick Stewart. *The Hollow Crown*, British Broadcasting Corporation, 2012.

Richard II. Directed by William Woodman, performance by David Birney and John McLiam, America's Music, 1982.

Richard III. Directed by Michael Bogdanov, The English Shakespeare Company, 1990. Films for the Humanities and Sciences.

Richard III. 1912. Directed by Andre Calmettes and James Keane, performance by Frederick Warde, Albert Gardner, and Carlotta de Felice, Kino Video, 2001.

Richard III. Directed by Jane Howell, British Broadcasting Corporation, 1983.

Richard III. Directed by Richard Loncraine, performance by Ian McKellen, Annette Bening, Jim Broadbent, Nigel Hawthorne, and Kristin Scott Thomas, MGM, 1995.

Richard III. Directed by Laurence Olivier, performance by Olivier, Ralph Richardson, John Gielgud, Claire Bloom, and Cedric Hardwicke, Criterion, 1955.

Rocklin, Edward L. *Performance Approaches to Teaching Shakespeare*. National Council of Teachers of English, 2005.

Rodenburg, Patsy. *Speaking Shakespeare*. Palgrave Macmillan, 2002.

Roper, William. *The Life of Sir Thomas More. Two Early Tudor Lives*. Edited by Richard S. Sylvester and Davis S. Harding, Yale UP, 1962, pp. 195–253.

Rosenblatt, Louise. *Literature as Exploration*. Modern Language Association of America, 1985.

Ross, Charles. *Edward IV*. Yale UP, 1998. Yale English Monarchs.

———. *Richard III*. Yale UP, 2011. Yale English Monarchs.

Rothwell, Kenneth S. *A History of Shakespeare on Screen: A Century of Film and Television*. 2nd ed., Cambridge UP, 2004.

Saccio, Peter. *Shakespeare's English Kings: History, Chronicle, and Drama*. Oxford UP, 2000.

Sams, Eric, editor. *Shakespeare's Lost Play*: Edmund Ironside. Fourth Estate, 1985.

Sanders, Wilbur. *The Dramatist and the Received Idea: Studies in the Plays of Marlowe and Shakespeare*. Cambridge UP, 1968.

Saul, Nigel. *Richard II*. Yale UP, 1999. Yale English Monarchs.

Scarisbrick, J. J. *Henry VIII*. Yale UP, 2011. Yale English Monarchs.

Schama, Simon. *Landscape and Memory*. Vintage Books, 1995.

Scholes, Robert. *The Crafty Reader*. Yale UP, 2001.

Schwarz, Kathryn. *Tough Love: Amazon Encounters in the English Renaissance*. Duke UP, 2000.

Schwyzer, Philip. *Literature, Nationalism, and Memory in Early Modern England and Wales*. Cambridge UP, 2009.

Schwyzer, Philip, and Willy Maley, editors. *Shakespeare and Wales: From the Marches to the Assembly*. Ashgate Publishing, 2010.

Schwyzer, Philip, and Simon Mealor, editors. *Archipelagic Identities: Literature and Identity in the Atlantic Archipelago, 1550–1800.* Ashgate Publishing, 2004.

Scott, Heidi. "Ecological Microcosms Envisioned in Shakespeare's *Richard II.*" *The Explicator*, vol. 67, no. 4, 2009, pp. 267–71.

Scott, William O. "Landholding, Leasing, and Inheritance in *Richard II.*" *Studies in English Literature*, vol. 42, no. 2, 2002, pp. 275–92.

Sebek, Barbara. "'After My Humble Dutie Remembered': Factors and/versus Merchants." *Emissaries in Early Modern Literature and Culture: Mediation, Transmission, Traffic, 1550–1700*, edited by Brinda Charry and Gitanjali Shahani, Ashgate Publishing, 2009, pp. 113–28.

———. "Canary, Bristoles, Londres, Ingleses: English Traders in the Canaries in the Sixteenth and Seventeenth Centuries." Singh, pp. 279–93.

———. "Different Shakespeares: Global Consciousness in an Early Modern Literature Course." *Teaching Medieval and Early Modern Cross-Cultural Encounters.* Edited by Karina Attar and Lynn Shutters, Palgrave Macmillan, 2014.

———. "'More Natural to the Nation': Situating Shakespeare in the 'Querelle de Canary.'" *Shakespeare Studies*, vol. 42, 2014, pp. 106–21.

———. "Morose's Turban." *Shakespeare Studies*, vol. 35, 2007, pp. 32–38.

Shakespeare Uncovered: Henry IV and V. Performance by Jeremy Irons, Public Broadcasting Service, 2013.

Shakespeare, William. *The Complete Pelican Shakespeare.* Edited by Stephen Orgel and A. R. Braunmuller, Penguin Books, 2002.

———. *The Complete Works of Shakespeare.* Edited by David Bevington, 6th ed., Longman, 2009.

———. *The First Part of King Henry the Fourth.* Edited by Samuel Crowl, Focus Publishing, 2009.

———. *Henry IV, Part I.* Edited by Claire McEachern, Penguin Books, 2000.

———. *Henry IV, Part II.* Edited by Claire McEachern, Penguin Books, 2000.

———. *Henry V.* Edited by Claire McEachern, Penguin Books, 2000.

———. *Henry V.* Edited by James D. Mardock, *Internet Shakespeare Editions*, 2012, internetshakespeare.uvic.ca/Library/Texts/H5/.

———. *King Henry V.* Edited by T. W. Craik, Arden Shakespeare, 1995.

———. *King Richard II.* Edited by Andrew Gurr, Cambridge UP, 2003.

———. *King Richard II.* Edited by Peter Ure, Methuen Publishing, 1961.

———. *The Life and Death of King John.* Edited by A. R. Braunmuller, Oxford UP, 1989.

———. *The Life and Death of King John.* Edited by Barbara A. Mowat and Paul Werstine, Washington Square Press, 2000.

———. *The Norton Shakespeare.* Edited by Stephen Greenblatt et al., 2nd ed., W. W. Norton, 2008.

———. *1 Henry IV.* Edited by Rosemary Gaby, *Internet Shakespeare Editions*, 2013, internetshakespeare.uvic.ca/Library/Texts/1H4/.

———. *The Riverside Shakespeare*. Edited by G. Blakemore Evans, 2nd ed., Houghton Mifflin, 1997.

———. *2 Henry IV*. Edited by Rosemary Gaby. *Internet Shakespeare Editions*, 2013, internetshakespeare.uvic.ca/Library/Texts/2H4/.

Shakespeare's An Age of Kings. Performance by Robert Hardy, Sean Connery, Judi Dench, Julian Glover, and Eileen Atkins, BBC Home Entertainment, 2009.

Shakespeare's Words. David Crystal and Ben Crystal, 2008, www.shakespeareswords.com/.

Sharp, Buchanan. *In Contempt of All Authority: Rural Artisans and Riot in the West of England, 1586–1660*. U of California P, 1971.

Shorter, Edward. *The Making of the Modern Family*. Basic Books, 1975.

Siemon, James R. "Landlord Not King: Agrarian Change and Interarticulation." Burt and Archer, pp. 17–33.

Sinfield, Alan. *Faultlines: Cultural Materialism and the Politics of Dissident Reading*. U of California P, 1992.

Singh, Jyotsna, editor. *A Companion to the Global Renaissance: English Literature and Culture in the Era of Expansion*. Wiley-Blackwell, 2007.

Sini, Matthew. "Transgeneric Tendencies in New Queer Cinema." *Refractory*, vol. 18, no. 6, 2011, refractory.unimelb.edu.au/2011/05/06/transgeneric-tendencies-in-new-queer-cinema-%E2%80%93-matthew-sini/.

Smallwood, Robert, editor. *Players of Shakespeare 6: Essays in the Performance of Shakespeare's History Plays*. Cambridge UP, 2004.

Smith, Alan K. *Creating a World Economy: Merchant Capital, Colonialism, and World Trade, 1400–1825*. Westview Press, 1991.

Smith, Bruce R. *Homosexual Desire in Shakespeare's England: A Cultural Poetics*. U of Chicago P, 1995.

———. *Shakespeare and Masculinity*. Oxford UP, 2000.

Smith, Matthew J. "The Experience of Ceremony in *Henry V*." *SEL*, vol. 54, no. 2, 2014, pp. 401–21.

Smyth, Adam. " 'The Whole Globe of the Earth': Almanacs and Their Readers." Singh, pp. 294–304.

Spenser, Edmund. *The Faerie Queene*. Edited by A. C. Hamilton, 2nd ed., Pearson, 2007.

Spevack, Marvin. *A Complete and Systematic Concordance to the Works of William Shakespeare*. Georg Olms, 1968. 2 vols.

Spurgeon, Caroline. *Shakespeare's Imagery and What It Tells Us*. Cambridge UP, 1935.

Stallybrass, Peter. "Against Thinking." *PMLA*, vol. 122, no. 5, 2007, pp. 1580–87.

———. "Syllabus: Reading, Writing, and Printing in England and America, 1450–2007." Department of English, University of Pennsylvania, 2007.

Stanislavsky, Constantin. *An Actor Prepares*. Translated by Elizabeth Reynolds Hapgood, Theatre Arts Books, 1948.

Stone, Lawrence. *The Crisis of the Aristocracy, 1558–1641*. Clarendon Press, 1965.

Stone-Fewings, Jo. "The Bastard in *King John*." Smallwood, pp. 50–67.

Stow, John. *The Annales of England*. London, 1592. *Early English Books Online*, gateway.proquest.com/openurl?ctx_ver=Z39.88–2003&res_id=xri:eebo &rft_id=xri:eebo:image:18449.

———. *The Chronicles of England*. London, 1580. *Early English Books Online*, gateway.proquest.com/openurl?ctx_ver=Z39.88–2003&res_id=xri:eebo &rft_id=xri:eebo:image:18151.

———. *Survey of London*. London, 1603. *Early English Books Online*, gateway .proquest.com/openurl?ctx_ver=Z39.88–2003&res_id=xri:eebo&rft_id =xri:eebo:image:18466.

Streuver, Nancy S. *The History of Rhetoric and the Rhetoric of History*. Ashgate Publishing, 2009.

Strier, Richard. "Faithful Servants: Shakespeare's Praise of Disobedience." *The Historical Renaissance: New Essays on Tudor and Stuart Literature and Culture*, edited by Heather Dubrow and Richard Strier, U of Chicago P, 1988, pp. 104–33.

Strohm, Paul. "Counterfeiters, Lollards, and Lancastrian Unease." *New Medieval Literatures*, edited by Wendy Case, Rita Copeland, and David Lawton, Clarendon Press, 1997, pp. 31–58.

Stubbes, Phillip. *The Anatomie of Abuses*. W. Pickering, 1836.

Suárez-Orozco, Carola, and Marcelo M. Suárez-Orozco. *Children of Immigration*. Harvard UP, 2001.

Sutcliffe, Matthew. *The Practice, Proceeding, and Lawes of Armes*. London, 1593.

Taunton, Nina. *1590s Drama and Militarism: Portrayals of War in Marlowe, Chapman, and Shakespeare's* Henry V. Ashgate Publishing, 2001.

Tennenhouse, Leonard. *Power on Display: The Politics of Shakespeare's Genres*. Methuen Publishing, 1986.

Theis, Jeffrey. *Writing the Forest in Early Modern England: A Sylvan Pastoral Nation*. Duquesne UP, 2009.

Thirsk, Joan. *The Agrarian History of England and Wales, 1500–1640*. Vol. 4., Cambridge UP, 1967.

———. *Economic Policy and Projects: The Development of a Consumer Society in Early Modern England*. Oxford UP, 1989.

Thomas, Keith. *Man and the Natural World: Changing Attitudes in England, 1500–1800*. Oxford UP, 1983.

Thompson, Ayanna. *Passing Strange: Shakespeare, Race, and Contemporary America*. Oxford UP, 2011.

Thomson, W. H. *Shakespeare's Characters: A Historical Dictionary*. British Book Centre, 1951.

Tillyard, E. M. W. *The Elizabethan World Picture*. Macmillan, 1944.

———. *Shakespeare's History Plays*. Macmillan, 1946.

Tinkcom, Matthew. "Out West: Gus Van Sant's *My Own Private Idaho* and the Lost Mother." *Where the Boys Are: Cinemas of Masculinity and Youth*, edited by

Murray Pomerance and Frances Gateward, Wayne State UP, 2005, pp. 233–45. Contemporary Approaches to Film and Media Series.

Traub, Valerie. "The New Unhistoricism in Queer Studies." *PMLA*, vol. 128, no. 1, 2013, pp. 21–39.

———. *The Renaissance of Lesbianism in Early Modern England*. Cambridge UP, 2002.

Traversi, Derek. *Shakespeare from* Richard II *to* Henry V. Stanford UP, 1957.

The Troublesome Reign of King John. Edited by Karen Oberer. *Internet Shakespeare Editions*, 2013, qme.internetShakespeare.uvic.ca/Foyer/plays/TRKJ.html. Queen's Men Editions.

The True Tragedy of Richard III. Edited by Jennifer Roberts-Smith and Dimitry Senyshyn. *Internet Shakespeare Editions*, 2013, qme.internetshakespeare.uvic .ca/Foyer/plays/TTR3.html. Queen's Men Editions.

The Unabridged Acts and Monuments Online. U of Sheffield, www.johnfoxe.org, 2011.

Underwood, Ted. "Where to Start with Text Mining." *The Stone and the Shell*, 14 August 2012, tedunderwood.com/2012/08/14/where-to-start with-text -mining.

Velz, John W., editor. *Shakespeare and the Classical Tradition: A Critical Guide to Commentary, 1660–1960*. U of Minnesota P, 1968.

———. *Shakespeare's English Histories: A Quest for Form and Genre*. Medieval and Renaissance Texts and Studies, 1997.

Vitkus, Daniel. "The New Globalism: Transcultural Commerce, Global Systems Theory, and Spenser's Mammon." Singh, pp. 31–49.

Wagner, Tony. *The Global Achievement Gap*. Basic Books, 2008.

Wallerstein, Immanuel. *The Modern World-System*. Academic Press, 1974.

Walpole, Horace. *Historic Doubts on the Life and Reign of Richard III: Including the Supplement, Reply, Short Observations and Postscript*. Edited by P. W. Hammond, Sutton Publishing, 1989.

Walsham, Alexandra. "Providentialism." Kewes et al., *Oxford Handbook*, pp. 427–42.

Warkentin, Germaine, editor. The Queen's Majesty's Passage *and Related Documents*. Centre for Reformation and Renaissance Studies, 2004.

"Waste, *N*." *Oxford English Dictionary*, Oxford UP, June 2004, ezproxy.chatham.edu :2104/view/Entry/226027?rskey=tZ6bxm&result=1#eid.

"Well Watch." *MarcellusGas.org*, 20 Dec. 2014, www.marcellusgas.org/well_watch/ well_watch.php.

White, Hayden. *The Content of the Form: Narrative Discourse and Historical Representation*. Johns Hopkins UP, 1987.

———. *Metahistory: The Historical Imagination in Nineteenth-Century Europe*. Johns Hopkins UP, 1973.

———. "The Politics of Historical Interpretation: Discipline and De-Sublimation." *Critical Inquiry*, vol. 9, no. 1, 1982, pp. 113–37.

Williams, Penry. *The Later Tudors: England, 1547–1603*. Oxford UP, 1998. New Oxford History of England.

Willis, Susan. *The BBC Shakespeare Plays: Making the Televised Canon*. U of North Carolina P, 1991.

Wills, Garry. *Rome and Rhetoric: Shakespeare's* Julius Caesar. Yale UP, 2011.

Wiseman, Susan. "The Family Tree Motel: Subliming Shakespeare in *My Own Private Idaho*." *Shakespeare: The Movie*, edited by Lynda E. Boose and Richard Burt, Routledge, 1998, pp. 225–39.

Wittek, Stephen. "Computer-Based Textual Analysis and Early Modern Literature: Notes on Some Recent Research." *Early Modern Conversions*, www.early modernconversions.com/computer-based-textual-analysis-and-early-modern -literature-notes-on-some-recent-research.

Wolffe, Bertram. *Henry VI*. Yale UP, 2001. Yale English Monarchs.

Woolf, Nicky. "US 'Little Rebels' Protest against Changes to History Curriculum." *The Guardian*, 26 Sept. 2014, www.theguardian.com/world/2014/sep/26/-sp -colorado-ap-history-curriculum-protest-patriotism-schools-students.

"The World of Shakespeare's Humors." *United States National Library of Medicine*, 19 Sept. 2013, www.nlm.nih.gov/exhibition/shakespeare/fourhumors.html.

INDEX